MYSTIC BARBER

His name is Andy Sinatra—and he can't sing a note. Usually Andy prefers to be referred to as the "Mystic Barber," but on my show he's better known as the "Mystical Tonsorial Artist from Brooklyn."

To describe the Barber as unusual wouldn't be giving you the full picture . . . Andy is in touch with other worlds. He's visited by Martians, who are identifiable because of their having no reflections —a point he's noticed when they come to his tonsorial parlor for a trim or a shave. Usually, his contacts aren't so direct, but are accomplished via telepathic communication. To make telepathy simpler, Andy insists that all beginners should have one of his inventions —a headband, a couple of inches wide with a pair of weird, bouncy antennae on it, for tuning in on the Venusian sending frequency. I've tried it, and nothing happens. But, you have to admit, it's kind of wild stuff.

COMPLETE AND UNABRIDGED

the way out world

LONG JOHN NEBEL

WILDSIDE PRESS

GENTLE READER . . . .

This is the Introduction—or, if you prefer, the Preface to the book. It was completed about two hours ago; I re-read the last chapter, made a few minor corrections, typed out the label, put it on the envelope, and after I complete this little bit it'll be on its way to the publisher.

To say it was a challenge is certainly an understatement. I've learned a lot—and, of course, this is pretty easy for me, because I know so little. I've learned that writing a book is not the easiest thing in the world. I've learned that you shouldn't end a sentence with a preposition—but I'll continue to. Dr. Edward Spingarn Professor of English, has many times told me that there's no such word as "enthused," but I'll let you in on a secret: I'm very enthused about the possibility of writing another book; but this time I hope, if some publisher will accept it, it'll be about "Hate Mail."

I'm indebted to literally hundreds of people, and naturally space does not permit the acknowledgment of all of them. Certainly Phyllis Rosenteur's, Stuart Daniels', and John Gudmundsen's encouragement was of great value. Jim Donnelly, "The Old Crusader," and Virginia Belmont of the Belmont Bird and Kennel Shop, were indirectly instrumental in helping me gather material. Monte Feuerstein and Hal Fleischer-of Cheers Steak House made it possible for me to have a restful place to sit down and enjoy a cup of coffee or a cocktail while attempting to get some off-the-air material from guests. And Barney Boyle of WOR-TV certainly deserves a word of gratitude for his help and encouragement. In the WOR family, I just couldn't fail to thank Ed and Pegeen Fitzgerald, Arlene Francis, John Wingate, and Galen Drake for the guests, material and suggestions they supplied to me—to say nothing of my pleasant memories of being a guest on their shows. George Brown, Director of WOR's News Department, has many times been a source of information about interesting people or exciting current topics that made interesting discussion material. And certainly Dorothy and Dick —in private life Mr. and Mrs., he being the noted *entrepreneur* (You're right; I got that word from a guest on my show), Richard Kollmar, and she the famous columnist Dorothy Kilgallen—have on many occasions earned my gratitude and respect.

And, of course, I could go on and on . . . but space is limited, and the memory is not what it used to be. So, to those whom I may have missed, many, many thanks also.

Well, that just about wraps up the opening pitch. I don't know if you're a letter writer or not, but if you are I'd certainly appreciate your opinion of the book—whether it's good, bad or indifferent; just send it to me, Long John Nebel, WOR, New York 18, New York.

And Anna is calling me, because I have about three minutes before show time. So long . . . and happy reading.

LONG JOHN NEBEL

"When you have eliminated the impossible, whatever remains, however improbable, must be the truth."
— Sherlock Holmes in *"The Sign of Four"*
(Sir Arthur Conan Doyle)

THE BIRTH OF A PITCHMAN

"HI NEIGHBORS, this is Long John Nebel. Tonight, I think we've got a really great one for you . . ."

And out there in the night they listen. Lying in bed, curled in a chair, driving a car, swinging on a porch—in every likely and unlikely place—the restless, the workers, the insomniacs, or just the "night people," wonder who will bring another fantasy to entertain them during the sleeping hours. Because that nightly greeting is an introduction to the most fantastic, fabulous and amazing people on earth, and I'm the lucky guy who plays at being their host. My guests come from a billion miles away, or a million years ago. They're the women who walk through walls, the men who raise the dead, even the children who read minds. The unbelievable is my business, and I always try to make it your pleasure.

Every midnight I sit down before a hot mike, twenty-four floors above the Square known as Times, and begin a conversation with a guest who has his own unique tale to tell. In much less than a year these round table discussions will total well over a thousand hours, and that's a lot of talking to do with some of the world's strangest people.

You might think that it would be more than enough for anybody, but the weird truth of the matter is that I switch over to television every Friday evening and do a full hour of the offbeat for the cameras. Sometimes the addition of the picture dimension proves very valuable, especially when the guest is an inventor of an "aurameter," or has pictures of "authentic and genuine flying saucers" to display. For the most part, however, I prefer the wide range of five hours' air time to sit and listen to the full, and usually remarkable, story. By the end of a conversation of that length every last bit of the story can be told. Although, I must admit that this is not *always* true. Not infrequently I've had to invite a guest back two, four, even a dozen times before the entire extraordinary "truth" was completely revealed—well, almost.

Everyone has his own bit, and this is mine. Curiosity about people, places, and, most of all, ideas. I have a mountain flooded with 50,000 watts of light. If you have a story, if you have something really interesting to say, no matter how strange, you can come to the top of my mountain, stand in the light, and people uncountable will hear you.

On good days, it seems like a million years ago; on bad days it seems like last night. Chicago, I mean; a number of decades ago. That's where it, and I, began. In Chicago, a pretty long time ago. Of course, that was when I was a kid; later I got older. I get older today, too, but what can I do—I don't smoke, drink (anything unless it's liquid), or run around with fast women (I'm a walker); so I get older. Except on *those* days— then I get younger. If any of this is confusing just hang on— that's the kind of book it's going to be.

My father was an advertising executive for a large candy firm and my mother was a dermatologist; I was a kid who ate a lot of chocolate creams and had a great complexion. My parents were fairly comfortably off and I had no serious complaints during those earlier years. As a matter of fact, sometimes I even had fun.

A couple of years rolled by, and by the time I was ten I had gotten into merchandising. I peddled hot firecrackers to cool friends. Later I was with my grandmother at Wisconsin Dells. This was one of those cases of being in the place, right or wrong, at the time, right or wrong.

My grandmother was a strict Methodist and a member of the WCTU; maybe I'd better enlighten you—that's Women's Christian Temperance Union. If I'm not mistaken, at one time she headed that organization in Wisconsin Dells—possibly heading a membership that totaled four, including Grandma—because, as I remember it, Grandpa was a man who always knew that herbs, barks and berries were of great value to the body . . . if they were properly fermented. As far as Grandma was concerned, card playing, dancing, attending carnivals or circuses was "worldly." And the devil promoted all of these things. Frankly, the card playing was of no interest to me; girls were nuisances (I was about twelve at that time—at the present writing I like to sit down and play a little poker, and the more nuisances the better). And I think at this point I should make certain that no one is under the false impression that my life has been devoted to body-building hobbies such as bar-bell lifting, swimming, tennis, boxing . . . in fact, there have never been any strong men or fighters in my family; I come from three generations of lovers.

However, let me hasten to say that a carnival was a big thing to me as a youngster, and a circus . . . well . . . at that time my idea of Heaven was a tremendous arena topped with beautiful striped canvas, with trapeze artists swinging, tight-rope artists walking, and wild animal trainers entertaining twenty-four hours a day. Being a boy from the "Windy City"—or as the Chamber of Commerce of Chicago preferred in those days, "The City of Go"—I was, if I may say with great deference to the kids of my age in Wisconsin Dells, a little "hipper."

All the kids had been talking about the circus that was coming to town. And these kids knew all the answers—such as meeting the circus when it arrived on the school lot that was rented to carnivals, circuses, chautauquas, etc. In those days the one-ring circuses were motorized; they didn't come into town by railroad.

On the morning that the circus arrived, I was over at the school grounds with the other kids at about five in the morning. Some kids were hauling water for the elephants, others were helping to unroll sections of canvas and to lace these sections

9

together, while yours truly was over at a cat wagon. And you know, there was something friendly about that moth-eaten lion. As I was standing there admiring it, a rather young, unkempt and in general dirty-appearing man climbed into the cage and, in a rough voice, hollered out some obsenities which caused the lion to move over to the other end of the cage. He then proceeded to sweep out the cat's living quarters. Later I was to learn that the chair, whip and gun manipulator—ballied on the colorful signs that could be seen in the windows of the barber shop, pool room and the combination furniture dealer and mortician—was the world's greatest wild animal trainer. Yes, they were one and the same: the wild animal trainer and the chambermaid to wild animals. And it might be interesting to note that all of the signs ballied "wild animals." It should have been "animal," because there was only one—and he wasn't wild. In fact, I know he wasn't wild because some thirty minutes later I had my hand in the cage, petting this lion's paw. And, minutes later, I opened the door to the cage and went in—minus chair, whip and gun. And this wasn't a matter of courage on my part . . . just plain, unadulterated stupidity. As far as I was concerned this was just a nice, friendly old giant cat.

In those day, circuses had parades; and in wandering around the lot I learned that one of the clowns was ill; this was about 12 noon. Being a pretty tall guy for my age, and a fair conversationalist, I approached one of the owners and suggested to him that I would possibly be the ideal temporary replacement for the sick clown in the parade and opening spec. Mind you, there was no loot involved in this—just glory. And as I look in retrospect, I don't think there was enough loot in the world to equal the glory and satisfaction that I received as I stood in my bright, shiny, red chariot, decorated with 24-carat gold leaf, controlling the reins of a beautiful white horse, as I became a "with-it" participant in that wonderful circus parade that went down Capitol Street in Kilbourne, Wisconsin (that was the name of Wisconsin Dells at that time), some 38 years ago, on a beautiful, hot, sunny afternoon in June.

That was the extent of my duties as a clown, and for the evening performance I drove the chariot again in the spec. When the performance was three-quarters over that night, they were starting to strike the top for the ten-in-one show. The tops that housed the various concessionaires and the grease joint were also being sloughed. By this time I had removed my make-up and I started to cut a jackpot with one of the owners, and learned that the next town they were to play was about 15 or 20 miles away; Baraboo, Wiscnsin.

It's interesting to note that Baraboo was the original home of the Ringling Brothers. The story goes that the good white fathers of that community taxed Mr. Ringling and his winter quarters right out of town.

After some ten or fifteen minutes of conversation, I sold him the idea that I should take over the clown's part in Baraboo, because by this time we knew he would be unable to work the date. I contacted my dad by phone in Chicago. He granted me permission to go with the circus for the next two weeks—naturally against the wishes of a lovely lady, my grandmother.

Instead of spending two weeks, I stayed with the circus for the balance of the summer. It's pleasant to remember that after my first week I was able to get on the payroll. I also became cognizant of at least one of the strange beliefs of Americans then, and possibly for centuries before, as well as today: the phenomenon of telepathy.

In the ten-in-one show, I became greatly impressed with a lady performer who had all of the beauty and charm of a Lillian Russell, and the fully-developed power of telepathy. And it seems like I'm hearing the talker make that introductory pitch for "Lady Ester" again . . . right now:

"Ladies and gentlemen. I'd appreciate it if you'll now gather over to this platform. Thank you. Will you be kind enough, please, to move in a little closer. Those ladies over there, would you please move in just a little closer. It is a rare privilege and a great honor for the Lamont Brothers to have this season, as a star attraction, Lady Ester. Lady Ester can read your mind without the aid of any mechanical or electrical equipment, or personal contact.

"She was the seventh born in a family of seven children. She was born on the 31st day of October—a day that we celebrate as Halloween. At the age of seven, Lady Ester was able to answer her mother's questions and execute her mother's desires prior to the time that they were orally stated. At the age of fourteen, she had completed her high school education. On her graduation day, she was giving the valedictory speech when all of a sudden she stopped. For a period of time that seemed hours, but evidently was just a matter of seconds, there was complete silence in that high school auditorium in Ashtabula, Ohio. Members of the audience began to feel sorry for this little youngster who evidently had forgotten the rest of her speech.

11

And just then little Ester said, in a quivering, faint voice, 'There's a bad wreck that's going to happen at the railroad crossing in a few minutes.'

"A very large percentage of the audience in that high school auditorium had heard reports of Ester's telepathic ability. This startling announcement therefore caused great unrest and concern for everyone. Seconds later, a blanket of silence covered the auditorium. In the distance could be heard the roar of an on-coming train. And then . . . a tremendous crash was heard! . . . the whining, screeching sound of the engine and the freight cars coming to a halt And, rather than give you any more of the gruesome details, let me say that Lady Ester, as a child of four-teen, had predicted, minutes before, one of the most tragic train wrecks in the annals of railroad history that occurred in that small community in Ohio.

"Yes, the lady whom I will have the pleasure to introduce in a few minutes . . . the lady who has amazed kings and queens, and three former presidents of the United States. Scientists in our major universities and colleges throughout the world have been unable to fathom this remarkable woman's ability. And now . . . I proudly present to you . . . the world's greatest mentalist—Lady Ester."

After this beautiful opening on the part of the talker, Lady Ester's husband would go among the audience and, by using a verbal code, would send back to this marvelous, mystical, mys-terious marvel of mental mysteries the birthdates and questions of members of the audience who had sprung a quarter to test the telepathic abilities of Lady Ester.

Ester's real name was Dianne Underwood, and her husband . . . well, I wouldn't want to be unkind and say that he was an alcoholic, but it was as unsafe to let this man remain un-guarded, without alcohol in some form, as it would be to take a car out when it's two below zero without alcohol in the radiator. I was always amazed and wondered why this lovely lady would bill herself as Lady Ester when she had such a beautiful name as Dianne. If I had anything to do with the act, I possibly would have billed her as Divine Dianne or Dianne the Divine.

As I got to know Dianne better, I was able to learn about some of the modus operandi employed by pseudo-mentalists. Using the phrase "pseudo-mentalists" leads one to believe that I think that there are legitimate mentalists. I don't, because I've never seen one—and I've talked to dozens.

One afternoon, while the big show was on, Dianne started to

tell me about the "science" of numerology. I think even Vincent Lopez would have loved Dianne, because even though she knew that she was involved in a gaffed act, she believed in numerology. Her legitimate name was spelled with two n's, making a total of six letters. Being somewhat of a Bible student, she became interested in Ester, and I'm pretty sure that in the Bible it's spelled E-s-t-h-e-r. She decided to bill herself as Lady Ester because her husband's name was Cy. She came to the conclusion that having five letters in Ester and two in Cy would bring the total to the lucky number seven. Being the seventh child in the family, she believed, through some mystical way, anything with the number seven would bring her good fortune. Dianne's life with Cy was certainly not a happy one. It was obvious to me, even as a youngster, that all the numerology in the world would not bring Dianne happiness. And yet, she was a "go-fer" for all of the prediction gaffs.

As an example, when we'd get to a town, if she heard that there was a great tea-leaf reader or a mitt camp (palmistry operation) in town, she'd spring for loot to get a little advance knowledge of the future. I remember one morning in Sheboygan, Wisconsin, she went into town to have her tea leaves read. About ten minutes before she did her afternoon performance, she told me that this woman—the tea-leaf reader—was the most remarkable clairvoyant she had ever met. Later that afternoon, after her performance, she saw me on the lot and called me over. I guess by this time I had become—at the age of thirteen—her father confessor. She was very unhappy and discouraged. When I questioned her, she told me that a woman in her audience bought four scopes that afternoon to have four questions answered. The woman, of course, did not recognize Lady Ester as a patron of the shop. The great clairvoyant tea-leaf reader was in the tip, looking for assistance from that mental marvel, Lady Ester!

Say, let me save you a trip to the archives in the public library. Don't bother to look up the facts about that "tragic accident" that occurred at a railroad crossing near the high school in Ashtabula, Ohio. It's not recorded. You know why? It never happened. That was just the talker's introductory pitch for Lady Ester.

And, wherever she is now, if she happens to read this book, I have only the fondest memories of the lovely lady. And if she's no longer with us on this plane, I have no doubt that she'll possibly get a chance to peek at the book. She's possibly a spirit entity acting as a spirit guide to some medium that I've interviewed in the past, or will in the near future. So again, Lady Ester, whether you're still with us in this incarnation or preparing for a new incarnation, I'm indebted to you for much knowledge and many, many pleasant memories.

In September, the great kick was over. I had found out three things: one, that I was hooked on show business; two, that psychic phenomena and the occult world in general were things I wanted to learn a lot more about; and last but not least, that selling is the greatest form of self-expression in the world—at least to me.

Soon I was making small loot with a door-to-door pitch pushing household items. Then I dropped the classroom to edge up into the business scene. Before I was seventeen I had promoted my way into the managership of a Wurlitzer piano store. With six feet already to my credit, no one doubted that I was in my early twenties.

Then I got another bug-bite: wanderlust; and I started to move East. To the Big Town, to Broadway. I became an usher in the New York Paramount, and followed that with an assistant-managership at the Winter Garden Theatre. By now, the glamour of the stage really had me going. I decided to put to test my long hours of tenor banjo practice. I hit the road with a fairly successful group and soon had an eighteen-piece crew swinging, with me up front. The band never achieved an international reputation, but I can make this one slippery claim to fame: I once followed Rudy Vallee into a major ballroom. Tired of the split-week bit, I went into the vaudeville hoofings.

During one dead season I grabbed off the management of a pair of Siamese Twins. Later I did a small magic gaff, which turned into a pseudo-mind reading act. When a couple of pretty good partners got married. I decided to get the tenor banjo out of the mothballs, form a group and go on the road again. A few months of one nighters, and I brought the boys back to New York for the taxi dance hall tour. However, by this time I really had passed the twenty mark, and so had the century. Things were bad, really bad, all over. One-time tycoons were working in stores that had no customers, former clerks were pushing apples on the streets for nickels, street peddlers had starved the year before. They were bad, bad days. But I was one of the lucky ones—I was young. Also, I hadn't even begun to take advantage of my greatest talent. It was then I found my field. I began to sell.

14

It wasn't easy. I got by. Looking back, I still get a kick out of how some guys kept themselves in action. Take the Chinese Corn Punk Pitch. This involved going down to Paddy's Market on Ninth Avenue and buying several cakes of yellow laundry soap for pennies. Then you went to the nearest Chinese Laundry and conned the proprietor out of his last week's Chinese newspaper. Now you headed for your pad, to slice the bars of soap into 1½" cubes. You cut the newsprint up into pieces of the right size and wrapped up the numerous little blocks of soap. A final touch of red ribbon for color, and off you went with your new product—Chinese Corn Punk.

Attracting a tip, you explained the wondrous benefits of this imported, oil-pressed Chinese Corn Punk. Extolling the great relief from pain it gave to all those who suffered from foot problems, you challenged anyone to try it on his or her corn. So great is the power of suggestion that not once did any customers ever deny immediate relief came to them from the magical remedy. Having made the turn, and blown the tip, you had a little loot to keep you in action for a few days.

Or course, there were times when you couldn't even spring for a couple of bars of soap. Times when you were really tap city, and had to dream up a gaff that didn't require capital. Then you turned to the Envelope Pitch. You didn't like it, but you were hungry, and what could you do?

First you found a hotel with a writing room. Picking up envelopes, you moved on to the nearest cafeteria, where you appropriated a couple of dozen paper napkins. Now the second were inserted into the first, and the envelopes were sealed. The napkins were to give the envelopes a little "body." Then you hit Forty-Second Street, and started to build your tip.

"Now, what am I talking about, friends. Step closer; I don't want to raise my voice. That's it. A little closer."

As the crowd bellied in, you would usually notice a woman on the edge of the group. This was good. It gave you a chance to hook the men.

"Gather in, friends. Ah, ladies, good evening. I'm afraid that what I have tonight is strictly for the men, but thank you for stopping by. Now, friends, when I say for the men, that's what I mean. That is, if you're among the lucky purchasers of the evening."

By now you had dropped to a near whisper, causing the tip to huddle about you. This you re-enforced.

"Friends,—I can't attract unnecessary attention,—just gather

15

in. What I have here is something every red-blooded American male wants to own—needs to own, given the opportunity . . . and this is the opportunity. I can't relate all of the remarkable details of these . . . pictures of . . . but I don't have to tell what they are; you all look like adult men. Believe me, when you see them, ten pounds of ice won't cool you off. The strongest, straightest pix you've ever seen in these United States. Now, let's move before we're joined by the law. I've only a few packages for an absurd one dollar, a buck, a skin . . . things are a little rough and I'm trying to raise some quick cash; otherwise they would go for the regular fin a throw. Important thing. Don't stand around. Take them home to your bedroom, pull down the shades, plug up the keyhole, and in the faint glimmer of a single lamp—look at the hottest photographs you've ever seen. Gentlemen, we'll have to hurry. One, sir. A dollar a copy. Three there. Buy and move on. One, there. Four there. All different. Right, sir. Two left. You, sir? Thank you. Thank you, gentlemen. Now go home and look at what you have had the good fortune to acquire, and I know you'll say to yourself— tonight, in Times Square, I met a young man and he did me— *good*."

Once I arrived in New York completely tap city, with just enough loot to pick up some very low line juice squeezers and a few "demo" oranges. On my first morning, it started raining. One day blown. I ate two, out of four, cans of beans. Two days. I ate another can of beans. It tasted pretty much like the other two. Three days. I ate the last can of beans and didn't taste it at all. Today, I'm still not a big bean man.

Finally, the rain stopped and the sun came out cautiously, like it was afraid someone would hit it in the eye. Down to my customers I went. I'd hardly gotten past assuring the small tip that I wasn't trying to sell them anything when John Law appeared. We took a little stroll. Half an hour later I was standing before the judge, hearing him say:

"You get off this time, but don't come back."

Grabbing my merchandise, I made a quick exit. Twenty minutes later I was working again. A couple of nothing sales and there was another cop. Off we went, to the courtroom, and—believe it or don't—there was the same judge. I thought for a moment that I'd really had it, but with a frown he told me to get out of his courtroom and not to come back, unless I wanted thirty days in the local sneezer.

Now, being pinched by the mendicant squad was nothing

new, but I decided I should be a little more cautious. This time in and out of court rooms was costing me too much of the long green. So, figuring it was a strictly down day, I stashed my tripes and kiester where you paid on the go-out instead of the come-in, and then went out to seek a solution to my monetary problems. An hour's concentration produced nothing but a tired head and an empty stomach, and so I decided to touch a pedestrian for a buck for something to eat. It was the only way for me to get it, since I was now completely tapped out.

An easy looking mark moved by and I hit him for a single, but this was just not my day. He was a detective. Off I went again to the courthouse. Naturally, I don' have to spell it out for you. My case came up and there was my good old "if-I-see-you-again-you-get-thirty-days" friend on the bench.

Let's face it, neighbors; I had no choice. I gave him a square count. What did I have to lose?

"Yes," I admitted, "I have been here twice before, today. But I obeyed your instructions. You told me not to peddle merchandise without a license. I didn't have gelt for the reader. In fact I was, and am, stoney broke. Also, I didn't want to disobey the court. So, when I got really hungry, I panhandled."

The judge looked at me for a long time. Obviously he was deciding whether to give me thirty rough ones, or send me to Bellevue. Finally, he spoke:

"Young man, I admire honesty. Maybe you guessed that and took a calculated risk. But that's all right, because I admire intelligence, too. I'm going to give you one more break, but, mind you, it's the last one. Get out of this court, and stay out. Understand me, this time I really mean it. Don't let me see you here again. Good luck."

And with that friendly warning, he leaned down from the bench and shook my hand, calling for the next case as he did.

Before I knew it I was out on the street, breathing the free, fresh air again; I became conscious of my hand. Opening it, I looked down at a folded dollar bill. The judge's contribution to one man's better times. I had been fortunate enough to run into, not a dispenser of law, but a judge of justice. Justice is what you get when you mix equal parts head and heart.

That's the story about the day I was arrested three times. But amazingly, that wasn't the end of the bit. Almost twenty-five years afterwards, a quarter of a century later, a guest walked into my studio to do a show. We got to talking and I found out that his father was the judge. When you think that in this city alone there are more than eight million people, it kind of makes you wonder. The circle often completes itself, even if it takes twenty-five years.

Going from one action to another, including fan magazine photographer and manager of one of the biggest camera stores in the country, I finally decided to set up my own operation out in New Jersey.

Soon I had 25,000 feet of floor space inside, and room for a thousand automobiles outside. The Long John Auction was under way, and so was I. You name it, I had it. Genuine (well, almost genuine) wall hangings from a Buddhist monastery. Watches, comforters, electric kitchen equipment, and on and on and on. If you didn't see it when you came in, it would be there when you walked out. The turnover was tremendous, the action was strong, and I was getting publicity. One mag did an exposé of the highway auction operations, singling me out as an honest practitioner. An *Argosy* article called me "the man who can sell anything." Luckily, Robert A. Monroe, then vice-president of the Mutual Network, saw the story and filed my name away in his mind. Later, driving toward his home at Croton-on-Hudson, he saw a tremendous crowd of parked cars. Getting closer, he saw a sign 41 feet long and 32 feet high. Simply and modestly it said, "LONG JOHN."

Hearing my pitch gave him the idea that I should be on radio. Shortly, that's where I was, thanks to him. Accompanied by a very talented guy named Charlie Holmes, I did a half-hour network bit in the late afternoon. What can I tell you except that the Charlie and John Show was evidently predestined to need the services of Frank. Oh, sure—you know Frank. Frank Campbell, the mortician? Let me let you in on the inside. Man, was it a deadly show! Then didn't even bother to embalm it. They just let it die. There were no services.

Then I got lucky again. Robert Leder took over as Vice President and General Manager of Radio Station WOR. He, and Robert Smith, Vice President in Charge of Programming, decided to give me another crack at the action. Generously aided by William McCormick, then Sales Manager of WOR but today Vice President and General Manager of WNAC-TV and WNAC, as well as the Yankee Network in New England, I was in again. This time with a slight twist. I interviewed people for three, four or five straight days to get the real story. You might say that I originated interviews in "breadth." Then

18

a better idea came along, in the very popular "Music from Studio X," and LJ was tapped out radio-wise.

The all-night session was being very capably handled, in those days, by top radio personality Jean Shepherd. His unfortunate mention of a product for which no commercial time had been bought made it necessary for management to make a change, and I had the privilege to be offered the midnight-to-five spot. Naturally, with Shep's talent and following you don't stay away very long, and soon he was swinging with his own show again.

My present all-night, every-night show began about six years ago, and has grown ever since. Today, we have a file of more than fifty "panelists" who appear on the program from time to time. From this larger group about twenty come on fairly frequently. Six or eight of these are what I call my "regular guys," although one or two are women.

Two or three "panelists" appear with the guest on each program. Many are specialists chosen for a particular show because of specific talents, education or interests. Several are very skilled in the art of extracting the inside story from a guest. Some are razor wits; others have a hammer-like humor. A few are so versatile they can appear on almost any show.

Although the program originally became famous because of the weird and off-beat people I had on, today the program covers every possible subject—bar none. The following list will show you the kind of action we have going during a given thirty-day period. It might be any time in a recent year; actually it is the schedule of the month of August, 1960:

1. European Society (also special report on execution at Sing Sing prison)
2. Modern Philosophy
3. The Fastest Gun Alive
4. Crafts and Hobbies
5. Yoga and the Far East
6. History of Submarines
7. Hillbilly Humor
8. Dangers of the Middle East
9. The American Consumer
10. India and World Affairs
11. Extra Sensory Perception
12. Woman's Place in the World
13. A Pastor and Witchcraft and Murder
14. American Politics

15. "One World" Philosophy
16. Houdini
17. Parapsychology
18. Literature
19. Notorious Trials
20. Weather Control with Thought
21. United Nations and Communism
22. Art of Pipe Organ Building
23. Worlds of Rome and Paris
24. Art Films—Voodoo
25. Spiritualism Colony—Exposed
26. Corporation Monsters
27. Sacco-Vanzetti Debate
28. Problem of Narcotics
29. The Civil War
30. Folk Music and Folklore

I should mention the three people around the show who help get it on the air. First is David Field. A degree in geology earns him the nickname—"Rocks." He takes care of all my recording equipment, and in general is my technical assistant. Then there is Anna Marie Goetz, who invented a combination crossword puzzle and anagram called the Long John Nebel Files. She is responsible for my answering those letters I manage to answer, and for keeping the office in some sort of order.

For two or three years, Paris Flammonde was my right-hand man. And occasionally he would sit in and do one of the all-night sessions as a panelist.

And so it goes, hour after hour, days upon days, years into years. One incredible personality exists and, nineteen hours later, another arrives. A merry-go-round of madness, and I love every minute of it.

I suppose to a few people it may sound a little dull, but, believe me, friends, this is a square count—life is never dull when you're hearing a man tell you about life on Saturn, or when Jackie Gleason comes swinging through the doors to argue with him. There's no monotony when this morning it's a private detective you're talking to, yesterday it was a psychiatrist, and tomorrow it'll be an Abe Lincoln—not the delicatessen store owner, but Abraham Lincoln, the former president. Of course, his appearance is made possible through a medium. You don't buy it? I don't either.

No, neighbors. It's never dull! It's exciting, and always new. I have to be frank with you, I'm a man who loves to do what he does—that is, talk to people. Rational, irrational, serious, amusing, simple, brilliant . . . they're all fascinating to me. Each one is a large or small mystery when they come in the studio, and sometimes they're more mysterious when they go out; but they all leave behind something I didn't have before . . . a little bit of knowledge.

You know, I was just thinking that I'm a pretty lucky guy. I can't honestly say that I'm making a classical buck, but I'll let you in on a secret: I haven't skipped any meals—or even postponed any—since I've been doing this bit. Yes, it's very true. I'm a very, very lucky guy, doing something that I get a charge out of, and at the same time I wind up with a shribe for doing it. Just in case you don't know, a shribe is a check.

And now let's actually get into the pitch. I'm going to try to tell you about the strange beliefs of many Americans today. The big cons, the little swindles, and in general the things I've talked about and have heard from my guests during the past five years. Always bear in mind I'm not a Hemingway, a Gunther, nor a Gehman,—just a guy who uses a single finger to punch the typewriter and the other hand once in a while to press the shift key and space bar. And any credit for perfect spelling or good punctuation goes to Anna Marie Goetz and Paris Flammonde. The grammatical errors you'll probably find are there because I insisted on letting them remain so you'll know your author is not a great brain, but a guy who has a thousand stories to tell. And after reading it, if you don't like it, don't ask your book dealer for a refund—just stay stuck. But do me one personal favor—don't let anybody else know that you didn't like it. Let the other marks get their feet wet. After all, the cost of the book isn't all the money in the world, and all of the profits go to a very worthy cause. The name of the cause? Oh, now you know? You're right. The John Nebel Foundation.

CHAPTER 2

> "All we know of the truth is that
> the absolute truth, such as it is,
> is beyond our reach."
> —Nicholas of Cusa

FLYING SAUCERS AND UFO

IT ALL began with Kenneth Arnold, back in 1947, but the groundwork came long before that. Of course, in earlier days they had other names, but UFO (Unidentified Flying Object) have been with us for millions of years, if you believe some saucerologists.

According to the English author Desmond Leslie, a visitor from Venus appeared in the year of 18,617,841 B.C.; his name was *The Sanat Kumara, The Lord of the Flame,* which you'll admit is pretty impressive. Accompanied by *Four Great Lords,* he stopped by to help primitive man become a superior creature. He was only partially successful. Leslie has claimed that later earthians developed a fair civilization of their own—two as a matter of fact: Atlantis and Lemuria. During this far out age the citizens had "air-boats" and "celestial cars," which were the saucers of their day. Back in those days, they even had death ray weapons. In other words, they were ahead of us, particularly in the science department.

Let's face it, if you're going to talk about beginnings, why be pikers? Other saucerites will tell you about later UFO and space ships to arrive on earth, after man got around to writing a little history. Where do they get their information? From Irish, Egyptian, Arabic, Chinese, and almost any other kind of legends you can think of.

Take the late Morris K. Jessup, for instance. His specialty was discovering Biblical "proof" of craft from outer space. In one book he points to evidence in *Kings, Exodus, Psalms, Revelations, St. Matthew, St. Mark* and *St. Luke*. The sub-title of his last book tells his story better than I can. It reads: "An original interpretation of Biblical phenomena which shows that miracles, prophets and mystical aspects of Biblical lore are directly related to UFO." What more can I tell you?

Some ufologists say the great Greek and Roman myths are really about saucers; more prefer the Aztecs and the Incas. Anywhere they find a "sun god," they have it made. "Moon goddesses" aren't bad either.

The first "scientist" to talk about space people was a mystic who lived in the 1700's, named Emmanuel Swedenborg, who wrote about "moon-men" and life on other planets. A few saucerites even claim that Ben Franklin was in touch with spacemen. I heard of another who thought that a man from another world had written the Declaration of Independence.

However, getting into the 20th century, I pass on to Nikola Tesla. This inventor of "alternating current," and other extraordinary things, is the patron saint of one school of saucer people which includes Otis T. Carr, Margaret Storm, and Norman E. Colton. However, I should make it clear that this is a different kind of saucer group. Its interest is not in visitors from other spheres, but in building "anti-gravitational," or "electrical propulsion," or "magnetic force field" space ships to fly to the moon, and similar vacation spots. But more about them in another chapter.

Now we come to the great forerunner of all the sighters, researchers, and contactees—Charles Fort. No man ever collected such a fantastic amount of "evidence" supporting the idea of something "in the sky" as he did. He reported snowflakes "15 inches across and 8 inches thick" and stones, even rocks, falling from the sky. Blue, brown and scarlet moons, and green, blue and black suns were mentioned in his papers. He recorded

23

"masses of jelly" dropping from the clouds, as well as fish, ants, toads, worms, and the like. But the items saucerologists like best are his stories of great black shadows crossing the moon, unidentified shapes against the sun, disappearing stars and flames exploding in the sky. After all, certainly a good percentage of these *must* have been space ships from Mars, Venus and Saturn.

So now that you have a little of the background material, I can say—

Flying saucers all began with the original Kenneth Arnold sighting of "nine discs" near Mt. Rainier on June 24, 1947. A sighting had been reported near Tacoma, Washington, three days earlier, but this was subsequently revealed to be an admitted hoax, and so serious ufologists date everything from the Arnold episode.

Flying over the 14,000 foot peak, the young businessman claimed he saw nine brilliant circular "things," about the size of cargo planes, off one of his wing tips. They were in formation and moving at very high speeds in "a diagonal chainlike line." He estimated them to be about twenty miles away.

Immediately prior to Arnold's experience the first "skyhook balloons" had been sent up, and they have been offered, by some, as an explanation. Others have said that a group of military planes were improperly seen. The most aggressive of the "sighting debunkers," Donald H. Menzel, Professor of Astrophysics at Harvard University, dismisses the Arnold incident as tilting snow-clouds or dust haze reflecting in the sun. But, no matter how you look at it, that was the beginning.

The next major event on the UFO calendar was the tragic case of Captain Thomas Mantell, U. S. Air Force. As usually told, Mantell was sent up, with a couple of other pilots, to investigate a crimson-glowing disc which appeared over the Goodman Field Air Base in Kentucky. One report said that the "saucer" was obviously a craft trailing a violent vermillion exhaust. The captain was still climbing at 10,000 feet when he radioed ". . . it looks metallic and it's tremendous in size . . . it's above me and I'm gaining on it. I'm going to 20,000 feet." That was the last ever heard from Mantell. His partner pilots saw him disappear into the stratospheric clouds. A few moments later he crashed to the earth and was killed. I have heard that the "saucer" was seen again about three hours later, but the Air Force released an improbable and curious explanation of the affair. They claimed that "Mantell had unfortunately been killed while trying to reach the planet Venus."

24

The "Gorman Case" was another interesting bit. This time a young North Dakota pilot, George F. Gorman, was about to land at Fargo. Suddenly he saw a light and moved toward it. It pulled away. After a moment it turned on him in a collision course, scarcely missing him. The attack was repeated, with Gorman just escaping with his life. And then the saucer disappeared, leaving the pilot convinced that "its maneuvers were controlled by thought or reason."

During this time, according to noted ufologist Major Donald E. Keyhoe, the Air Force established agencies to investigate saucers and UFO (Unidentified Flying Objects); among them were "Project Sign," "Project Saucer," "Project Grudge," "Project Twinkle," and "Bluebook." Over the years Keyhoe has taken the position that the Air Force has been withholding vital information regarding UFO from the public. There seems to be evidence on both sides of any argument, since the Air Force has both admitted OFU may exist and denied the possibility.

Possibly the high point in flying saucer history from the conservative point of view was the month of June, 1952. Sightings around the world increased considerably and particularly in our own country. First "discs" in Washington, where it all started. On the 12th another sighting. The next evening several thousand people claimed they saw a big oval craft, trailing a fiery exhaust, over Indianapolis. Captain Richard Case, piloting an American Airlines Convair, is quoted by Major Keyhoe as reporting that it was "a controlled craft of some sort."

Later that night two Pan American pilots, with more than ten years flying time, spotted six "disc-machines" glowing red-hot. These flew in tight formation and moved at about 3,000 miles per hour. A few days later six saucers were seen over Veronica, Argentina.

Three days later reports came in from Boston; a couple of days after that a great silver disc was seen over East Germany; and on it went. Then it really struck home.

Very early on the morning of July 20th, seven "blips" were caught on the radar screen at Washington National Airport. Jets were ordered up to investigate when the radarscope saw the "blips" accelerate from 125 miles per hour to 500 mph, turning at 90° angles as they went. At one point they just stopped in mid-flight and shot off in the opposite direction. One high speed checking device registered them at more than 7,200 miles an hour, for a brief time.

All of this extraordinary activity continued for more than two hours before the jets that had been ordered up arrived, during which time the saucers swept back and forth across the American capitol. When the planes finally arrived, the "things" disappeared; when the ships departed, the saucers returned. At last, at dawn, they left permanently. Permanently?

On the evening of June 26th, the late Capt. Edward J. Ruppelt, former Head of United States Air Force Project "Bluebook," says it was about 10:30 P.M., the saucers returned. For an hour they were tracked by radar and then the orders went out for a jet group to investigate. Again, there was considerable delay in getting the ships airborne, and by the time they got up the saucers had gotten lost.

There was a furor, but the Air Force dismissed the events, at least to the public, as natural phenomena, mass hysteria, misidentified orthodox craft, clouds, dust, and whatever else came to mind.

All kinds of people had all kinds of opinions. One of the more interesting ones was expressed by Dr. Herman Oberth, father of German rocketry and co-creator of the famous "V" rockets of World War II. His position was that flying saucers do exist and that they are intelligently controlled, possibly being interplanetary, probably being inter-stellar. The noted news analyst Frank Edwards also supported this argument.

The years went by and thousands of sightings were reported in this country; tens of thousands around the world. The vast majority always seemed to have logical, even obvious, explanations; but there were inevitably a number left which defied the debunkers.

In 1956, reports Major Keyhoe, the crew of a westbound Navy Super Constellation, crossing the Atlantic, had an amazing experience. Piloted by a naval commander with more than 200 Atlantic crossings and ten years' flight time behind him, the ship was returning to the U.S. some thirty airmen who had been stationed in Europe. Without warning, a cluster of lights was seen below on the ocean surface. Suddenly, one of these lights broke away from the formation beneath and hurled upward towards the plane, flashing past it by inches. Revolving, it began to pace them some hundred yards away, and they saw that it was a monstrous craft, in diameter some four times the breadth of the Constellation's wing span. Constructed like two facing saucers, its center measurement seemed to be about thirty feet, and the rim glowed scarlet as the surface shone metallically.

After a short time the enormous saucer accelerated upwards and disappeared, and when the men looked below they discovered that the others, on the water, had also gone. The officers and men were later questioned exhaustively; but neither they, nor the public, ever received one word of explanation. What can I tell you but to draw your own conclusions.

Almost since the beginning of saucerology the rumors of Air Force and governmental suppression of information have persisted, although you constantly hear that people in the highest places are "in contact" with the UFO. A letter expressing interest in the subject, from Vice President Johnson, was published in the November, 1960, issue of *Fate* Magazine by Curtis Fuller.

The National Investigations Committee on Aerial Phenomena, headed by Major Donald E. Keyhoe, has an executive board crowded with notable persons. The late psychologist Carl Jung expressed some acceptance of them. But all of these advocates for either the open-minded approach to, or the acceptance of, flying saucers have had to face the "official" stand, well supported by the press, that "there ain't no such aerial phenomena."

Gray Barker, the ufologist, has asserted that great pressures have been brought to bear on certain of the saucerologists, his most famous story being about the "three men in black" who supposedly silenced forever the considerable activities of the noted saucer researcher Al Bender.

What can I tell you, neighbors? When you listen to some of the distinguished promoters of ufology, you wonder. When you listen to their opponents you wonder again. It would be easy for me to say to you—"who's got an opinion?" But as we now move from the incredible to the fantastic, I'll admit for neither the first, nor the last, time—I don't buy it.

By now, I should have made it clear that there are two different kinds of flying saucer people. The people I've talked about in the last few pages, such as Major Donald E. Keyhoe and Captain Edward J. Ruppelt, people who might be called the "serious saucer investigators," make up the first type. The second group comprises the ones I'm going to tell you about now; they are the saucerites who claim to have made contact with craft and beings from other planets and galaxies. They're usually called "contactees."

In 1949 a couple of rather vague, half-hearted claims were heard in the UFO circles, but the first important "contact" report came from Daniel W. Fry. It went something like this when he told it to me.

On the Fourth of July, 1950, Dan Fry was working at the White Sands Proving Grounds in New Mexico. Getting a little restless during the evening, he took a long walk out into the desert. After about an hour he thought he saw stars disappearing, and, staring at the part of the sky where this was going on, he began to realize that "an ovate craft about thirty feet in diameter" was approaching him from that direction. Its flight was silent and its color silver-violet. Moments later it landed and Fry went forward to investigate, but a voice from inside told him not to touch the ship as it might be dangerous. Also, and I must admit this is pretty far out the voice referred to him as "pal." As the "conversation" continued, Fry became aware that they were communicating telepathically, which was perfectly natural. The invisible space person reported that the ship was a cargo carrier, remotely controlled from a "mother ship 900 miles above the earth."

"Alan," as the voice was called (as a matter of fact this is the favorite spaceman name), mentioned two reasons for being near the earth. One was to "collect atmosphere," and the second was to contact properly receptive people so that ideas could be exchanged. By this he meant so that he could show these particular earthians how stupid they were and how great all of the space people were. Let's face it, neighbors, the sad truth is that all space people are always superior.

Dan Fry apparently made a great impression because he was invited on a stratospheric joy ride. Entering the saucer, he found an oval room about seven by nine feet, with four contour chairs. Seating himself, he was immediately on his way to New York, which, according to Alan, was about a half-hour trip. In other words, they would be travelling at some 8000 miles an hour. The trip itself seems to have been on the dull side, but his host filled him in on some interesting "historical facts."

Alan told Fry that originally there were two great civilizations on Earth—Lemuria (Mu) and Atlantis. Both were very advanced and very competitive, and eventually approached the verge of war. Neither could win, but they fought anyway and the world was almost brought to an end. The handful of people left divided into two camps. One group gathered at the top of the world and began to build again; this became Tibet, birthplace of all modern civilization. The second camp took four of the most advanced space craft, and although none of the ships had ever gone higher than a thousand miles above the earth, they were used in an attempt to reach another planet. According to space history, three made it, but one was lost forever in infinite space. And, as Dan Fry tells it, the second group drops back to visit the first now and again, which after all is the neighborly thing to do.

Fry also had some highly complicated and rather unusual "scientific theories" which were collected in a slender book a few years ago, but a couple of my scientist friends tell me that what is scientific in Dan's theories is not very unusual, and what is unusual is not very scientific. But I wouldn't know, since I even have a hard time understanding this typewriter I'm using.

Speaking of "Understanding," that is the name of a large, loosely knit organization which considers Dan Fry its leader and guiding light. The last time I heard from Dan, he told me that there were "43 clubs, or 'Units'." "Understanding" sponsors lectures on saucerology, contactology, and brings out small publications from time to time. The lecture portion of "Understanding's" activities, which is by far the largest of the operation, is not a purely spiritual undertaking. Always present is the down to earth miracle of the separation of the silver and the palm, or in translation a dollar and a half or more door charge. If you take that as an average admission, for a lecture in a hall of about 150 people, and not a few halls from two to five times that many seats, the take is two hundred and twenty-five dollars. Deducting fifteen for the room, ten for the mailing, and half-a-yard ($50.00) for the speaker (which all but the really top names are very happy to get), the promoter walks away with 150 for a couple of hours' work—and that takes very little "Understanding."

A couple of years after the Dan Fry story came out, another name exploded on the saucer scene. Today he introduces himself with this business card . . .

Construction Engineer   Analytical Research
Author of Books on Extraterrestrial Beings and Travel
"ABOARD A FLYING SAUCER" $3.00
"VOICE OF THE PLANET CLARION" $1.25
"FACING REALITY" $5.00
Reader, Analyst and Appraiser of Unseen Human Vibrations
TRUMAN BETHURUM
P. O. BOX 1028
PRESCOTT, ARIZONA
The Earth Holds No Secrets From Those Who Know!
APPRAISAL BY SPECIAL APPOINTMENT ONLY

A Californian with little formal education, Bethurum spent most of his working life as a semi-skilled laborer, but that was before the great event. Since then he has been many things, only a few of which are listed on the card above.

It began on Sunday, July 7th, 1952, as he was driving a truck across the desert out of Mormon Mesa. It was early evening, the weather was hot, and Bethurum decided to stop roadside and take a nap. Several hours later he awoke to the sound of foreign tongues" and, peering out of his cab, saw a number of "little men, all less than five feet," clustered around his truck. The strangers, wearing slate uniforms with black caps, had olive skin and jet-black, crew-cut hair.

One of the miniature men spoke to him in English, which surprised Bethurum. Why he expected little men in the middle of both the night and the California desert to speak a foreign language has always been beyond my understanding, but since "Understanding" is Dan Fry's pitch, not mine, what can I say?

Deciding to move with the action a little, he left his truck to join the crowd, and to his "amazement" there was a genuine, 100% really round flying saucer a few yards away. He guesses that it was some 300 feet in diameter, and about 18 feet through the center. It looked like polished silver metal. But the wildest part was that it was just "hung three feet above the ground."

If you hadn't noticed, I might point out that both Fry and Bethurum saw their saucers in July (Dan on the 4th, Truman on the 7th), on both occasions it was evening, in each instance the night was very hot, and both times it was on the desert. Both ships were silvery, both metallic, both were roundish, and so on. But back to the story.

"Have you a captain?" asked Bethurum.

"Surest thing you know," came what I think was a weird kind of answer. But maybe it figures, since the "captain" turned out to be a real swinging chick named "Aura Rhanes."

Over the following few months, Bethurum was visited by the "scow," as the space people called the saucer, several times, and on each occasion he was given a bit more "information" by the beautiful leader of the expedition. He found out that they came from "Clarion . . . a planet beyond the moon," where no one ever had problems and everything was great. According to her, there are a number of populated planets where various people are able to fly through the universe without regard to space, time, heat, cold, or apparently anything else. He also discovered that we are still in kindergarten as far as the science department is concerned, that space people don't want to have their pictures taken, and all like that.

On one visit, "Aura" told him how her people had the power to knock an enemy into "a state of non-existence," but then she assured him that such victims weren't hurt. If you can figure out that gaff, you are better than I am.

By now Truman had been visited by the strange grandmother-gal ten times, and was anxiously awaiting her return, but a full three years went by before he heard from her again. He never explains why the long vacation period.

In November of 1955 she reappeared, but this time without her saucer. Twice she visited the contactee "astrally," meaning only her "spirit body" came to him, and on these occasions she brought a message. (Personally, if she ever visits me, astrally or otherwise, I hope she leaves the "spirit body" back on the planet Clarion and comes down with the physical body; because this gal, according to reports, is built like a brick house—and every brick is positioned in such a way that it's an anatomical master-piece.) He was to collect some friends, the ones with money, and assemble sufficient funds to buy up a large section of land. On this property he was to establish a "Sanctuary of Thought," a commune of "peace, brotherly love," and gaffs like that. Eventually he got together enough loot to pick up the land and get the movement under way. Of course, once it was in operation Bethurum naturally required regular "contributions," which he suggests in his publications ought to be about a sawbuck. He also feels that this sum should be supported by an extra six pieces of green a year. For the true believers he has made several of his "spiritual books" available. One forty-page bit goes for a buck and a quarter, another costs a trey; and the third one you can have if you want to spring for a fin. Bethurum is also available for "readings," "analyses," "appraisals," and other gaffs for a spiritual (sometimes known as a "good") price. But, let's face it, friends, when you are being put on the inside track by one who receives "unseen human vibrations," you have to pay for the privilege of getting with it. And, although you may find it hard to picture, there are always those who want to get "the message" and to a number of people one of the contactees with a pipeline into the unknown is Truman Bethurum.

Shortly after Bethurum's original adventure, another West Coaster began to make a big name for himself. And, as far as

31

I'm concerned, although I don't buy any of these bits, this man's was, and is, the most imaginative, the most beautiful, and the most fascinating of them all. His name is Orfeo Angelucci.

In a manner of speaking, Orfeo's first experience took place even earlier than Kenneth Arnold's.

In August of 1946 Angelucci lost some mold cultures which he had sent up in Navy-type balloons to test the effect of high altitudes upon them. Since they were the work of many months, he was quite upset, but his disturbance was suddenly interrupted by the sight of "a craft" in the sky. Although at the time he had no idea what the strange ship might be, he was told later that it had been a flying saucer. This happened in New Jersey; later he moved to the West Coast where he continued to live for several years.

The actual contacts began in the summer of 1952, when he was living and working in Burbank, California. Getting off the evening shift, it was about half-past-midnight as he drove homeward. Gradually, he became aware of a dim red glow ahead of him. It seemed a dozen times larger than a traffic light and oval in shape. The more he watched, the brighter it got. Although he varied his speed, it always maintained the same distance between them. Orfeo followed along until he found himself on a side road with the glow hovering about thirty feet away, and he stopped. Suddenly, the egg of light leapt upward into the sky. As it went, two brilliant green balls of fire flashed from it and shot toward Angelucci, stopping only a few feet away from the amazed contactee. By now the red glow was gone.

As he studied the new emerald lights, which were each about three feet in diameter, they pulsated. Then, unexpectedly, a strong masculine voice came from the globes of fire. It told him not to be afraid and to get out of his car. He was reminded of the balloons and the unknown craft, and was told that he had been watched ever since that time. Suddenly his attention was drawn to a "crystal cup" sitting on the fender of his automobile. It contained a golden, bubbling fluid which he was told to drink. Downing the liquid, he was immediately rewarded with a wonderful sense of well-being and health. Almost a sensation of radiance. Say, it just dawned on me. Maybe I'd better tell Jackie Gleason about this fluid. And as the interplanetarians say, "To your radiance, Jackie."

As Orfeo just stood there feeling great, the two green discs began to expand until they merged into a three-dimensional screen upon which appeared the head the shoulders of a terrifically good-looking man and woman. Through telepathy he was told that he was one of three persons on Earth who would be contacted by the space people. The other two lived in Rome and India. Each had been selected because, he was told, the meek and humble would inherit the contacts. (To give you a square count, I have not always found this to be the case with the saucerologists.) As the thought waves continued, he was made aware that the strange discs were powered and controlled by tapping the cosmic magnetic force and might be considered "synthetic brains." Further, he found out that the images and voices, which were described as "essentially etheric," were being directed from a "mother ship" far up in the stratosphere. The purpose of the space people, they revealed, (and this came as no great surprise) was to aid in the spreading of the "universal brotherhood of compassion and understanding."

After a few more communications, the couple bid Angelucci goodnight. The screen resolved into the two green, pulsating globes which began to "hum" and, flaring into an "irridescent emerald flame, they shot upward and disappeared in the pitch black sky."

Shaken and bewildered, Orfeo drove home, and collapsed into his bed, where he remained for two days. Unlike other contactees, his reactions to his experiences seem to be just about what one would expect of the average guy. He didn't act like he'd just run into a movie star or congressman.

A couple of months later, Angelucci was returning home one evening. Suddenly, as he crossed a dark, empty lot, he became aware of a great luminescent "bubble." He estimated its height at thirty feet, with a base of about the same measurement; it formed a semi-sphere. In its side opened a door.

Entering, Orfeo was faced with a circular room eighteen feet across, and mostly built of something like glowing mother-of-pearl. Seating himself in the nearest chair, he relaxed with that old feeling of well-being, as mystical music, playing his favorite melody, filled the compartment.

A slight change in pressure made him realize he was in the air. He relaxed as the wall in front of him began to roll back, and he found himself staring out of a nine-foot circular window. Below, in all of its glory, spun the Earth. Stars forever twinkled in the background. He realized that he was thousands of miles above his planet, soaring through space. Tears filled his eyes as he gazed at the wonder of the universe. A voice spoke:

"Weep, Orfeo. Let tears unblind your eyes. For this moment we weep with you for Earth and her Children."

After a short time, the contactee had another fantastic experience. Into his field of vision floated a titanic dirigible-like ship which he pictured as about ninety feet in diameter and over a *thousand feet long!* This was the unbelievable "mother ship."

Swooning under the impact of what was happening to him, Angelucci heard the mysterious voice continue touching one great truth and another. It spoke of ethics, aesthetics, science, medicine, and finally, inevitably it turned to the subject no saucer story neglects—religion. However, unlike the "reports" of many of the contactees, Orfeo's tie-in with religious ideas is tasteful and inoffensive, except possibly to the very sensitive. It certainly is extraordinarily imaginative.

Then, without any warning, the voice announced:

"Beloved friend of Earth, we baptize you now in the true light of the worlds eternal."

Instantly Orfeo was blinded by a burst of white light, almost losing consciousness! He felt "aware" of many previous incarnations and by the time he was completely himself he was lying in his own bed in his own home on his own planet, again.

Later the owner of the voice, who was named Neptune, visited him in person for a brief period and then vanished, possibly to the other side of the universe.

Now Angelucci had a quiet period. No space ships, no contacts, no action, no nothing. Well, that's not exactly true. During this time he participated in a "Flying Saucer Convention," which also included such famous saucer names as George Adamski, George Van Tassel, and Truman Bethurum. As might be expected, the pitch was a red one. And for the unintiated, on a midway that means a real success.

One afternoon, as he lay on his living room sofa, Angelucci fell into what can only be called a trance state. But as he sank deeper and deeper, he also felt himself wake wider and wider into another strange and unknown world. An astral world, a spiritual world. Looking down at himself, he found that his sickly, frail figure had been replaced by a perfectly formed Adonis-type body in a gold and white toga kind of thing. As his eyes wandered about the room, he heard the sound of distant thunder. Then a door across the chamber opened, and a gorgeous gal walked in. Her hair was long and golden, her eyes were large and blue.

Let me interrupt this tale for a moment. My friends claim that I've been in the trance state for years. But I've still got this sickly, frail body. In fact, when I go to the beach, the guys throw sand on me and great-looking chicks walk by—and I mean right by me. And now back to the Angelucci story.

Orfeo flipped when she called him Neptune, but out there on other planets somebody can be you, you can be somebody else, someone can be himself. You know, I don't know what that last sentence means. But for real, that's what Angelucci told me.

Lyra, which was her name, was followed in, unfortunately, by a golden boy who went by the name Orion. As they tried to explain a few things to him, he got the idea that this was what was left of a world of a long, long time ago. The way his space friends told it, once upon a time the good guys and the bad guys had it out, and the bad guys, led by Lucifer, lost. Earth, he was told, was composed of many people who were Luciferians, and many who were not. As for Lucifer himself, he's right here on Earth in an unidentified form—but the space people were not able to divulge who he was at this particular time.

I must admit, neighbors, that this part of Orfeo's story had me going for a while. As a matter of fact, some of us used to sit around just guessing who Lucifer might be impersonating today, and offering evidence to back up our opinions.

Among the wild experiences enjoyed by the contactee were super-suppers, profound philosophy, and a moment of mystical communion with Lyra which made old-fashioned earth-type sex dull as rocket-wash. But Orfeo does admit that as long as one is hung up on earth the usual relationships between men and women are approved. But back to the other worlds of Orfeo Angelucci.

After a week of this visit to a small planet, the happy contactee found himself awakening from his lengthy nap on his own drawing room couch. Actually, at that time he remembered nothing of his astral adventure. It did not all come clear to him for about six or seven months.

At the conclusion of this "first phase" of Angelucci's story, he had a "vision" of the Lord. Not a visitation, mind you, just a personal insight. A short time later he was visited for the last time by the original voice, Neptune. And that was that—for the moment. However, once the story was circulated, the Angelucci clan began to grow. His name rose rapidly to the top ranks of saucerologists. Lectures, articles and books came from him, and it was all of this action that led him into the second, and even more amazing, phase of his fabulous adventure.

CHAPTER 3

"A new, unnatural cross between
A mystic, monster, and machine."
—Sir Alan Patrick Herbert

FIVE-INCH BLONDES AND
THREE WILD GEORGES

ORFEO ANGELUCCI had become an important name in the flying saucer field by 1954. His book dealing with his original contacts with people from other planets had attracted a great many followers. But after much publicity and many lectures, his health began to fail him again, and he decided to retire to a small cottage in the High Desert, near Twenty Nine Palms, California, home of the celebrated "lady" of like nomenclature.

One evening, a few weeks prior to Christmas, he drove into that small community to have dinner in the town cafe. Entering the restaurant, he was struck by the dynamic presence of a young man seated there.

"Hello, Orfeo," greeted the stranger, who announced that he might be called "Adam."

Ordering two steaks and dismissing the waitress, the young man offered Orfeo "a very rare champagne." Handing Angelucci an ivory-colored pellet, he pointed to one of the water tumblers, and the contactee dropped the tablet into it. Orfeo was fascinated as he saw the glass become a goblet of bubbling amber nectar, and he recognized it as the magic potion of before. Drinking it down, he began to feel the same strange and wonderful sensation of well-being.

Soon Adam revealed that he was a physician from Seattle who, although less than forty, had but a few months of life left —at least on this Earth. He admitted that when he learned his fate he left his practice for a period of contemplation and decision. As Adam spoke, the two men became aware of a third, empty, and unused tumbler on the table. It began to glisten and suddenly filled with the golden nectar. Staring at the glass, they heard the soft hypnotic strains of etheric music—and they were stunned. Before them, a vision was beginning to form in the image of an exquisite miniature woman dancing in the glass. She was radiantly beautiful, magnificently formed, and no more than five inches tall. Her eyes were a brilliant emerald green, her hair was long and golden, and her flesh was tinted ivory and rose. She was barely concealed by a transparent silken robe.

Incidentally, on the air I quickly reminded Orfeo that I thought we had run up against a minor semantic difficulty because, as I often say, it's a family show. And I suggested to Orfeo that the robe was possibly translucent, rather than transparent.

Her whole body pulsated, faster and faster into a frenzy of excitement and passion. The music grew wilder and madder. A collision of cymbals! A crush of drums! And the tiny creature dropped to her knees, exhausted. In moments she began to fade. In a minute she was gone—completely.

Then Adam began his fantastic tale.

One evening, as he was walking in the desert, he reports, he became aware of a yellow-orange light circling overhead. Music floated down from it. As he stared, the light dimmed and disappeared; but simultaneously a voice from nowhere spoke:

"Adam, may I speak with you?"

He was astonished, but that was nothing to what he felt as he saw a mist began to form in front of him. Soon he realized that it was taking the shape of a shimmering silver dome-designed spacecraft. It was solid and real, and so was the inescapable "beautiful woman" who stepped out.

I should mention immediately, for the benefit of the prophets out there, that the gal was not Orfeo's friend of other worlds,

Lyra, and she was not a large economy-size version of the five-inch blonde. But, nevertheless, when she invited Adam for a trip into "a new estate," he accepted gratefully, and they entered the spaceship.

As the flight got under way, she told him her name was Vega. Prattling on, as women will, about the great mysteries of the universe (and she had the answers to many of them), she remarked that they were traveling at ten million miles an hour. You have to admit that's fast. But, I understand, it's rough on gas.

As they sped from one solar system to another, during which time Vega was more than a little friendly, she admitted that neither her people, nor her "peers," had achieved the speed of light. (Naturally, you have to expect pseudo-science once in a while, even from space people.) After a while he discovered that Vega was from Alpha Centauri, where they're—wouldn't you know it—many centuries ahead of our world.

During these intimate hours with Vega, she assured Adam that, although they were playing around "an outpost of love," soon they wouldn't even remember each other. However, she did guarantee him that before long he'd run into another woman of her race, and that she'd be the greatest. His anticipation was a little dampened when she also told him that the new girl, who'd be named "Launie," would be considered somewhat "retarded" among her own kind. Vega, in a flash of amazing modesty, added, however, that compared to "Launie," even she was nothing.

Finally, after passing from one experience to another, Adam's saucer was ushered into an enormous "mother ship." This mechanical monstrosity was shaped like two facing saucers, and was some ten miles in diameter. It housed half a million persons.

In this fantastic craft, or floating city, which he called "Andromeda," the physician from Earth encountered an endless series of amazing things, places and people. One of the most important of these was a girl named "Lily," with whom he became pretty involved. All of which was somewhat confusing, since he was on the lookout for this chick named "Launie," who had been strongly touted to him. Later, it turned out that "Lily" was "Launie," "Launie" was "Lily"—and, like I said before, I don't dig that any more than you do. He also got to know some of the top men around the action, meeting Orfeo's friend "Neptune" and other such people.

Then came the last of the out-of-this-world females Adam was to meet. Her name was "Aleva," but that ended up, unfortunately and obviously, as "Eve."

These two entered upon the adventure to end all adventures. This was the most. Adam and his gal took a space ship, and traveling at 50,000,000 (that's fifty million) miles an hour, plummeted into the center of the sun! That's the way Orfeo tells it. Adam and his fair-faced friend zoomed into the sun and out again. And let's face it, neighbors, that's a pretty wild stunt.

Eventually, Adam got back to Earth and, I suppose, died. Orfeo wrote the story, which made for his second successful book.

Today, Angelucci still lives on the West Coast. He writes and lectures, and tells his extraordinary tales. Once in a while he gets to New York, and we have lunch and chat. And every time I'm more impressed than before. He's one of a kind in a life made up of one-of-a-kinds. But what else can I tell you about the amazing and charming guy named—Orfeo Angelucci.

* * * * *

"I am George Adamski, philosopher, student, teacher, saucer researcher." That's the way George introduces himself in one of his early books, and who's going to disagree? He lives *near* the famous astronomical observatory at Mount Palomar, California, conducting his investigations of ships from outer space with two telescopes of his own—a 15" housed one and a 6" portable job.

In his version it all began on October 9th, 1946, during a shower of meteors over San Diego. As the atmospheric disturbance came to a close, he and his party suddenly (remember, it almost always happens "suddenly") noticed a gigantic dirigible overhead—but it disappeared almost at once.

Less than a year passed George had his second sighting. On this occasion he witnessed 184 "bright objects" wheeling about the sky, reversing in mid-flight, and speeding off in the opposite direction. He later ascertained that there were really 204 of the "things."

He continued to notice various of these phenomena through his telescopes and photographed many of them—more than 500, he claims,—although he does admit that not more than a dozen of the pictures offer "proof that these craft were different from recognized Earth craft." During these years Adamski wrote many articles and gave many lectures on flying saucers, interplanetary travel and the possibility of life on other planets. As a matter of fact, it must have become obvious to the saucer people, or anyway to the professional saucer sighters, that things were getting a little monotonous. After all, how many sightings is the public going to read about before it gets bored with the whole deal? True, Dan Fry had created a little stir with his bit in 1950, but that hadn't turned into action. Then things began to move. First the original Orfeo Angelucci tales, then Adamski's "man from Venus" report.

It was noon, Thursday, November 20th, 1952, and George was cruising out on the desert near Parker, Arizona, with some friends. George Hunt Williamson, who has built a reputation in the saucer and occult fields, was there along with four or five others taking scenic photographs. Unexpectedly (which is almost the same as *suddenly*), an enormous, cigar-shaped, silver ship appeared above them, and hung motionlessly. In a few moments Adamski "got the feeling" he should go "down the road" to meet some space people. Leaving the group, he ventured along the sand. Before long he saw a circular "scout ship," obviously from no local airline, and standing nearby was a man from another world. The stranger was small in stature, light in weight, slightly oriental in appearance, long-haired, and as pretty as a picture—a picture of "an unusually beautiful woman," that is.

Exchanging some fast sign language, Adamski discovered he was from Venus, that his saucer came from a huge "mother ship," and other fascinating "facts." After a while they got tired of talking and the spaceman took off, leaving behind, silhouetted against the golden desert, the strong silent figure of George Adamski—friend to men from other worlds.

But that was only the beginning. The world was to hear much more about space ships, space men, and life on other planets. And from whom? George Adamski, of course.

On February 18th, 1953, he was picked up at his Los Angeles hotel by Firkon, a Martian, and Ramu, a Saturnian. They took him to meet their friend, and his, Orthon—the man from Venus.

Soon George was being treated to a tour of inspection of a space craft which was not too different from the one Dan Fry rode in. And like that fortunate gentleman, Adamski found himself suddenly airborne. A huge chart flashed and flickered, a huge panel of buttons were pressed and punched, and it was wild. About eight miles up they approached a 2,000 foot long, 150 foot thick, cigar-shaped "mother ship." Naturally, they flew right inside and landed.

He finally ended up in a Radio City type lobby with a Bardot-

41

built blonde Venusian chick. Her eyes were "gentle and merry." The second was even greater, and was a brunette whose eyes, according to George, promised anything but mere gentleness and merriment. Her name was Ilmuth—which, let's face it, sort of killed the whole thing right there. She was strictly from Marsville. Far out, that is.

But then came the big moment. George Adamski met a portrait. A "symbol of Ageless Life." Which he tells us left a far deeper and more profound impression on him than the super-sexy set of space gals. And although he devotes three pages to them and only a half page to it, I certainly don't doubt it.

Most of the time on the "mother ship" was spent asking questions. He discovered, along with other contactees, the following: All other planets have superior architecture, science, engineering and medicine to that of the earth; people of this planet were the only ones in the Universe capable of "evil," war, crime, emotional imbalance, and everyone else is just about perfect. Furthermore, he found out that the ship he was on was at that time 50,000 miles above the Earth. Given an opportunity to visit the immensities of space, George thought it looked like "billions upon billions of fireflies . . . flickering everywhere, moving in all directions as fireflies do."

As they started back to George's personal planet, he was introduced to a great sage, a universal wise man, who was almost 1,000 years old. It was from him that Adamski received the real message. It went about like this.

In space there are innumerable planets, pretty much like the Earth. Each moves around a sun, pretty much like our sun. In each case there are twelve planets in a system. Twelve such systems are whirling around a sort of super-sun, creating what our scientists call an island universe. Twelve island universes spin about something else, and twelve of these swing around . . . and so on, without end.

Many planets are populated, but most are so advanced that we Earthians couldn't possibly understand them. Fortunately, however, and so maybe we'll get to visit the rich relatives yet. Another very encouraging thing to know is that we're not the stupidest people in the universe—just in this solar system.

After assuring George Adamski that the space people were only coming to Earth to help us—which is, I believe, what every conqueror in history has told the victims—they brought him home.

A couple of months later he ran into Firkon, on the street as it were, and they stopped in a small cafe to chat. Frankly, when I heard the Martian's order, it broke me up. Peanut butter on whole wheat bread, apple pie and black coffee. How American can a foreign planet spy disguise himself?

Finishing their snack, they hopped out to another and much larger model of flying saucer. But the quick spin up to the mother ship was pretty conservative from a contactee point of view.

These neighborly visits continued until August 23, 1954, when Firkon admitted to Adamski that the visit of the moment was to be the last.

During his adventures, Adamski "took many photographs" of the craft, which is pretty exciting—until you see the pictures, and then you pays your money and you takes your choice.

Over the years, Adamski has sold many thousands of books, and given hundreds of lectures in the United States and elsewhere. He's one of the really big men in the flying saucer field. He tells great stories. Too tall to see over, but not too thick to see through. But it's a pretty good living.

* * * * *

The first contactee I ever met was George Van Tassel, owner and operator of Giant Rock Airport, a private landing strip at Yucca Valley, California.

One night he and his wife were sleeping out in the middle of the desert when he was awakened by an odd man in a ski-type uniform. Having identified himself as "Solganda," the spaceman, he told George to follow him, which Van Tassel did. In moments they were standing beneath a flying saucer hanging above the earth. Overhead, in the belly of the ship, was a hole, and as he moved forward with Solganda, both were caught up in an anti-gravitation stream and lifted into the craft.

Looking about, George observed that there were a couple of pilots at the controls of the ship, but this small crew was bypassed without a word. With a "snap of the thumb"(!) seats appeared out of the wall, with a second snap a cabinet opened up and displayed expansion-contraction uniforms which adjusted to fit all sizes.

Conducted below the deck, Van Tassel was permitted to see the counter-wheeling rotors, which were the propelling machinery of the ship, functioning.

After this extremely brief visit he was escorted out of the

saucer and back to his wife and desert bed. As he left, Solgandâ assured him that they would be back. But that was in 1953, and at this writing the good contactee was strictly a one-time man in the contact department. But never fear, if he lost out on the physical meeting level, he really started to swing on the telepathic plane. In fact, you get the impression that he operates with an almost "open line" to the etheric spheres.

Regardless, from his telepathic contact with the other planets, George Van Tassel has been able to collect the information which forms the contents of his several books. (Unlike the traditional messiahs, who had disciples to write their teachings for them, the contactees, taking no changes, almost always write them themselves. Usually several volumes at several bucks apiece.)

Actually, it makes little difference which one of Van's volumes you read, because, for the most part, if you've read one you've read them all. There are literally hundreds of phrases, sentences, and even paragraphs, that appear word for word in all of his writings. Let me quote the dedication to one of them, "Into This World and Out Again,":

"This book is dedicated to the people from other life levels in space. The 4th density center of the Quadra-Sector, Blaau. The Council of Twelve Lords in our solar system. The Council of Seven Lights on Shanchae. The Space Station Schare (Share-ee) and all its complement of guardians. Also the active participants in the reception of this information at the College of Universal Wisdom."

I think that it's only fair to tell you at this point that if you understand the above passages it'll be a waste of time for you to read further. You already have the message clasped in your hot, damp little kooky hand. However, I must admit that you "ain't heard nothin' yet," because if that dedication ain't nothin' I don't know what isn't.

One of George Van Tassel's major activities is the operation of the "Universal College of Wisdom," and its through this organization and its publication, "Proceeding," that he's able to spread the message. And quite a message it is.

To begin with, he's sort of rewriting the Bible. Particularly the Book of Genesis. Some of that enlightened Van Tassel material instructs that Man was created of the Adamic race. He was a spaceman. Eve was the highest form of animal. Instead of Adam mating with one of his own kind, and Eve mating with one of her animal kind, they mated with each other. This was the original violation. To quote Van Tassel, "not in eating the apple; it was in eating the *wrong* apple."

At one point a little later, he comments that "the space people were the first human forms of life to occupy the Earth." In other words the "humans" were space people. But elsewhere he takes the opposite position when he insists that "the Earth people (not the space people) are called 'humans'."

With regard to Jesus Christ, George asserts he was the last space teacher to be introduced to Earth via normal birth, adding however that *"Joseph was a foster father to Jesus. There was no blood of Joseph in Jesus."* Which certainly seems to contradict his claim that it was a "normal birth." On another occasion he claims that *"Mary volunteered for the assignment* (!!!) *of bringing through birth—to the Earth—a true son of our Adamic race* (that is, the space people.). *Jesus also accepted the assignment knowing beforehand what his earthly birth would entail* (reincarnations carefully woven in later on). *Mary became pregnant and was landed on the Earth by one of our ships."*

By this time, I feel pretty sure that it won't come as any great surprise when I tell you that, according to Van, the Star of Bethlehem was a flying saucer hanging around to keep an eye on everything. It should also be noted that this same craft has been orbiting about the Earth for many thousands of years, and will be the method employed to return Jesus to this planet for the Second Coming.

If, at this point, you feel that he has thrown in everything but the Great Pyramid of Gizeh in Egypt, you're wrong. He has that, too, describing it as being some 25,816 years old (but of course that was a couple of years ago).

And then there are George's "little men" who live below the surface of the moon. Or—

"Contrary to the opinions expressed by our scientists, the center of our planet consists of a sun. This sun, as the core, rotates in the opposite direction to the moving crust." Or—

Space people maintain a space station that has orbited Mars for thousands of years. Ten miles in diameter, it is noted by our astronomers as a Martian moon. Or—

There are many visitors from Venus wandering about the Earth without being recognized. Or—

Light does not travel at approximately 186,000 miles per

second, as our scientists have believed for some time; it travels at either 202,000 miles per second, or at 388,000 per second. (I must admit that I can't remember if it travels at any of the other available speeds in between.) Or—

Some of our top scientists, government officials, teachers, are from outer space, but their minds have been "blanked" until their comrades take over.

One would imagine that the creation of a new version of the Holy Scriptures would be enough for one man, or a contact with people from outer space, or being the recipient of fantastic and revolutionary extra-terrestrial information; but none of these have fulfilled the need, or possibly he would call it "the work" of George Van Tassel. As has been mentioned before, he operates an airport and has established and is building the "College of Universal Wisdom." But there is more. Van is also responsible for the plans for a "rejuvenation machine," and for the efforts which are supposed to lead to the building of a great laboratory near the "College" to house it. But this remarkable device we'll discuss later in the book, along with the other amazing machines of our time. At the moment we've been concerned with George's activities where they were involvd with the extraordinary flying saucer phenomenon. And I suppose we've touched on most of his action in this area—but not quite. Annually, George Van Tassel promotes and directs the topper of them all, his "Interplanetary Spacecraft Convention."

From all over the country, and even beyond, come the messiahs of this and almost any other world you can think of, and many you can't. There are lectures, talks, classes, conferences, pamphlets, books, magazines, records and tapes for those who would like to convince—and for those who would like to be convinced. And who pays attention to such nonsense? Some of the top newspapers in the country and magazines like *Life* and *Harpers*.

And so George Van Tassel seldom leaves the close comfort and security of his airport and immediate followers, but he's not resting. There's always something new. In 1960 he suddenly appeared, buttoned, bannered and boosted, running for the presidency of the United States. This year America, tomorrow the world? Who knows what world he, and the "space people," have in mind? Certainly not this one. But you can't deny that a man selling a mixture of unequal parts of mysticism, occultism, religion, contactology, ESPology, and plain social politics is merchandising a strong mixture. And there are an awful lot

46

of people who don't agree with me when I tell George Van
Tassel that I don't buy the bit.

* * * * *

George King of England—is what he calls himself, and you
can't be sure whether he's pausing after "George," or after
"King," but it doesn't really matter because after about three
minutes you get the idea strong and clear. This is the third and
last of the trio of Georges who wield great influence around the
world where flying saucer people meet.

King claims that his first contact came during May, 1954,
as he stood in his London flat washing dishes. Before this, he
says, he had never heard of saucers. And then that afternoon
came the voice:

*"Prepare yourself, you are to become the voice of Inter-
planetary Parliament!"*

And, for the moment, that was all there was; but eight days
later the real action began. He was in his apartment again when
he heard a "rustling" and, looking up, he saw a ghost-like thing
passing through the closed door. It was the "projection" of a
famous living Earthian, who told the ex-cabbie what the contact
was all about. He was to be the representative on this planet of
the people from other worlds.

Today, if you ask George why he was selected above all
others to perform this extraordinary task, he mumbles something
about having once taken a couple of courses in Yoga, and that
he "supposes the space people thought he was the right man for
the job," and all that gaff. But if you press him he falls back
on the most often heard phrase in the entire history of saucerology, the mystical and the occult:

"I'm sorry, but I'm not permitted to divulge that information
at this time . . ."

Since that second contact, the first physical one, King has
been in constant touch with the space men. He speaks to them
telepathically almost daily.

At first the word was delivered via lectures, with a few
trances thrown in when things were slow. But when the ball got
rolling he was able to form the "Atherius Society," which was
named after the "main communicator." The purpose of the
group was to pass along the messages the spiritual Mr. King received from outer space. This being mainly accomplished through
personal appearances and a little magazine named "Cosmic
Voice," which is sub-titled "Mars and Venus Speak to Earth."

47

This incredible thirty-two page pamphlet comes out six times a year and is edited by the King of the contactees, George. It carries material that's often unbelievable, and usually massively tasteless, but it is well-designed to appeal to the gullible, the lonely, the old, the tired, and the foolish.

In the "Cosmic Voice," the British contactee has announced that his mother *Mary* (please note) *King* has met people from Mars and Venus, entered their space ships, and taken trips in same. One issue describes such a blasphemous caper somewhat as follows:

Mary King was flying high in a Martian spacecraft when she was told that she was to meet two Venusians. Suddenly they appeared and she recognized one as . . . "our dear Jesus." According to this offensive "report," Christ called her "little sister of the Earth," and asked if she had brought along a book by her son, George. Fortunately she had thought to do so, and so Christ took the volume and said:

"Oh, Supreme Master of all Creation,
Higher than the Highest,
Mightier than the Mightiest,
Greater than all Greatness,
We bring to Thee this offering in great Love and humility
From our beloved brother of Earth—George—
The one Whom Thou didst choose to be a leader
Among men of Earth, in this their New Age."

In conclusion, Jesus told her to tell George that . . . "this Book is now and forever will be—Holy."

Upon her return to Earth, her son interviewed her about her trip.

"He did speak to you about the time when you were alive when Jesus was on Earth and He also told you of your contract with Jesus in those days?" (I don't have to point out that this is a slightly leading question.)

"Yes, definitely," she replied. *"He told me who I was in a former incarnation; it explained my intense love of the Master Jesus."* (The implication here is both too obvious and too offensive to explain.)

"He also mentioned," King continued, *"the fact that I had had a previous incarnation in a certain place?"* (Follow the leader!)

"Oh, yes, definitely true," she replies unexpectedly.

And on and on it goes, building the myth higher and higher. While King admits that he has no saucer of his own, and that he has had no invitations to go flying about in one, he still has collected a library full of information unavailable to Earthians. For instance, he tells us that Juperterians don't "breathe as we do." Of course, if you wish a further explanation, you'll have to get it from him. The Saturnians have a somewhat simpler situation; they have "still bodies," and they live several dozen lives, which is pretty impressive when he adds that any one of these life-spans is about 60,000 years long.

As far as space travel is concerned, it will all seem quite clear to you, if you understand that the larger craft achieves the velocity of "V-12!" Which means, of course, the speed of light to the twelfth power. Naturally, he doesn't mean that it flies that fast in this dimension. This is in the 16th or 17th dimension—but I suppose that was automatically understood.

During an appearance on my radio show, George King had what I consider a wild exchange with the great comic Jackie Gleason. I think that it put contactees of his type in their proper perspective. It came about in this way.

On a previous occasion, having stopped by during one of the saucer broadcasts, Jackie had made an offer of $10,000 cash to anyone who could produce conclusive evidence that there was higher intelligent life on other planets. Without mentioning the famous comedian's name, I told King that such an offer had been made and that if he could fulfill its demands, I'd have that small fortune for him by noon the following day. First King asked what I meant by "evidence," and then said that it made no difference, since he could not accept the challenge even if ten million dolars was offered. At this point a call came in on my private line and I had it transferred to the "beeper phone" (an arrangement which permits both sides of a phone conversation to be broadcast). It was Jackie Gleason wanting to discuss the entire matter with the English contactee. Their exchange went exactly like this (and I'm quoting from the tape):

GLEASON: How are you?

KING: Very well, thank you.

GLEASON: Are these people from outer space good friends of yours?

KING: I believe that they are friends of mine, yes.

GLEASON: Could you call upon them for assistance? For in-
             stance, if you were in some sort of legal difficulty,
             embracing some part of their recognition of you,
             would they come to your aid?

KING: Under those circumstances, they would help, yes.

GLEASON: If I were, for instance, to say to you that you are
             a bare-faced liar, now you know you could sue
             me for libel, right?

KING: Yes, yes.

GLEASON: Now do you think that you could get any legal
             assistance from them in a case like this?

KING: No, I don't.

GLEASON: Why?

KING: Why should they help?

GLEASON: Well, you're championing their cause.

KING: No, no, I'm not. I'm trying to give a spiritual
             message, which I believe to be good for all
             people . . .

GLEASON: Why do we need a spiritual message from some-
             one in a flying saucer?
             Don't we have enough from Christ, Buddha,
             Moses . . . men like that?

KING: Do we live by those teachings?

GLEASON: Yes, I do.

KING: You do? Then you're the first Christian I've
             ever seen.

GLEASON: You mean that no one lives by the laws of
             Buddha, or Christ, or . . .

KING: I never met anyone.

GLEASON: By the way, do you know that every time you are
            uncertain when you say something, you cough.
            Do you know what that means psychologically?
            In other words, you cough every time you tell
            a lie.

KING: Do I?

GLEASON: Now, George, look at the juicy opportunity you
            have. Here's a guy that you're talking to that's
            got a lot of dough. You can sue me for maybe a
            million dollars . . . and maybe get it. And all you
            have to do to get it is to bring one of your friends
            from Mars to O.K. this thing. And then you win.

KING: I've already answered this question. There isn't a
            man on Earth who could do this.

GLEASON: In other words, you have absolutely no proof
            from these people whom you are championing?
            You have absolutely no backing from anybody
            from outer space for what you say?

KING: Just a moment, please. Just one minute.

GLEASON: I'm waiting . . . and cough a little bit.

KING: I shall put this phone down in a moment.

GLEASON: Yes?

KING: I'm a guest here, you see.

GLEASON: Not in my house, you're not a guest. I think
            you're a phoney!

KING: C L I C K !

And so ended the conversation between one of America's
best-known comics and one of England's best-known contactees.
The last I heard, George King of England was still table-

51

hopping from religion to space travel to religion to yoga to life on other planets to religion to ESP to contact with Martians and Venusians to religion, because that is what Mr. and Mother King are selling—a 20th century Messiah with a 21st century religion. It has a little something for anybody, and in the long run a lot of nothing for everybody—except, of course, George King and his Mom.

* * * * *

As one hears the various stories which gather followers unto the different contactees, it becomes apparent that each one has specialized in one or two particular slants, but none ever approached the absurdity, conscious or unconscious, of the tale of "Bo, the 385-pound Venusian Dog," as related by the Ozark farmer Buck Nelson.

Colorado-born Nelson, who tells his story with more vanity than grammar, and less conviction than confusion, has been a rural and urban laborer for most of his life. Finally, after having traveled in all of the states and several foreign countries, he settled down in the back hills of Missouri.

I first met Buck at the Van Tassel "Fourth Interplanetary Space Convention" on May 11th, 1957. At that time he was selling small envelopes of . . . but I'll hold that, since it would be getting ahead of my story.

It seems that on an afternoon in July, 1956, Nelson stepped outside his house and saw three immense "disc-like objects" hanging overhead. As he signaled at the ships with a flashlight, he was struck by a "ray," and he describes the effects:

". . . I had suffered, off and on, from lumbago in my back and neuritis in my side and arm, for fifteen years. When I started to get up, easy-like, I was surprised because I felt no pain."

From then on, apparently, Buck was visited by the space craft quite frequently, and on one occasion he made his initial contact. A saucer arrived, landing in his back pasture, and three men and a giant dog got out. One was a late relative and expatriate named "Bucky," who was, at that time, residing on Venus. The second member of the crew seemed to be an apprentice, and the third was 200 years old, but looked 20. But the star attraction was "Bo"—a 385 pound Venusian shaggy dog.

This canine monster was left with Nelson, and it was during this period, when he was dutifully brushing and combing the great space hound, that he was able to collect the considerable amount of shaggy Venusian dog hair that he later offered for sale to the public at the Fourth Interplanetary Space Convention at Yucca Valley, California.

It was not long before Buck Nelson, like almost all of the other saucerologists, decided that his stories should be spiced up with a touch of religion. To begin with, in an atrociously badly printed little booklet about his "adventures," Nelson is compared to "JOHN THE BAPTIST." Eventually, this messianic complex hit its high point when Nelson announced that he had been given "THE TWELVE LAWS OF GOD . . . ON VENUS." When you read them you find that they're rather badly re-written Biblican commandments. Why Buck didn't feel that Moses had done an adequate job, no one has discovered. Although there is a good deal more to Nelsonic theology that is unlike the scriptures promoted by other contactees, none of it is particularly exciting or imaginative.

It is my impression that Buck Nelson has made very little money out of his wild, if somewhat crude, stories, but there are those who believe in him, many for just that reason. Frankly, I suspect that he would change this aspect of his activities if he could, but it just didn't seem to be in the cards that he should make out in the way that Adamski, Van Tassel, King and several others have. Maybe his very nearness to the earth, to the hills, is part of his appeal. But to me there is something rather pathetic about this 60-year-old, fragmentarily successful contactee—Buck Nelson of the Ozarks.

CHAPTER 4

"Is life, then, a dream and delusion
And where shall the dreamer awake?"

SATURNIAN LOVERS AND VENUSIAN MISTRESSES

HOWARD MENGER's story begins when he was ten years old, at which time he was living in High Bridge, New Jersey. It was 1932 and, according to the contactee, he and his brother had been sighting "discs in the sky" all summer long. Eventually one of the weird objects landed in a nearby field so that the children were able to see that it was a glimmering metallic circle. Other "discs" hovered above, but soon all vanished in the distant sky.

Not long afterward, Howard was walking in the local woods when suddenly he saw "the most exquisite woman" he'd ever seen. She was haloed by the sun and her long golden hair. Her skin was lily-petaled and her eyes were flecked with gold. Through her translucent ski-suit she was really stac . . . that is, she was possessed of aesthetically stimulating and artistically valid contours which activated the spiritual impulse to an accentuated degree. Or, to put it in Howard's words, "It was a tremendous surge of warmth, love and physical attraction which

54

emanated from her to me." Which, let's face it, is a pretty good reaction for a ten-year-old lad to feel. If Lolita had known about this, she could have gone around with guys her own age.

The conversation with the girl in the woods was pretty brief, and then she departed.

In 1942, while serving in the U.S. (not Royal Neptunian) Army, Menger saw "discs" again. But like other illogical contactees, he assumed that only he had had the sightings, so they went unmentioned. During this same period he visited Juarez, Mexico, on a pass. While in this small, but notorious, south-of-the-border community, he was accosted by a man in a cab who had shoulder-length blonde hair. Understandably he declined the invitation.

Later Howard, who by this time had acquired a wife and son, was approached by a man wearing an army uniform. This stranger mentioned the girl on the rock in the woods, the queer fellow in the cab, and told Menger how the space people had been in contact with the Mexicans for centuries. After passing along a bit more of this inside material, he, too, disappeared. Shortly thereafter Howard was sent to Hawaii.

On this traditionally romantic island things began to look up interplanetary-communication-with-the-space-people-wise. Following his arrival, Howard discovered a number of caverns along the shore. One evening, finishing his work, he had a psychic impulse to visit them. As he arrived at the beach caves in a "borrowed" jeep, he saw the figure of a (surprise!) magnificently beautiful brunette, with great dark eyes, emerge from the shadows. She was dressed in an almost transparent pair of pajamas with a tunic top; the pink and misty material revealed the slow sensuous curves of her flawless body. Her lithe movements made him feel like . . .

The point I'm making is that when Howard talks about having a "physical contact," he doesn't beat around the bush—it's physical as all get-out.

Anyway, this wild chick identified herself as being from Mars, tossed off a couple of offhand prophecies and melted into the great beyond, or beside, or behind, or—she vacated the scene.

Not long after this, Menger got the telepathic message to go rendezvousing around the caverns again, and let's face it, with the chance of meeting one of those blonde Venusians or brunette Martian females, it didn't require much persuading to flip him on his merry way. Unfortunately, the visitor turned out to be a

Venusian man. He came loaded with off-beat information, telling the Earthian that there is no death; disappointingly Howard discovered that the spaceman meant "spiritual" death, which he had known all along. The stranger further asserted that names were of no importance, that our side was going to win the war (I don't know what the space people told the Germans, Italians and Japanese during the war), that Germany was very advanced technically, and things like that.

Finally the war ended, Menger was discharged, and he returned to the New Jersey countryside and a livelihood of sign-painting. One day in June of 1946, although living several communities away, he had the impulse to visit his old woodland haunts, where his first contact had taken place. He had spent an hour or so wandering about the glade and was preparing to leave when he suddenly saw a "tremendous flash of light" and felt "heat on the back of my neck." Overhead was a spinning globe of radiance whose brilliance began to diminish until it took the form of a metallic, bell-shaped craft which slowly descended, coming to rest on the ground nearby.

A moment passed and a trap-door opened. Two well-built men with long yellow hair emerged wearing slate blue ski-suits. They were followed by a (surprise! surprise!) beautiful woman. Not just any beautiful woman—this was the lady of the woods. Amazingly, she looked just the same as she had on the first occasion, in 1932. However, this was understandable to Howard when he was told that at that time she was over 500 years old. Laughing, teasing, and winking her way through a very mystical conversation during which she told him, in effect, that this was only the beginning, she went the way of all space people—into thin air.

The months went by; Howard was introduced to various space men and women, as well as to their main landing strips in his part of the country. He discovered that the site of his original meeting with the Venusian gal was "Field Location No. 1" (why not "Field Location No. 384", I'll never know). Then he was directed to "Field Location No. 2". At these two interplanetary airports he met a number of the outer-worlders. For a while they were mostly Venusians, then Martians started popping up fairly frequently, and in general things were booming on the flying saucer front. Howard's numerous contacts brought him many and various assignments in the name of interplanetary friendship. Some of these were: gradually moving toward vegetariansm, carrying messages and running errands,

56

purchasing earth-type clothing for space women (they don't use brassieres, he discovered), shearing off the long locks of the Venusian males, distributing dark glasses, conducting courses in the use of slang, briefing the strangers on our customs and habits, procuring special foods—usually fruits and grains—and occasional tools.

On the first occasion that he was permitted to photograph a space ship, the pictures turned out so badly that Howard was afraid to show them to people. They looked almost like they might have been "faked"! Of course, this was obviously ridiculous, but you know how people will gossip. However, on August 2nd, 1956 Menger had a chance to shoot a saucer with a Polaroid camera. Several space men also posed for him. The pictures Menger has taken at one time or another of craft are space-ship-like, but are certainly not startling: the shots of space people turn out to be mere blobs of light on the negative. So much for the Menger space photo library.

It was about this time that Howard discovered his occult powers, the most impressive of which was his ability to "teleport" (meaning to project a physical body instantly from one point to another with the implication that the object dematerializes at one point and re-materializes at another with no passage of time). No example of this remarkable power is quite so fascinating as what is usually called "the Menger teleported pipe story." It goes like this:

Howard's sister-in-law, Mary, was sitting in the Menger living room when she heard a knocking on the door. Knowing that Howard was many miles away that evening, she wondered who it might be. She opened the door and was, to say the least, surprised to see Menger standing there. He said nothing, but handed her a briar pipe and then "disappeared." The time was about 8:20 in the evening when the apparent apparition appeared. A few minutes later, at what Mary estimated to be 8:30 P.M., the telephone rang. She answered it to hear Howard on the other end of the line.

The verification offered by Mary that Howard was just under a hundred miles from the house was that his voice sounded distant, and that she "knew" that he was supposed to be that far away at that time, and besides which Howard said he was. Menger had suggested that the phone company could verify that he was where he said he was, but obviously the phone company is in no position to tell who phones from a diner in the hills of Pennsylvania on some indistinguishable night.

In listening to Howard you realize the importance of the pipe. He had brought it with him, and left it with Mary, to "prove" that he had been to his house; and therefore had actually "teleported" himself over a distance of 80 miles.

But now, let me turn away from Howard for a moment and tell you something of Marla Baxter, who became the second Mrs. Menger. This attractive young lady was originally seen by Menger when she attended a flying saucer lecture conducted by George Van Tassel. His first glimpse of her struck him with the realization that she was the materialization of a prophecy made by the Venusian girl of his childhood, who had promised him that one day he'd meet one "who is my sister." "She will work with you and be with you for the duration of your life span. She is my sister from Venus, and incarnated on this planet some years ago in your state of New Jersey."

As he stared, Howard had no doubt that this was the right girl, particularly since she closely resembled the space girl of the woods. The strong mutual attraction was not unexpected, since Howard had only recently learned that he was himself a Saturnian serving an earth-existence. As a matter of fact, they had had a pretty good fling on Venus one existence back. Unfortunately, just as things were beginning to really swing, Howard had to pop off to Earth to jump into the body of a one-year-old boy, naturally named Howard Menger, who had just died.

In Marla's version of their relationship she refers to Howard as "Alyn." As you may have begun to realize, that name, with various spellings, is extremely popular among contactees. Describing their initial meeting, the subsequent rendezvous, the contacts of "Alyn," and so on, Marla always parallels, and often almost duplicates, the experiences Howard relates.

Some time after the relationship had been established, Marla received a different kind of visitation. Having just bathed, she was lying naked on her bed with a small towel thrown across her body. Suddenly she became aware of "someone" in the room. When she turned no one was there, but later that evening, when talking with "Alyn" (Howard), he complimented her on her appearance earlier. He apologized, but told her that he just couldn't resist an occasional astral projection.

One night as she prepared to retire, "Alyn" (Howard) visited her. Sitting on the living room couch, he confessed that he was really a Saturnian, that she was a Venusian, and that Saturn should be in the House of Venus . . . oh no . . . that's astrology . . . that comes later. He spoke persuasively about the eternal, natural law which drew them together, of the great work they had to do, and all that jazz. If you're a man, you know more or less what I mean; if you're a woman, you know exactly.

At one point Maria considered leaving the group "Alyn" (Howard) headed, but a final decision was brought about one night when he visited her. They were speaking and, without warning, "the very next sentence was a soul-searching kiss." As they embraced, she tells of how he "began to grind his teeth, and turn and twist and stretch. He appeared to be getting taller and stronger . . . his facial contour seemed to change . . . his voice was different—deeper and lower . . . he had ceased to be "Alyn" (Howard) and had become a Saturnian (Marla never makes it clear how, since she had never seen a Saturnian before, she knew one when she saw him) . . . after a short time, there was a short exhalation of breath, and he grew weak and sort of collapsed to his regular height . . . and was himself again." Which is one way of putting it.

Tragically Howard lost his son around this time, and shortly afterwards divorced his wife, Rose. As soon as he was able, he married his Venusian lover. That was in the summer of 1958.

Getting back to Howard, I should say something of his "first trip to the moon the second week of August, 1956." But, understand, he was not the only lucky one; other contactees had the opportunity, too. One of them gave Howard a "moon potato" which, according to Menger, contained six times the normal amount of protein. This lunar vegetable probably was the most publicized "proof" of flying saucers ever offered. The story was that it had been dehydrated, but to my skeptical eye it just looked and felt like an ordinary stone. Anyway, I can tell you this much: you might have baked it, or fried it, or boiled it, but no one could have ever mashed it without a sledge hammer.

Earlier I mentioned the various West Coast saucer conventions, but until the appearance of Howard Menger no such activity had been conducted on the Atlantic side of the continent. But the Saturnian from High Bridge changed all that. Under his direction, an interplanetary carnival was held on his farm. Everyone was under the impression that this affair would be conducted like the Van Tassel, and other such, conventions in California. That is, that there would be no admission, or gate fee, but that all of the profit (we never doubted that there would be a profit) would be derived from concessions, book selling, merchandising, and similar action. Unfortunately for me, since I had mentioned the affair many times over my radio show, this was not how it turned out. In what appeared to be a pretty unexpected switch, the management slapped on a "two bucks a head" tab for every person who arrived. Naturally the great majority of people who had driven all the way out to this farm in New Jersey from New York City, New York State, Pennsylvania, Connecticut, and elsewhere, came up with the loot rather than turn around and go home, having made the unusually long trip for nothing. The fair attracted a couple of thousand cars with one, two, three, and often four persons per vehicle. Two bucks each. That isn't hay—it's clover. Not that I begrudged Howard cashing in on his publicity, he worked hard enough to get it. And, after all, if one desires to put oneself on exhibition for a fee, fine, but I've always thought that it was not really giving me and my listeners a square count not to announce his profit plan in advance.

Finally, the boom began to diminish and Howard slowly withdrew into seclusion with his wife Marla. And although he brought out a book about his "adventures," he did little or nothing to promote it—and kind of left his publisher, noncontactee saucer man Gray Barker, holding the promotional bag.

A year went by, and from Howard and Marla nothing but silence. I'd been lucky enough to see my radio show grow rapidly, and had moved into the television area, too. One day I was visited by "Mr. Lester," who told me that Howard wanted to come out of "retirement" and would like to appear on my TV show. I assumed that at this rather late date Menger wanted to promote his book, or make a comeback with some new tales, or the like. Since he had given me many great shows in the past, I thought that it was probable that he'd come up with another wild one. Anyway, I felt that I should gamble on it. But if I thought he was merely going to be the old, improbable, even amazing, Howard, I didn't guess the half of it.

A couple of days prior to Menger's scheduled television appearance, I had George Adamski booked for the all-night radio session. When the West Coast prophet arrived that evening, I discovered he was to be the featured guest at a large flying saucer rally in New York on the night of Menger's TV exposure. Obviously, one event was in direct conflict with the other. The solution was unique in the annals of even flying saucer history. As a matter of fact I can compare it only to those other well-known conventions.

On the evening of the Adamski lecture, the audience arrived

to find television sets stationed at all the most easily viewed points in the great ballroom. The program opened with well-known saucerologist Courtland Hastings speaking and introducing George. George presented the first half of his address to the large audience. Concluding the opening segment, he returned to his seat, and Hastings announced that the time had arrived to turn on all television sets. This was done, and that entire audience viewed Howard Menger on "The Long John Nebel Television Show." At the conclusion of the broadcast, Adamski concluded his lecture for the end of a contactologically eventful evening.

But what did Howard say? What was the show like?

Answer: Howard said nothing, and unsaid most of what he had originally claimed. The show was a disaster. The show was sensational. All depending upon your point of view.

Where he had once sworn that he had seen flying saucers, he now felt that he had some vague impression that he might have on some half-remembered occasion possibly viewed some air-borne object—maybe. Where he had once insisted that he had teleported himself, he now speculated that strange things did happen to people and if it hadn't actually occurred to him, well, that's the way the story crumbles. Where he had formerly stated that he had been to the moon, he now suggested that this had most likely been a mental impression of the other side of his consciousness.

In other words, Howard Menger backed up, and backed up, until he fell into a pit of utter confusion and finally sank forever into the waters of obscurity.

And where did his thousands of believers and followers go? Some, feeling that he had been "silenced" by space people or officialdom, still hold onto the myth, but the vast majority turned to where the light of fantasy still burned brightly and became disciples of George Adamski, or Van Tassel, or King, or anyone else who happened to be available with a completely unbelievable story.

And on and on could go the tales and the portraits of the men and women who claim to have sighted, contacted, flown in, traveled to other planets, systems and galaxies in flying saucers.

Still undescribed are Gabriel Green who "ran" for the presidency of this nation in 1960 on a "space ticket," and John Otto who turned a major radio station silent for one minute listening for messages from outer space and then came up with a recording no one has been able to decipher to this day. On the West Coast are many others, not the least followed of which is George Hunt Williamson, friend and co-contactee of George Adamski. He's the author of a work bearing the intriguing title, "The Saucers Speak—A Documentary (!) Report of Inter-stellar Communication by Radiotelegraphy."

To some of the etheric enthusiasts the most convincing of all of the tale tellers is Reinhold Schmidt. He says that in November of 1957, just outside Kearney, Nebraska, he encountered a grounded space craft. From this silver saucer two men emerged who spoke English with German accents. The earthman was shown the interior of the vessel and met many space men and women. Among themselves they all spoke High German. Finally, Schmidt was returned to his car, and the saucer departed. Quickly the contactee reported the entire incident to the local authorities, who rushed to the site of the landing and investigated. All agreed that every evidence was there (except the actual craft) to support the Schmidt claims. Headlines hit the street with the banner "Spaceship in Kearney."

Suddenly, the contactee was approached by the local authorities to deny his original assertions and say that none of his story had ever happened. When he refused he was tossed, summarily, in jail. From all sides he was bombarded with pressure and "faked" evidence to support the denials that anything unusual had ever taken place in Kearney. He was also questioned by two Air Force officials, who offered no explanations in return. After which he was offered defense counsel, against what he wasn't certain, who immediately demanded that he admit that none of his tale was true.

A few hours later, according to Schmidt, he was illegally confined to a mental hospital while the authorities attempted to coerce his relatives into committing him. Fortunately for our hero, they were unsuccessful in the long run, for, although they managed to keep him locked up for almost two weeks, the combined effort of his employers and family finally got him released.

Three months later he had anther contact with the saucer and its occupants. This time he was given a brief ride and an information-pumping session. He promised to try and get the desired information and was taken home.

And, like many of the other stories, so goes the one related by Reinhold Schmidt, complete with hidden saucers under the Great Pyramids, ten-minute trips around the world, and that kind of stuff.

Somewhat less dramatic, somewhat less physical, than his West Coast competitors is John Mittl of Pennsylvania. A vegetarian and recluse who petitioned long and hard to be on the all-night session, he told an interesting tale, but hardly soared to the heights of imagination attained by Menger and Angelucci. Mittl described many "contacts" achieved under dreamlike astral conditions. He spoke freely of etheric type saucers and other such things. However, it appeared that he was not really in his proper field because I recently got a brochure from him announcing that he was available for lectures on special theories of diet and nutrition.

Speaking of brochures, pamphlets, and mailing pieces and such, a few of the organizations that specialize in such activities should be mentioned.

One very active group is *The Planetary Center* in Detroit. It sends out frequent mimeographed bulletins which are just chock-full of lively space news. Sometimes the subscribers around the country receive special material. For these it was formerly the custom to forward contributions to the group headquarters; however, a recent bulletin regretfully announced that they had been informed by "the Michigan Securities Exchange Commission" that they could no longer function as a tax free society, and so the latest word is that in theory all printed material will be sent without any desire for financial support in return. Laura Mundo, who is one of the co-founders of this effort, writes extensively about her saucerological activities, her associations with contactees, and the like. The material printed as her exclusive work is a mish-mash of all sorts of little bits of information pasted on religion——as she sees it.

A kind of mysterious figure in the ranks of contactees is Dr. George Marlo of St. Louis. He seems to have entered the field rather late in its development since I didn't hear about him until the end of 1959. At that time I received a message from an Ottmar Kaub, who was "Secretary to Dr. George Marlo, Director of U.F.O. Research, with 60,000 members world-wide, who has been on the space ships known as flying saucers more times than most of the contactees of the world." The letter continued and revealed that "The Brothers and Dr. Marlo" were inviting me to take a saucer ride at some early, but undecided, date. Then, rather unexpectedly, I must admit, Mr. Kaub devoted the remainder of the letter to promoting a violin that he had "invented, designed and built."

Later a second letter arrived, which opened with the line:

"Dr. George Marlo has asked me, his secretary to . . . etc." and it was signed "Dr. George Marlo." Whether this indicates that there are two Marlos, one secretary and one employer, or that the doctor fired Kaub and became his own secretary, or whether he is a dual personality, I don't know.

Less than a year ago, several more messages came from Marlo and Kaub, one announcing that the time for the trip to outer space had been just about set. From other sources I discovered that a date had been "set" several times, but always postponed. However, one invitation read, in part:

"Among those accepting so far are Gray Barker, Ray Palmer, Jack Benny, Art Linkletter, Jack Paar, and Arthur Godfrey."

In a conference call with Jackie Gleason, Gray Barker told the great comic that Marlo's saucer was supposed to pick up various people around the country and take them to an island off the coast of Brazil. After a conference everyone was to be returned to his or her home. Since that time I've received at least two dozen letters from Marlo and company, but to this time no saucer junket has come off, and I'm afraid that the good doctor has sort of faded from the light.

Borderline Science Research Associates was another of the saucer groups regularly issuing printed material. Under the directorship of Meade Layne, longtime saucerite, *"Clips— Quotes and Comments,"* the voice of the organization, came out on the first of every month. Although much preoccupied with saucerdom, it also speculated about and offered opinions on many other of the occult or legitimate sciences. There was also Max Miller's *Saucers* and *Space Craft Digest* and dozens more, but the furthest out of all was probably James W. Moseley's *Saucer News.* The wildest, not because it told the most fantastic tales, but because it told the impossible as though it was reporting unusual, but unquestioned, fact. On the other hand, even more fascinating was its manner of exposing complete absurdities as though there could have ever been any question as to the ridiculousness of the assertion. An interesting example of this concerned a man named Less Childers.

This contactee began his pitch with the claim that he was a royal prince of the planet Tythan located eight-and-a-half light years away. Naturally, when he arrived on earth he put aside his real name for a while—Prince Neosom. Things were pretty rough during the earlier part of his life here. "The Three Men in Black," sometimes mentioned by Gray Barker, have killed him three times, he claims, which isn't bad—even for a Tythanian.

On one of these occasions he was shot in the back of the neck, taken to a hospital, and died. When the intern stepped out of the room for a moment, space people from a saucer hanging over the city brought him back to life and he vacated the premises. Understandably, he explains, there are no records of this since the hospital people would never admit losing a body!

At one point in his adventures he married a woman named Beth, and before the ceremony was over he had promoted her to the rank of Princess Negonna. Interestingly, Moseley's journal asked, ". . . what happened to Childer's first wife and five children? Perhaps they were sent to Tythan, or possibly the Three Men in Black got them."

Since I've not heard of him for some time, maybe he returned to his home planet and is trying to convince them that there are people on a little bit of rock in the sky eight and one-half light years away, a place called Earth.

In one issue of *Saucer News*, a Richard Ogden lays claim to the title of the man who can "prove that we have visitors from outer space." To support his contention, he makes a series of twelve prophecies. The first one is that "in the 1960 presidential election, it will be Stevenson vs. Nixon. Nixon will win." Obviously it is unnecessary to go any further. (Moseley by the way, predicted Stevenson by 1,860,000 votes, in the same issue.)

Not infrequently saucerology has been guilty of the worst possible taste, often in the area of religion, sometimes in the realm of sex. The crudest and most offensive example of the latter related to a blood mark that appeared at Gray Barker's bookstand at the Giant Rock Spacecraft Convention in September, 1960. When the sample was analyzed by a firm in Hollywood, their conclusion was that it was a specimen of "menstrual discharge." A good deal of speculation was bandied back and forth across the continent, among saucerites, regarding the mystery of its appearance, its meaning, purpose, and the like. The only constructive comment forthcoming from the entire sordid affair was Barker's observation:

"There seems to be a great deal of sex connected with saucers, and an occurrence such as the Giant Rock 'psychic blood' phenomenon would, in our opinion, be typical of the Space People, especially when we consider the low level of intellect they have demonstrated so far through the contactees."

Which, coming from one of the leading researchers and writers on the subject of saucers, is pretty interesting.

Dan Martin is one of the more recent contactees, but his story essentially falls into the Adamski or Angelucci category, although he does add a twist by introducing Mercurians into his claims.

Actually there are dozens of other amazing people to talk about and thousands of other stories. When I rush past someone like Dan Martin with thirty-two words, it's only because I've already overloaded the space allotted to flying saucers, not because his "report" is lacking in power to astonish. In the magic world of ufology and flying saucerdom there are people and places and things and dimensions and universes you couldn't even dream about, let alone imagine, but someone has dreamed about them, or imagined them—unless, of course, it's all true.

Unfortunately, there have been times when I've been a little unhappy with some of the stuff that has been shoved at me in the name of space people. These times have fallen into several main slots. Occasions when a contactee has offended my intelligence—not by being incredible, but by being unbelievable without being fascinating—but this has been rare.

Another area of offense has been religious. I recall unfavorably the evening when one of the people I've mentioned earlier argued with me because I wouldn't permit him to announce over the air that "Jesus was the pilot of a flying saucer."

A third bit that has always bugged me is the "I cure incurable diseases" pitch some of them toss around.

And lastly the racist propaganda which keeps cropping up from one group to another. In this area, regrettably, I'm unable to name names and cite occasions, since the allusions are always so carefully phrased so that the offenders could easily deny the intention of their remarks. But the meaning is there, never doubt it. As is usually the case, the unfavored parties racially speaking, are the Jews and Negroes, and the theme of both Fascism and Communism seems to echo from behind the scenes on more than a few occasions. But it's all part of the action.

And that's the way they come, and stay, and go. Each one has his reason for being in on the operation. Ufologist or saucerite, everyone is serving his own purpose. Either he's spreading a message he believes, or a message he doesn't believe but can sell, or he's making a market for a book—or he's very sick. Everyone has his private drive.

But man is a stargazer. He swings on the unknown. It frightens him, but it fascinates him. He gets hung up on it, and in a way so have I. Although I've heard the weirdest and the wildest, I'm always waiting for another saucer story, a little weirder and a little wilder. I don't buy any of it—but I'm a sucker for a guy with a far-out gaff.

CHAPTER 5

"Yes, an' no, an' mebee,
an' mebbe not."
—David Harum
(Edward Noyes Wescott)

THE $20,000,000 TICKET TO THE MOON
PLUS SOME IMPOSSIBLE INVENTIONS

"THE OTC-X1 Circular Foil Craft" is almost certain to go down in history—somewhere. Fact or fiction, farsightedness or fraud, I can't pretend to judge, but fantastic, fascinating, and incredible? Yes. As the cataloger of the impossible in this country, I give you a square count, neighbors—there was never anything like the story of the OTC-X1. There were never—well, hardly ever—people like unbelievable "scientist" Otis T. Carr, and the promotional wizard Norman Colton.

I first encountered Carr when he was operating out of Baltimore. Of course, since then he has managed his way across the continent to Apple Valley, California, and back again, leaving an unbelievable series of adventures in his footsteps.

For a quarter of a century this remarkable gentleman served in the capacity of night clerk for innumerable hotels. He chose this manner of making a living because it permitted him time to experiment and meditate. Years were spent in the study of the laws of physics and metaphysics, chemistry and alchemy, biology and technocracy; and, on occasions, he discovered and invented laws that were all his own. These latter included concepts of antigravitation, electromagnetism, neutron accumulation, and other pretty esoteric-type bits.

It doesn't take too much imagination to visualize the young O. T. Carr clerking, as he actually did, in a hotel where the great inventor Nikola Tesla lived. We can picture how the eager young man took every opportunity to talk with the genius who conceived of alternating current and other modern miracles. There they would sit, among the dozens of pigeons Tesla had flying in and out of his room, discussing the abstractions of the universe, with Carr running out for peanuts for the birds, and back for more speculation. And, according to OTC., during all this time Tesla was revealing fantastic scientific secrets which he never told to another soul.

And the years went by for Otis Carr.

Eventually he began to get things under way, establishing, at least in name and on stationery, "OTC. Enterprises, Inc." The purpose of this corporation was to design, construct, manufacture, promote and merchandise the "OTC-X1 Circular Foil Spacecraft."

According to inventor Carr, he had discovered how to capture and utilize the "gravity factor" in revolving machines. He said he could control "free energy," which was "everywhere," and 'build a ship to go to the moon. Or, as stated in "Information Bulletin No. 3," dated December 23, 1957:

"Any vehicle accelerated to an axis rotation relative to its attractive inertial mass, immediately becomes activated by free-space-energy and acts as an independent force. We have shown that a charged body, so accelerated, indicates polarity in a given direction. The dip needle points, say, up toward the top of the body. But mount this whole rotating body, with its spindle, on another platform and rotate this platform on a spindle, then, if the counter-rotation is greater than the initial forward rotation of the body, a dip-needle on the second platform will point *down* while the first dip-needle points *up,* indicating the *complete* relativity of polarity. When the exact counter-rotation matches the forward rotation, the body loses its polarity entirely and immediately becomes activated by free-energy (tensor stresses in space) and acts as an independent force."

On the other hand, it might be put this way:

"Mxhyn ppfgdnt llojwnzx osossenfoump mxmhsgsred alal . ."
but I'm afraid I'm merely echoing Carr.

The first "OTC-X1 Circular Foil Spacecraft" was conceived as 45 feet in diameter and 15 feet through the middle. Accommodating three passengers, its flight range was to be 1,000 miles from earth. OTC Enterprises, Inc., loudly announced that it would deliver a fully completed OTC-X1 from any place in the country, orbit one or more times outside the earth's atmosphere, and land it wherever specified.

The price on delivery? A mere 20,000,000. Twenty million bucks. Naturally, quantity buying offers its advantage here, as elsewhere. Each additional identical unit is only $4,000,000.00. All deliveries within twenty-four months.

One of the more refreshing aspects of the Carr bit is its flexibility. On one promotion piece we were told that the forty-five foot diameter was a minimum, and that breadths of one hundred feet were likely, too. Yet, the smaller need was also considered with the "family-size ten-foot diameter" model the corporation was projecting, which was to sell for less than the price of an automobile. With the midget model, you would be able to spin your family across town, about the country, or even around the world, whenever you desired.

It's quite possible that you're saying that this was some small crackpot company, a couple of thousand dollar operation with big ideas, but if so you're very mistaken. This was, and at this writing is, a big-time, top-level action.

Take, for example, one of their many promotional brochures. This is an 8" x 11" piece, printed on high grade textured stock in four colors. The legends on the jacket read "OTC Enterprises, Inc. . . . Brings you *Atoms for Peace* . . . The Gravity Electric Generator, the Utron Electric Battery, Solar Energy Devices, Electro-Magnetic Machinery (and) Free Flight in Space." These are thirty-two beautiful pages rife with elaborate diagrams, graphs and renderings, including a 40" x 8" foldout. It's a brochure that ranks with the best that Madison Avenue has to offer, and it's one of many.

Another of these extraordinarily powerful pieces is executed in black and white, and genuine silver. This particular bit is on the "Utron Electrical Accumulator" and is so titled, with a sub-title "The Geometry of Space in Fourth Dimensional Physical Form." On the center-fold are four illustrations of the "accumulator" in excellent artwork. The shape is that of two cones placed base to base. Each cone is perfectly round and the line of one side in relationship to its opposite side is a ninety degree angle. Therefore, if the object is viewed from the top, or bottom, one has the point centered, and the edge forms a complete circle; however, if it is viewed from the exact side, with one point on the upper right and the other on the lower left, it takes the shape of a perfect square. To wit, it is both a perfect circle and a complete square. According to Carr, this proves that he has solved the age-old, and presumably unsolvable, problem of "squaring the circle."

And who is the man behind this sensational promotional and public relations job? Who is the man who is often called the "brains" of Otis T. Carr? His name is Norman Evans Colton. What is he like? That's very, very hard to say; it's almost as hard to answer as the question—"What does he think?"

Norman is a small, well-dressed, dark-haired, blue-eyed man with a very charming manner who moved from association with a public relations firm to the far more demanding and infinitely more exciting position of "Director of Sales Engineering for OTC Enterprises, Inc." This title, however, means even more than it may seem to, for covered by Colton's broad administrative command is everything, apparently, other than the actual "scientific theorizing" which makes all of these wonderful things possible(!).

When I first brought the OTC story to my radio listeners, both Otis and Norman appeared, sharing the time available in explanation of the OTC-X1 and allied experiments. However, from that time forward it has been Norman who seemed to be the dynamic force. Certainly it was he who most eloquently spoke for the new world of OTCism. He answered questions in a manner which was, if not intelligible, entertainingly confusing, generally leaving the interviewer with the feeling that no one in the world really could understand him, but that it was the world's fault and not his.

Then came the night of the conversation between the eminent physicist Dr. Wallace Minto and Norman Evans Colton. It's completely impossible to tell you how unbelievable the discussion was, but this was the general effect of a small portion of it:

MINTO: What you have stated is in direct opposition to Newton's Third Law of Motion.

COLTON: Dr. Minto, we are in favor of bringing many of the more old-fashioned scientists up to date. You might

	say that Mr. Carr would like to see some of them repealed and revised versions introduced.
MINTO:	But Mr. Colton, modern science still accepts as true the scientific law referred to.
COLTON:	And it's a good thing that all the old traditions aren't lost.
MINTO:	I'm afraid I don't quite see the connection, but let's touch on something else. How does this utron accumulator, that powers the craft, work?
COLTON:	Very hard, especially if you speak softly to it. Seriously, though, when the full absorption effect of the accumulator permits the concentration of the anti-gravitational free-energy available you inaugurate a series-reaction of natural responses and a remarkable, but scientifically valid, phenomenon occurs—it goes up.
MINTO:	I'm afraid that I'm forced to be blunt, Mr. Colton; none of that makes any sense.
COLTON:	Exactly. It is the new approach that will win the pathway to the stars. The basic principle of anti-matter and anti-sense will serve to open an entirely new universe of speculation. The word is out, it's on the wing. The word is "OTC."
MINTO:	That's a word?

With all respect to the distinguished Dr. Minto, I have to give you a square count, friends, when Norman starts to roll no one can pin him down. He's really fantastic when he gets swinging. Straight talk, crooked talk, single talk, double talk, and triple talk. Weave them all together, and you have the technique Colton uses to blanket any conversation with whole cloth and a yard wide. This is an intriguing and a charming guy, but I have to admit that I don't buy a single word he says. Maybe it's because he's just a little too good.

Then came the trip.

I received word from Norman that a great event was to take place on Easter Sunday, in an amusement park called Frontier City, in Oklahoma City. A prototype of the OTC-X1, six feet in diameter, was to be launched, proving the power of the utron accumulator.

I landed in the western metropolis with several friends of mine to discover that the spacecraft was hidden away on the outskirts of town and no one was being permitted to see it.

Sitting in that early morning restaurant a thousand miles from Broadway, with the rain pouring down on the gray dawn highway outside, this report seemed a little ominous. However, several of us were more curious than tired, and we decided to drive out to the mysterious "hangar" and see what was going on.

We wheeled through the torrential storm of thunder, lightning, and rain, along semi-lit streets, and eventually pulled up in front of the place where the model of the spaceship was being kept. Our reception was hardly cordial, but my friends and I worked our way into the abandoned warehouse they were using for the OTC-X1. I must admit that we didn't make any startling discoveries. The prototype was in a small room guarded by four burly men. We were permitted a quick look and then abruptly ushered out.

The next day I was informed that Colton wasn't in town, but that Carr had been around, but unavailable, for several days. He had asked us there, but where was he?

Now, none of my boys are "private eyes," but it didn't take them long to find Mr. Carr; he was in semi-seclusion in a local hospital. I went over and found out that he had had some trouble with his throat and was having it checked. I thought it was pretty peculiar when he told me that he wouldn't be able to attend the launching of his own spaceship on the following Sunday. However, he assured me that he would be there in spirit and in voice—he had prepared a tape recording to be played on the evening following the "launching of the prototype." For some strange and psychic reason a dark feeling came over me and I began to doubt that I'd ever have the great and interplanetary privilege of seeing the model OTC-X1 take wing (which would have been pretty clever for a ship that didn't have any—wings, that is).

Then came Sunday morning. Launching time was set for three o'clock in the afternoon, at Frontier City. We arrived at the historic site about noontime and began checking around. We discovered that there was a central headquarters for the OTC operation located near an amusement-park-type ride which was a larger version of the OTC-X1. A beautifully designed and executed device of polished aluminum, it was intended that in the future it would simulate an actual flight in the full-sized craft, but at that moment one could merely enter it and look around—for a quarter.

An associate of Carr's gave a rather lengthy lecture, which was not what anyone had come for, but the crowd waited

73

patiently. At last three o'clock came, three o'clock went—and nothing happened. The prototype didn't even show up. Four o'clock came, looking for three o'clock, saw the direction it had taken, and followed along. Five o'clock trailed after them a little later. Nothing had happened. No launching, not even something to launch. And it was long, long after launch-time. In fact, it was almost time for dinner. Finally came the announcement. There would be no take-off today because of "technical difficulties." No one could find the switch. Or possibly someone pulled a switch. Well, regardless, after a thousand-mile trip, I was just a little irked at its all adding down to a small nothing.

I had made some excellent tapes of the people who had shown up for the occasion, but I wanted the story I had come for, or an explanation of why I wasn't getting it. I decided to go back to the abandoned warehouse. When we arrived, there was a flag-draped truck, with a huge winch, standing at the doors. Inside, the model sat on the floor. The room was jammed with the press, who listened attentively as Norman Colton described how a "mercury leak" had delayed the scheduled testing. He added that they hoped to have it repaired and ready for flight in a couple of days. But it never happened, and after another day or so of useless waiting, I took my miracle-seeking caravan back to New York town.

During this period and for six months following, another dramatic announcement originated from Colton and Carr. They would "fly to the moon," they said, "on December 7th, 1959." Even I was offered a seat on that spectacular expedition, which I had to decline because of a luncheon appointment. When it's a choice of luncheon or launchin', I dig food to fantasy every time.

According to Norman Colton, the OTC-X1 would travel to the moon in five and a half hours. Naturally, the trip back, being a downhill slide all the way, would be a little shorter.

December 7th trotted by breathlessly, and nothing occurred. To this date the OTC-X1, wherever it might be, is earth-bound. Or if it finally hit the air, I never heard about it. And since I never recognized "modesty" as being Carr's outstanding virtue, I must take it for granted that no such flight ever took place. Later on, Otis T. Carr was brought into court, in the State of Oklahoma, on charges which I believe were, in effect, the disposing of stock under improper conditions. If I'm not mistaken, he was fined some $5,000. And that was that.

74

Naturally, you understand that this was what is commonly referred to as "bad publicity." I say "commonly" referred to, because some pretty shrewd people have questioned whether there is such a thing as "bad publicity," that is, so long as "they spell the name right." Actually, I think it's obvious that some publicity is destructive, but it takes a wise man to know when what is which. The effect of Carr's Oklahoma involvement with the law was to attract more people, to stimulate the general interest, to convince a number of people that the great man was being "persecuted."

It was after Carr got clear of "gross intimidation" that rumors spread widely and wildly to the effect that Carr and Company had received a very large grant from one of the most famous institutions in the land. Fifty thousand was spoken of, a hundred thousand was mentioned, a quarter of a million was wondered about, a million was whispered—as far as I know, no such grant was ever forthcoming. However, it must be conceded that if such grapevine gab didn't convince some worthy institution that such an endowment should be offered, it was a powerful persuasive to innumerable potential investors in the OTC-X1.

Then, having swept across half the country, from Baltimore to Oklahoma City, the Carr-Colton operation continued the sweep, swinging all the way to Apple Valley, California. In this charming little West Coast community, Otis T. Carr leased a building, erected an enormous highway sign (sporting, I'm told, the original OTC-X1 prototype), and stepped up his expansion program. One gathers that the town, if somewhat befuddled by the builders of spacecraft and anti-gravity motors, nonetheless took the OTC clan to its collective bosom.

Carr and his various projects received great publicity in the papers in his area of the country, while in New York the district attorney's office indicated that they were interested in the organization's stock procedures in Gotham. At this writing, although there seems to have been some push and pull between the Carr-Colton contingent and the D.A.'s office, nothing has been brought to any concrete action.

Meanwhile, back at the ranch country of the desert valley community, Carr sailed along happily. At the end of August, 1960, the front page of the *Desert Valley News-Herald* announces that Otis will begin his operation and hiring and all that, on September 15th. The three main projects mentioned are the OTC-X1, the Carrotto Gravity Motor, and the display ride model of the ship.

Also broadly announced in that issue of the newspaper is the "International Space Craft Project Convention," scheduled for the first few days of September, and sounding like a direct competitive enterprise to George Van Tassel's bit of the same general name. Among those listed as being expected to appear are—Gloria Lee, author of some way-out mystical writing; John Otto, certainly not the country's most scientific investigator of saucers and contactees; Reinhold O. Schmidt, contactee and president of International Space Craft Project; Dan Fry, whom you'll remember from earlier in this book. The report on this convention is, by the way, concluded in what is a very (unintentionally, I think) funny way. After mentioning this Space Craft Project, and all of these very esoteric people, it suggests that since the visitors will be out in a particular location for the affair, they might want to run up the canyon and take a look at a tourist "gold camp" where they can play at panning for that ever-precious metal. Of course, Carr takes the position that there's plenty at the end of the rainbow—which end he hasn't said. But one thing we know—he claims he has the transportation to get there.

And so one of the world's most extraordinary corporations rolls along, to the delight of all (excepting the SEC, and a couple of DA's); even those who have invested, both lightly and heavily, in the outlandish speculations of oracular Otis still, with rare exceptions, confidently support OTC Enterprises.

But, if I were to credit this amazing attractiveness to one person, if I were to credit a single individual talent with the success of the entire bit, I wouldn't name Otis T. Carr, oddly enough, but Norman Evans Colton—who may well be the greatest salesman I ever met. I don't buy his product, but how that man can pitch!

* * * * *

The years bring more and more fantastic discoveries of science and technology into reality. The number of things invented by man now reaches well into the millions, but there's always something new, something never thought of before—at least as far as the public is aware. The smallest thing can make a man more money than he ever thought existed; a hair pin, a bobby pin, a safety pin, a staple, a paper clip; and what are all these things—little bits of wire. Well, in my time I've seen some strange things introduced onto the social scene. Inventions beyond the wildest imagination of most people. But they're believed and bought by the ever-fascinated fellow—not you, of course; I mean the other guy.

His name is Andy Sinatra, and he can't sing a note, but when you hear his rather unusual flutter-frequency and hesitatingly-husky voice, you're not certain that he can talk, either. That is, until you find out that his conversations are often held with people from the misty worlds behind the mirrors. Then you understand. Believe me, if you don't understand, you've got problems.

Usually Andy prefers to be referred to as the "Mystic Barber," as cutting hair is his method of acquiring a livelihood; but on my shows he's better known as the "Mystical Tonsorial Artist from Brooklyn."

To describe the Barber as unusual wouldn't be giving you the full picture; but, on the other hand, it would require photography to present an accurate representation. He isn't a tall man, and leans toward being a little on the round side. Actually he doesn't really lean, but he does carry his right shoulder a bit higher than the other one.

Andy is in touch with other worlds. He's visited by Martians, who are identifiable because of their having no reflections—a point which he's noticed when they come to his tonsorial parlor for a trim or a shave. Usually, however, his contacts aren't so direct, but are accomplished via telepathic communication. Not the ordinary, run-of-the-mill, everyday, man-in-the-street, common-garden-variety, down-to-earth, two-feet-firmly-planted-on-the-ground, common sense kind of telepathy—his mental relationship with the mysterious ones are the extraordinary, miracle-of-the-mill, once-a-year, pie-in-the-sky, vision-of-paradise, up-in-the-air, walking-on-clouds, extra sensory kind of telepathy. And, believe me, there's a difference. I don't know what it is, but if they were the same the disappointment would be more than I could bear.

Naturally, this special order of mentalism requires a little unusual effort to be achieved. This, the Mystical Tonsorial Artist has accomplished via his headband inventions. Although they have an over-all similarity, each one has its own particular and unique characteristics. However, all are worn in approximately the same manner, and that is around the head, just above the ears.

One of these bands, which is a couple of inches wide, and has a pair of weird, bouncy antennae on it, is for tuning in on the Venusian sending frequency. Of course, Sinatra hastens to assure us that he no longer needs this instrument to get the message, but, in turn, insists that all beginners should have one to make the telepathy simpler.

Another band serves the opposite need. That is, Friend Andy has become so intimate with the people from outer space, and proficient in the use of telepathic communication, that he suffers from a constant bombardment of extraterrestrial messages; therefore, to provide himself with periods of relief he devised another headpiece to black-and-block out the thoughts at appropriate times. This band is also decoratively constructed, like the first, of bits of wire, glass, tops of tin cans, and other valuable minerals of earth.

There are several more bands in Sinatra's collection, but these two give you the general idea. As a matter of fact, just for the sake of authenticity, I've had one made up identical to his "receiving" set, but, of course, I consider it all plain nonsense. That is, I can pick it up, and put it on my head, the way I'm doing . . . *hnjje ptnnygh oooops rerewonson th tr th oopsam gadabamm ononontotoont p* . . . and then remove it, and absolutely nothing happens. But, you have to admit, it's kind of wild stuff.

On one occasion I had a man named Gist Talmist on the program with an invention called the "psygistograph." This particular creation seemed to be composed of an umbrella with no fabric, various strings and wires. I have no doubt that its purposes were many and magnificent, but after five hours' conversation with the deviser of this machine I was still unable to understand, and more unable to convey to others, its functions. However, it may be that in machines, as in men, "they also serve who only stand and wait."

However, if there are inventions that just sit there and do nothing, there are others that are a positive explosion of activity, devices that flash and flicker and—do nothing. As a matter of fact there are a number of such examples of imagination, but the greatest of these madnesses is the *Spectro-Chrome* gaff created by a small, transplanted Indian who prospered in this country under the name "Colonel" Dinshah Pestanji Ghadiali. This particular confidence man, who has been reprimanded by the law to the extent of suspended prison sentence and a very heavy fine, started his extraordinary pitch immediately following the First World War.

Invading a field that was already heavy with a host of medical quacks, he proceeded to make himself one of the most successful of these connivers. This he achieved by inventing a worthless contraption called the *Spectro-Chrome Machine* which did nothing but blink various colored lights. Each of the many hues was possessed of powers to "cure" particular disorders and/or diseases. Brilliant red restored virility, violet "de-sexed" one. At one point he was imprisoned for some time for conviction on a Mann Act charge, which, one would imagine, would have a rather negative effect on his "medical" career, but he continued to work very successfully following his release. Many, many thousands of the Ghadiali contraptions were leased and sold; thousands more paid for "instruction" classes, and books. When being tried for his questionable activities he was confronted by a number of witnesses who asserted that their relatives had died while following the treatments of the occult operator. Yet, regardless of the obvious nonsensicality of the invention, and notwithstanding the disastrous testimony of government witnesses, over a hundred persons came forward to claim that the quack had "cured" them with his gaff of a thousand lights.

The one thing the Ghadiali machine couldn't cure was gullibility.

Dr. Wallace Minto, physicist and chemist, has been on my radio show several dozen times—often as an orthodox scientist discussing physics, astronautics, chemistry, biology, and other serious areas of investigation, but more frequently he has taken to the microphones in defense of, and to expound upon, telepathy, clairvoyance, psychometry and aura readings. His interest in the off-beat, particularly the "psychic", amounts to fascination; and of the various categories mentioned I imagine the one that occupies his greatest attention is "aura reading."

Now there are only a few mechanical instruments associated with aura reading, but those that are are wild. Of the highly technical and intricately complicated versions none compare with Dr. Minto's machine.

My television show for one week was going to be dedicated to the proposition that all auras are created—by the mind that sees them. But Minto was going to appear on the show to establish that the little haloes of many different colors actually did exist. It was his theory, and that of many other people who buy the aura action, that each person possesses a personal nimbus which is composed of one, or more, colors. The radiations, as well as being tinted, are supposed to vary considerably in width, distance from body, and so on. By weighing the implications of the various colors and measurements, a professional aura reader purportedly can diagnose illnesses, attitudes, emotions and characteristics.

A black aura is found only about the physical being of a corpse.

Normally, auras are read without any mechanical aids by those "possessed of the power," but Dr. Minto devised a method by which such examinations might be conducted on a more "scientific" level. He employs an aura meter. Unfortunately, when he brought it to my television show the cables carrying current all around the studio interfered with the function of the device, but it was a remarkable thing to see. Covered with dials, and knobs and switches, it gave the impression that it could not only read auras, but could also serve as a small Univac, on the side. Of course, as far as I was concerned, there was no doubt as to its efficiency. In point of truth, to my mind it had but one minor flaw—I don't believe in auras.

Another aura meter which is really fascinating is the one conceived and merchandised by the Rev. V. L. Cameron, of Elsinore, California. This one consists of a cylindrical "handle" about 1″ in diameter and 4″ long. From this hilt a wire angles down an inch or two and then arcs up and away for almost a foot. At the end of this tension wire is connected a "head" in the shape of a slender rifle cartridge. When held by the grip, the rest of the assembly tends to bounce and "rock" freely up and down and from side to side. Presumably, by following the action of the aura meter, one can deduce certain things about people, find water and precious minerals, and in general have a rollicking good time. If you're not really able to achieve your desired heights as an aura reader with this unique (and, by the way, beautifully designed) instrument, then Rev. Cameron has something else to aid you in your endeavors—a pair of aura goggles. These made it possible for anybody—well, almost anybody—to see auras. Naturally, in my modest manner I have to admit that I'm not anybody; as a matter of fact I don't know anybody who's anybody. But if somebody is anybody they can see auras with the Cameron Aura Meter.

It's the opinion of most of his critics that, like Nikola Tesla, the late Wilhelm Reich suffered a mental deterioration during the latter part of his life, and this seems both more likely and kinder than the other negative position that he forsook truth to become a successful charlatan. Regardless, there is little question that, unless one entirely rejects all of psychoanalytic theory, and psychoanalytic philosophy, Reich began with a brilliant mind.

His early work may well rank second only to the master's, Freud, with whom he had a severe and permanent argument in the early Thirties.

However, it's not ideas, per se, with which we're concerned in this chapter, but inventions. And his invention was the "orgone box." Actually, to give it the dignity accorded it by its creator, it's called he "Orgone Energy Accumulator." This compartment consists of "plyed" sheet iron and wood, constructed to resemble a standing coffin, with door, or a phone booth. Of course, this was the simplest form of accumulator; more complicated ones were devised composed of up to more than a dozen layers of metal "wool," "rock," wood, metal, and the like.

The theory of therapy behind these apartment compartments was that they collected "orgone energy," which was the scientific basis for sexual vitality. Having absorbed this condensation of sexuality in his accumulator, the "patient" proceeded to deposit himself in the box for a while and derive the benefits of the "life force." As propounded by Reich, this was the cure-all, the panacea for every ill of man—and woman, because it would lead to complete and successful orgasms; he held that the achievement of total orgasms would dissipate all neuroticism, and, in general, restore the average unhealthy, or unhappy, person to the height of well-being.

Unfortunately, since his death, although orthodox scientists tend to view most of Reich's later theories—particularly the orgone accumulator—as nonsense, not all do. And it's difficult for the layman to know if he really went off the track, and if he went off, when; and having determined when, how far.

I should also mention that the same once eminent Dr. Reich subsequently added another machine to his catalog—this was a gun-like "rainmaker." It never achieved the fame of the accumulator, but several were distributed around the East Coast, and success-claims were made for them. Recently, they seemed to have passed out of interest, but the popularity of the "orgone box," while diminished, still brings its message to the public. But more on Reich later.

Another box which has been rather widely acclaimed was created by Thomas G. Hieronymous, and promoted by editor John Campbell Jr. It's commonly referred to as the "Hieronymous machine," but often classified as being of the "psionics" type. According to Campbell, "psionics" is a new science which combines electronics and psychic phenomena, but when the original device was constructed the inventor wasn't informed of this new area of investigation. Hieronymous asserts that his machine, patented in 1949, analyzes the "eloptic" (a combination of electric and optic) radiation in minerals. This, of course, is a previously undiscovered type of emanation, but one which is supposed to be very important.

In appearance, the instrument may be about the size and shape of a shoe box, and contain some wires, resistors, and so on. A selection of unknown mineral is placed on the specimen plate, and by moving the calibrated dial the composition of the mineral is established. At least, that's what Hieronymous claims.

Campbell has commented rather caustically on the original device, holding that his improved and modernized version is the one that really works—at least for him. One of such late-edition psionic machines represents an excursion to the farthest outposts of "science." With this instrument, the electrical insides may be removed and replaced with a simple schematic of the original "guts," and it works perfectly. A specimen is placed on the specimen area, the dial is adjusted, and the free hand is placed upon a plastic plate. When the plastic plate gets "sticky," you have it made.

Oddly enough, Campbell has admitted on occasions that his model doesn't work too well for people of either analytical or mystical turns of mind. He also refreshingly reveals that he intuitively feels that the device operates beyond all known dimensions, but that the inter-relationship of various things have something to do with its function—providing, of course, that you believe that it does function. Amazing to tell, there are hundreds of persons who claim at least a fragmentary knowledge of some of the sciences, who not only accept, but vocally support, this ridiculous curiosity.

It's quite possible that the following report may not really belong in the same category as the foregoing as, I understand, there are some very reputable scientific persons who support the contention that it's based on fact. Yet, I must confess that, although I have no answers for a couple of the points I'll mention, I can't accept this one either. The purported science is titled "Bio-Rhythm." Fathered by a Dr. William Fliess, the theory of bio-rhythmics is based upon the conviction that our life is strongly influenced, if not controlled, by the cyclic fluctuations of our cells. The supposition is that there are three separate orders of cells, and, therefore, three distinct cycles affecting us. In each set, it's the ebb and flow, the building up and dissipation of our cells which determines our physical, emotional and intellectual tempers.

The first of these cycles reflects the physical welfare, strength and endurance characteristics; and it's designated, for no understandable reason, as the "male substance." Why the "physical" is considered masculine in nature is a mystery, since most modern biologists hold that the woman usually has a higher degree of physical endurance, lives longer, and in general gives the impression of being, if less strong, more "physical."

The next aspect consideration in bio-rhythmics is the one governing sensibility, nerves, feeling, intuition, and creative ability, and is described as being "female." The reason for this interpretation is even more mysterious than the former, since it's generally understood that men don't "bounce back" emotionally with quite the verve possessed by women; certainly, while they may not be as maudlin as women they're just as feeling; and lastly, but indisputably, men are, excepting for motherhood, almost exclusively "creative."

The third, and final, of the cycles is the one dominating the intellect, intelligence, memory, logic, reason, and ambition. This area is left un-sexed by the bio-rhythmers.

Each of the three cycles operates on a different schedule. The first, which is designated with *red* ink on their graphs, functions on a twenty-three day sequence. The second, indicated by *blue,* has a twenty-eight day pattern. The last projects itself over a period of thirty-three days. Each of these cycles is subdivided into a period of "unfolding" and a phase of "regeneration," which are exactly half of the full time span.

Now, the machine that explains all of the strange and prophetic things is called a "Bio-Rhythm Computer." There are large ones and small ones, but the popularly available models are of two types—identical, except for the metal employed in the casing. One is shelled in stainless steel, and one in gold plate. The former costs $35.00; the latter $45.00.

Visualize a disc two inches in diameter and slightly less than half an inch deep. This computer is set internally to your birthday and locked closed. Now, by looking at the back, which is a series of white dials marked in three languages, you can see the days of the year. Turning the dial, by means of a small ridge on the clear plastic cover, sets the computer to the date you wish to know about—either in the past, present, or future—but within the year. Then reversing the computer you find three "travelling" circles, one inside the other, which have been adjusted by the manipulation of the back. One hand is red and white; one, blue and white; and the last green and white. In order, as explained before, they represent the physical, the emotional, and the intellectual. A spin of the dial and you have all of the answers. At least, so the bio-rhythmics assure us.

I will admit that I paused to wonder when Mr. George Thommen, representing the device in the United States (it's quite well known in Europe), told me on the night of November 11th, 1960, that Clark Gable would have a severe "double critical" day on the 16th of the month. This "double critical" kind of indication, he had told us, meant that the subject was in his "most vulnerable" condition. Just a day or so before his prognostication, Mr. Gable had had a heart attack, but the papers had reported that he was well on the road to recovery. Tragically, on the day noted, the "King of Hollywood" died.

By going back to a point about three weeks prior to his appearance, Mr. Thommen demonstrated another curious accuracy. He drew up a chart for Paris Flammonde, saying that he had had a "critical" day on a particular date. Upon hearing the date specified, we both recalled that Paris had had a fairly severe accident around that time. He had scalded his arm rather badly. We checked the calendar and found out that it was the very day designated.

Naturally, with my almost inescapable scepticism, I don't buy bio-rhythm, but apparently many, many people do—and on the first hearing, too.

And there aren't dozens more, not scores more, not hundreds more, not even thousands more,—there are probably tens of thousands more insane, impossible, improbable, unlikely, questionable, possible and, maybe, even probable inventions waiting for the people who believe easily. And buy even more easily than that.

CHAPTER 6

> "I believe the future is only the past
> again, entered through another gate."
> —*The Second Mrs. Tanqueray*
> Sir Arthur Wing Pinero

A BACKWARD LOOK AT
BRIDEY MURPHY AND REINCARNATION

NO CASE, in our time, made such an impact for and against reincarnation as the one filed "Bridey Murphy." Beginning as just another off-beat book, one of hundreds in that year of 1956, it zoomed steadily to the top of the best seller lists and stayed there. Every magazine and newspaper ran articles on the book, its heroine, or the general subjects of hypnotism, reincarnation, pre-natal regression and anything else that could be tied in with the publicity-valuable Bridey theme. Radio and television programs soon evidenced the effect of the fad, as did comedians of every size, shape and delivery. It was a real wild brainchild, this "search for Bridey Murphy," begun by Morey Bernstein and carried on by half the country.

I don't doubt that many of you never actually read the book, although all of you must have heard the jokes and seen the strained cartoons. Others of you have probably forgotten the details. They went something like this.

Morey Bernstein, a very successful businessman from Colorado, who had been an amateur hypnotist for some time, began a series of "age regression" tests on a young housewife who is usually called "Ruth Simmons." The first of these experiments took place late in 1952, and set Bernstein and "Ruth" off on an amazing adventure both in the psychic field (we've been assured) and in the realm of public attention.

Now the term "age regression" merely means that a subject is put into a deep hypnotic trance and told to recall, and then relive, previous periods of her life. Eventually, the regressionists claim, a person can be reduced to a state of infancy where she behaves as though she were only a few months old. In a few rare cases, the most famous of which is the Bridey Murphy affair, the position is taken that the subject can then be projected past the "birth moment" into a state called "pre-natal regression." In this condition she is supposed to be re-living another life. Oddly enough, this "other life" is almost never one immediately preceding the present one, but rather an existence the subject went through a hundred or a thousand years ago. Very frequently, in fact in ninety percent of cases, even though in life the person is a clerk, or a plumber, or a housewife, when regressed to another time he, or she, turns out to be Moses, or a great Indian prince, or Prime Minister of England. However, in the Murphy report, this wasn't the case.

On the first occasion, Bernstein put "Ruth Simmons" into deep trance and immediately began regressing her. Seven years old, then five, three, and one—at each level stopping to ask her general questions, and then retreating in time again. Having achieved this degree of recession, Bernstein then directed her to push even further into the darkness of her memory—back to other times, to "faraway lands."

"Bridey Murphy" spoke, for the first time, at that moment. At least according to supporters of the story. "Miss Simmons" announced that she was four years old, living in County Cork (Ireland), and that her name was "Bridey." Her parents were Kathleen and Duncan Murphy, and her brother was named after his father. Some years before, while she was almost an infant, another brother died; she had always been the only daughter in the family.

"Bridey" told Morey Bernstein that her address was "The

Meadows," that her father was a barrister and that she had bright red hair and was named after her grandmother. Later she spoke of trips taken by the family to "Antrim" by the seashore and passing references are made to the "loughs," "Carlingford," "Foyle," and "Munster."

At fifteen the colleen of almost a century and a half ago was attending "Mrs. Strayne's Day School" and less than a year later she had met a young man named Brian MacCarthy. The two young people apparently got involved pretty quickly and they were married when Bridey was seventeen and he was just under twenty. Brian's father was also a barrister, while her new husband was attending Queens College in Belfast. It was to this town that they went to live.

In her unfamiliar surroundings, she made friends with "Mary Catherine and Kevin Moore," attended "St. Theresa's Catholic Church" (although she had been born and raised a Protestant she followed the ways of her husband), and read the *Belfast News-Letter.*

During the years that followed she became deeply impressed with the parish priest, Father John, and relied much on his counsel.

Speaking from her trance state at a point in her life when she was about forty-seven, she refers to "trouble" of a political nature. One gets the idea that she means unrest in public sentiment and an anti-English attitude in the southern Irish. Curiously there also seems to have been strong opposition to speaking the Gaelic language. At another point in her digression, Bridey speaks of Irish history and legend, referring to a great warrior named "Cuchulain."

Having reached her sixty-sixth year without producing any heirs or heiresses, Bridey Murphy fell downstairs, broke several bones, and "sort of withered away"—that is to say, she died. Her husband Brian survived her.

One might think that here this remarkable story would end, but it doesn't. Fortunately, Morey Bernstein pursued the mystery even further. He questioned Bridey intently about the period that followed. The after-life. Death.

As she replied to his queries, Bernstein described "Ruth Simmons'" voice, in the Irish girl's brogue, as "pained" and "plaintive." However, according to Bridey there was no pain. No grief. No emotional attachments, nor marriage, nor family, nor friends. No rules, laws, nor regulations existed, and no one ate, slept, got tired, or had sexual relations. One moved from one place to another (although all places were really one) by willing it. Certainly it's easy to understand why Bridey evaluated the place, or state, as "no better" than the one on earth. And it's obvious she had good reason not to like it, as she admitted.

Immediately following her demise, Bridey saw her body. For a while it remained in the house with Brian, although, at her request, no wake was held. Later it was "ditched," that is, buried.

She hung around the house for a while in spirit form, but when Father John finally died she departed for Cork, and her childhood home. Here she saw her brother Duncan, whom she described as being "so old." Actually, he was about seventy, according to the dates she had supplied. Of course, he was still alive, and so she decided to stay in his home. She tried to contact him on many occasions, but he never became aware of her. Curiously, although she "met" Father John, after his death, she was never joined by either Brian, her husband, or her brother Duncan.

Bridey remained in this "spirit world" for a long time, although time seemed to mean nothing, but she never succeeded in contacting or "speaking to" people on earth. She did try on numerous occasions, but without any success. Apparently, her failures were to be blamed upon living people who didn't listen for spirit voices. She never remembered whether any of the other "spirits" were able to make contact. Eventually she was reborn in the United States in the Twenties.

Bridey Murphy is supposed to have lived from 1798 to 1864.

That, in a very much more expanded form, is the essence of the tapes of "Mrs. Ruth Simmons," as recorded by Morey Bernstein. Tapes upon which she speaks, or is purported to speak, as the colleen Bridey Murphy. The hypnotist made these recorded sessions the hub of his extremely successful book, in which he suggested the probability that the material substantiated the claims of those who believed in reincarnation. Citing "Bridey's" use of words like "brate" for wishing cup, "ditch" for bury, "lough" for river or lake, noting the names of places and people, and generally arguing that "Ruth Simmons" couldn't have known of many of the things referred to by Bridey Murphy, he concludes with reincarnation.

He offers the opinions of several reputable scientists and medical men in favor of the rebirth idea, plus the convictions of several mystics such as Steiner and Cayce.

A newspaper editor became interested in the story and decided that an investigation should be made of the matter by an independent agency. The matter was turned over to an Irish legal firm and such people as they chose to assist them.

According to Morey Bernstein, many "facts" came to light indicating that Bridey had actually lived in Ireland at the time she had designated.

It was ascertained that a man with the name of Bridey's father-in-law, and two more with the names of grocers mentioned by her, had actually existed during the proper years and had been engaged in the work she ascribed to them. Her references to myths and legends were correct, and so were comments about a book, various geographical locations, language usages, and proper names.

Later a couple of reporters were sent to Ireland to get more material on the Bridey Murphy story, but the results were very superficial. Assistant Editor William Barker of the Denver *Post* went over for several weeks to look into the case, coming back with interesting conclusions.

He believed that Brian wasn't a "barrister," but a clerk who worked for a tobacco company, possibly a hardware firm, and maybe Queens College. Further, he was of the opinion that her father hadn't been a barrister either, but rather a farmer. Apparently, according to Barker, the lower class Irish girl was always embroidering her story so as to make her family appear far more important that it actually was. Nonetheless, in summing up his discoveries, the reporter is clearly convinced that a dozen or so of his points come close to proving the Murphy tale.

The next development in this increasingly spectacular case was the interest of the Chicago *American* in the early summer of 1956. This was the first big debunking. The story claimed that "Ruth Simmons" (whose real name, by the way, is Virginia Burns Tighe) had constructed "Bridey Murphy" and her Ireland from subconscious memories of her youth in Madison, Wisconsin, and Chicago. The report asserted that "Ruth Simmons" had had an aunt more Irish than the Blarney Stone, who had filled her with wild and fanciful tales of the "ould sod" when she was a child. A subsequent article asserted that the "real" Bridey had been found in the person of "Bridey Murphy Cockell," who had lived just across the way from "Ruth" in Chicago.

A Denver *Post* reporter tried to discredit the Chicago *American* story with an article which attempted to refute the refutation. *Life* magazine got into the act a couple of times. And back and forth it went.

Now, years later, looking back over the affair, one has to admit that it's almost as confused a mess as it was when it was at its height. Many of the fundamental facts have gone unproven. No record of any "barrister" named Duncan Murphy, with or without a wife Kathleen, living in Cork at the end of the 18th century, has ever been located. No evidence that they, nor anyone, had a daughter Bridget Kathleen Murphy, nor that such an offspring married a Sean MacCarthy . . . naturally, all that would obviously follow from the original "fact" is set aside when it's necessary to discard the original "fact." There are simply no traces of the birth, marriage, death, parents, or friends of Bridey Murphy.

On the other hand, when Bridey mentions two grocers named Farr and John Carrigan it stirs the interest, since gentlemen with those specific names were the only ones in all of Belfast in the food business. Her designating "The Meadows" as the place she lived is supported by the discovery that a particular area of Cork went under that name at that time. She makes accurate reference to "Queens College," proper use of several uncommon words, and informed allusions to mythic stories of that period.

So, neighbors, what do you end up with? Fact or fake? Reincarnation or remembrance?

One thing you can be sure of—if it was a fake, Morey Bernstein did not perpetrate it; because this is one of the most honest and sincere men ever to operate on the periphery of the field of psychic phenomena. To be involved in any fraudulent activities would not prove to be of any value to him personally, as it is reported that he's a millionaire—a brilliant man and extremely successful in the normal channels of commerce.

Take another striking example of regression experimentation. The case of Lord Thomas Grover, the pre-natal life form of a young man who was called merely "George." This gentleman was brought to me by a hynotist named Edward Sunwall, who was able to put his subject into a very deep trance state and regress him to a point prior to his birth, or it so was claimed. In this previous incarnation "George" was an English nobleman living in London in the 16th century.

I must admit that I was very impressed with the first "performance" of the regression staged for my radio show by these two young men. Following an opening interview which established that Mr. Sunwall was a businessman by profession and that "George" was an unemployed actor, the induction got under way.

Physically, "George" was about twenty-five years old, pleasant looking, with fairly even features. As he dropped deeper into trance, the face became more relaxed and lineless, until it was a countenance at peace. He even looked several years younger. In the first questioning stage, "George" identified his age as about six. In response to Ed's questions, he named a couple of classmates, described the schoolroom he was in, and the like. The most interesting thing was the speech pattern, which was that of a small child—the pronunciation, and the vocabulary, and the phrasing.

The regression was continued until the subject was supposedly about two years old. The effect was really amazing. "George" was baby-talking in the most convincing manner. Which, coming from a husky, if reclining, young man, was amusing and surprising. The lines of the face, the motions of the mouth, the entire effect was amazingly infantile.

Finally, Edward Sunwall told the subject to "go over the hump," meaning that he should jump from the two-year-old state to a pre-natal consciousness. Slowly, the face began to alter. Lines returned to the forehead, and the corners of the nostrils down past either side of the mouth. The eyebrows seemed to more aggressively project over the eyes, which narrowed. The nose gave the effect of becoming more prominent. The mouth looked as though it had thickened and the corners turned abruptly, and sourly, downwards.

As the face changed so measurably, the voice continued to mumble unintelligibly, but the tone of it dropped at least an octave. By the time Sunwall posed his first pre-natal question, "George" seemed to have assumed a striking, but arrogant and commanding, appearance. His voice was of that quality when he spoke.

He described himself as being in his middle thirties, of poor health, and a member of the House of Lords. Apparently he had a home in London and a country castle. Both were described in considerable detail. Although he was of a high social position, it soon became obvious that his education and culture were sadly lacking. He had never heard of the major poets and authors of his time, and the name of the Prime Minister of England was unfamiliar to him. He complained of the gout and of a general dissatisfaction with life. As I recall the interview, he died at a fairly early age.

Following his death, he spoke of having watched his body being burned, and so disposed he wandered off into the spirit life.

The most amazing thing about the sessions I observed with "George" was the extraordinary change that took place as he moved, in his trance state, from his present personality to the early childhood, and then "over the hump" into his "Lord Grover" life. The face, attitude of the body, and the voice ran an entire gamut. And while I don't buy this bit any more than any other, still, it was really something to see.

Needless to say, there are many theories of reincarnation, but, in general, they fall into several major categories. Some believers hold that as we die we immediately pass into another existence; that is, we're conceived again, but without any memory of what went before. And following each death there is a total loss of any connection with former lives. In this version, there is no definite pattern from one life to another. A variation on this theme is that once one dies he moves to another existence, either immediately or after a stay on a spiritual plane, and is rewarded either for a good previous life, or punished for a bad one. If the former earth time has been exemplified by behavior of a "high moral order," then the following incarnation will be appropriately elevated. If one has left an undesirable record behind him, then he will become an inferior man—or possibly even an animal.

From time to time speculation runs rampant among reincarnationists regarding sex. Believers seem about evenly divided on the two major aspects of this consideration. First, that in going from one life to another an individual maintains the same sex; and second, that sexual relations are to be found in the "in-between" phases, and on the "higher planes," and generally are described as being even superior in quality and kind to what is available on earth.

Of course, the entire idea of reincarnation (and transmigration) is very ancient. Among the earliest records are those which refer to the Egyptian beliefs in this philosophy. As a matter of fact, one of the major aspects of the mystical tradition of that time and place was the repeating life concept. It was a popular conviction in Greece, and carried over into Roman culture.

The concept of rebirth is common to the Christian Bible, the Talmud and kabala. A number of the saints obviously preached it. It's part of the dogma and/or lore of Brahmanism, Buddhism, Confucianism, Hinduism, Islam, Taoism, Zoroastrianism, and many other theological and theosophical orders of thought.

Of course, almost every group supporting the idea of reincarnation views it in a different manner. As a matter of fact, about all you can find among them that is similar is the assertion that we each live more than one life. For instance, the established average time between births ranges from a mere twenty-five years to a millenium—a thousand years. The reported number of lives one has to go through ranges from seven to seven hundred and seventy-seven. In the larger number, the word is that the first seven hundred are lived in bleak and black ignorance, the next seventy in knowledge and culture, and the last seven in bliss and wisdom. After that, either they don't tell you what happens or they simply say that you are absorbed into the supreme cosmic consciousness. Whatever that is.

As is the case with most off-beat, occult, or mystical gaffs, the arguments presented to convince the non-believer of the bit are long, complicated, and pretty difficult to understand. They'll say, for instance, that "the idea of immortality demands it." Usually they completely overlook the possibility that the listener may totally disbelieve in immortality to begin with. Secondly, it's quite possible that if he does accept the promise of more life after death, he will, in all likelihood, expect it to be in heaven, or an equally orthodox other-life place. Why should he consider another existence on a physical level in a material body the inevitable result of dying?

Another writer will claim that the "nature of the soul" requires it. Well, again the reincarnationist is assuming that his audience believes in the existence of a soul. Then he's assuming that the hearer means the same thing by the word soul that he means. And even if he gets by these two barriers, how in (or out of) the world is he going to prove that "the nature of the soul requires it?"

And one after another they attempt to solve mystical problems and answer mystical questions with even more mystical replies. When confronted with objections to the idea of reincarnation, the rationalizations are really wild.

And yet, recognition of the exponents of these far-fetched phantasies comes from surprising sources. Recently the memory of Leon-Denizarth-Hippolyte Rivail, better remembered as Allan Kardec, was noted by the Brazilian government by the issuing of millions of postage stamps featuring his portrait and the words: "First Centenary of Organized Spiritism."

Kardec, born in France just after the turn of the 18th century, was the originator and organizer of a pseudo-religious sect based, primarily, on the idea of reincarnation. He was a powerful and prolific writer, a phrenologist, hypnotist, psychic investigator, and general double talker. In a number of books he transcribed —the actual writing being done by spirits—he brought to the world his, or rather the "true," facts about reincarnation, the spirit world, and what have you.

He had no success in England, nor in the United States. But France, and the South American countries, found him to be just what they had been waiting for—and he really began to grow. In one of his volumes he lists categories of medium types, among which are included "Calm Mediums," "Mediums for Trivial and Obscene Communication," "Illiterate Mediums," "Mediums for Apparitions," "Touchy Mediums" and on and on.

According to Kardec, reincarnation is all part of God's plan by which He means for Man to eventually reach perfection, even though he may have a pretty rough trip. There's no choice about the whole thing as he tells it; an individual progresses whether he likes it or not. Even though it's only an inch each life, Man must move up the ladder; he can never move back down. Finally everyone makes it, or so the "Spiritism" spirits claim.

Unlike many of the reincarnationists, Kardec drew a rather bleak and forbidding picture of the after-life. He saw it as an almost endless and completely lonely journey through time, where once one died he lost all memory of his friends, relatives, and/or loved ones, never to know them again.

He was ahead of his time, however, in terms of imagination. He visualized Mars as a virtual penal colony of spirits who were of an even lower order than earthians. Jupiter supposedly housed a spiritual civilization of superior souls. The Sun was the resting place of radiant non-physical wraiths.

This was the man honored with a postage stamp all his very spiritistical own.

Almost a hundred years after Kardec and half-way around the world, an incident occurred which seemed far more persuasive to the doubting mind than the story of Kardec—or so it has been reported.

In the late 1920's, a child named Shanti Devi was born in New Delhi, India, of unexceptional parents. At the age of seven or eight, she began speaking of a small town named Muttra where she had lived previously, describing her "former home," the community, and the like. As the next couple of years went by, the little girl's "memories" continued to pour out. Among the various experiences reported by the child was that she had been raised to adulthood in the hamlet, married, bore three children whose names she mentioned, and even identified her own other-life name.

We're told that on the occasion of a visit to her father by a man who had come to discuss business she immediately identified the stranger as "my husband's cousin." It was quickly established, although the man didn't recognize Shanti, that he did live in Muttra, did have a cousin who had lost a wife ten years before, and that the wife had had the name Shanti claimed she formerly had.

Upon being taken to the town of Muttra, she instantly knew her "husband," his mother and brother, all the town landmarks, pointed out her house, and greeted her ancient father-in-law. She also conversed freely in the local native dialect, although she and her parents knew only Hindustani. Without hesitation, she recognized her two oldest children, but curiously not the one which had caused her death.

As reported, the story was fully documented by Indian authorities, who never found nor offered any explanation for the extraordinary case. Shanti is grown, of course, and when last heard of worked in New Delhi, having decided to live but one life at a time.

Reincarnationists find almost unlimited sources to quote from in support of their multiple-life theories, but the favorite references are statements of famous men. For example, they'll cite Napoleon's exclamation: "I am Charlemagne! Charlemagne! Don't you remember who I am? Charlemagne!" Or they'll tell you of Sir Arthur Conan Doyle who said: "The balance of evidence shows that Reincarnation is a fact." Or even the practical-minded Henry Ford's observation: "I believe that we are here now and will come back again."

And these are but three of scores they have on file who've indicated that they were inclined to believe in the repeating life concept. As a matter of fact, there are lists of names of famous people who were followers of the word which add up into the hundreds. And although I don't know exactly what the basis for their inclusion in these lists is, you'll find such differing and unexpected personalities as Alexander the Great, St. Augustine, Balzac, Edgar Cayce, Cicero, Confucius, Dante, Edison, St. Francis, Gandhi, Goethe, Hegel, Hermes, (!), Hugo, Leibnitz, Plato, Shakespeare, Voltaire, and the names are almost endless. But again I must point out, I have no idea of what kind of flimsy evidence was used to justify the inclusion of many of the notable people.

There has always been a ready acceptance in the East of the general concepts of reincarnation, while in the West the tendency has been, at least for the public at large, to doubt it. In India, for example, the advocates of the previous life theory have innumerable reports to bolster their contentions. Earlier I told of the case of Shanti Devi, but that's only one of many. Another is the story of Jagdish Chandra, born in 1923, who lived in Bareilly, India. It was his assertion that he had previously existed in Benares, and he proceeded to relate many details to prove same. We're told, as we are in most such cases, that the story was verified by "authorities." Who the officials were, I don't know. But the point is that, in that particular country, tales of reincarnation are quite common and readily accepted.

Generally speaking, throughout recorded history, there has been a tremendous inclination and desire to believe in reincarnation, or metempsychosis, or palin-genesis, or pre-existence, or whatever you wish to call it. It's claimed that, in the second five hundred years of the Christian era, over a hundred thousand persons were executed for supporting the philosophy. At one time or another, most of the major religious movements have endorsed the basic principles of re-life. The figures vary widely as to the number of people believing in reincarnation in the United States today, but a million would probably be a reasonable, if not conservative, estimate.

It's easy to understand how the least fortunate, starving people of the underprivileged countries of the world might well have sought and accepted the idea that they would be given another go at life. Another time around when the chips wouldn't be stacked so terribly against them. But it's even more interesting, and maybe a little sad, that in this, the most prosperous nation on earth, a million persons are so dissatisfied with the lives they're leading, or have led, that they feel a great need to come back and do the bit again. For obviously this isn't the religious fervor of after-life, heaven, or union with God; this is the drive to return to earth, not merely one time, but hundreds of times—the need to hope that once more will the individual be, not rewarded with the glorious life eternal, but subjected to the troubles and ignominies, pains and disappointments, frustrations and foolishnesses of this world.

CHAPTER 7

"Healing is a matter of time,
but it is also sometimes a
matter of opportunity."
          —Hippocrates

EDGAR CAYCE, PSYCHIC DOCTOR, AND
JOHN R. BRINKLEY, KING OF THE QUACKS

EDGAR CAYCE was the greatest healer of them all. Of course, I mean in modern times. But, come to think of it, if one accepts all of the claims made in his name, he compares with any healer of any time.

He entered upon this earth at Hopkinsville, Kentucky, on Sunday, March 18th, 1877; he left this life from Virginia Beach, Virginia, on January 3rd, 1945; and in between that arrival and departure, according to his unlimited legion of followers who still survive (and many insist because of him), Edgar Cayce (pronounced Casey) performed some fifteen thousand miracles.

From the very beginning, his life took most curious turns. For several weeks following his birth, he's reputed to have cried

98

almost constantly. The reason was a mystery until a local Negro nurse was called upon. She immediately solved the problem by pricking each of his nipples with a sterilized needle. Milk flowed for a short time, stopped, and that was the end of the matter.

As quite a young boy, he was amply supplied with sisters, but had no boys to play with. However, one day a boy appeared and they spent the day together. Time went by and other children came to him. His companions were phantom boys and girls.

While he was still young, Cayce lost his grandfather. Well, actually "lost" wouldn't be the right word. The old man died, but the boy kept in touch. He used to meet his grandfather in the barn or down along the woods. Naturally, these occasions went unmentioned.

Early in life he discovered that sleep was a great power to him. The first evidence came to light one night when he was studying a lesson under the supervision of his father. Over and over again Edgar tried; over and over again he failed. Slapped and admonished by his father more than once, he finally begged for a few moments rest. Receiving this, the boy fell forward on his books and napped. A short time later, when his father returned and awoke him, the lesson began anew. This time, however, it was all different. Edgar sped through it like a little wizard. He even asked his father to try him on other sections of the school book. Parts he hadn't even read yet. And he answered every question. Soon it was obvious that by some unknown means he had absorbed the entire volume as his head lay resting on it.

What was the key to this wonder? Well, in later years, Edgar Cayce explained it in the following manner. A couple of days earlier, he had been sitting in a little lean-to he had built. Without warning, he looked up and there was a woman. For an instant he thought it was his mother, but immediately he realized he was wrong. The woman spoke in a soft and musical voice, saying that his prayers had been heard. She offered him a wish.

Amazed, the boy stared at the creature when he saw that from her back swept two large graceful wings.

He replied that most of all he'd like to be able to help people, particularly children. And suddenly, even more suddenly than she'd arrived, she was gone. From the moment of this vision forward, he felt that he had been ordained by the unknown to do great work. From a more practical point of view, he never again had to read a book to know its contents, he just went to sleep on it.

Later in his youth, Edgar Cayce suffered an ordinary accident with rather strange results. While playing baseball one afternoon, he was struck on the base of the spine by a thrown ball. At the moment he didn't seem to be too severely affected by the unfortunate blow, but as the hours went by he began behaving most curiously, singing, giggling, laughing, squinting and tossing things about. By the evening, when he was put to bed, he had turned completely serious. In a semi-coma condition, or shock state, he began prescribing for his own disorder. He told his parents to apply a poultice to the back of his neck. This was done and the boy went to sleep. In the morning he awoke, feeling in excellent health, and remembering absolutely nothing. This was the first—this self-cure—of many thousands which were to follow . . . or so his disciples claimed.

During his adolescence he confused and confounded his family and friends developing his extraordinary "talents"; but when he was about twenty-three he suddenly was afflicted with aphonia. That is, he lost his voice.

At the time he was acting as a salesman, and he had just arrived at a small town some fifty miles from his own home town of Hopkinsville. He'd been suffering from severe headaches for a number of weeks, and he had taken a sedative powder and gone to bed. The next time he became conscious he found himself in his own bed in his parents' home. He had been found wandering around the other town in a dazed condition by a couple of family friends. They brought him home. But having awakened, he tried to speak—but the voice was totally gone. Physicians reported that he was fine except for the loss of vocal power. Days passed. It didn't improve. A specialist was called in, but he offered no helpful suggestion except to name the problem—aphonia. One doctor after another, one month after another, went by; the voice did not return. Finally, and reluctantly, Cayce decided his illness was incurable.

It was obvious that his job as a salesman was finished, but he had the good fortune to be offered a position in a local photographer's studio. Working as an apprentice, he spent most of his time in the dark room, and so he was not required to speak. The clock continued and things were about as good as they might be. Cayce even began to look toward having a studio of his own.

One day a noted hypnotist arrived at the town opera house; his name was Hart. From the descriptions we have of him, it seems obvious that he was pretty good at his "profession." After Hart had been in town for several days, he heard about Cayce's problem, and although he made no claim to be a therapist he became interested in the case. At the time, the medical value of hypnotism was being much discussed and it was not long before he was challenged to try his skills on the voiceless young man. He accepted on a fair, but rather practical, basis. If he succeeded in his attempt to return Cayce's voice, he would receive $200.00; if he failed, he'd receive nothing.

The first attempt got under way. Hart put Cayce into a light trance, and into a deep one. He made a post-hypnotic suggestion that the voice would return to normal when the subject awoke. To the disappointment of all, when Edgar came out of the trance, the condition of the voice had not changed. The hypnotist made several more efforts, but always failed. Cayce, he said, was going into trance easily enough, but not deep enough to accept an effective post-hypnotic suggestion. He was certain, however, that sooner or later he would. But before this ever happened, Hart had to move on to keep his commitments.

During the experiments, a professor of psychology at a local university had been attracted to the case. This gentleman had spoken with Cayce and Hart and was quite familiar with the situation.

One of the leading physicians advocating the use of it for therapy was a New York doctor named Quackenboss. After an exchange of letters with the professor of psychology, his interest in the case became so great as to make him decide to visit Cayce. He arrived in Hopkinsville and began his attempts immediately, but, sadly, with no more success than Hart had achieved. The doctor returned to the North, leaving behind only the thought that Cayce's trance problem seemed to be that after a certain point he rejected all further suggestions from the hypnotist. Quackenboss offered the final idea that possibly someone should try to get the subject to "take over" himself while he was still in trance.

The only "resident" hypnotist in Hopkinsville was a fragile little man by the name of Al C. Layne. As a last resort, Edgar agreed to permit Layne an opportunity to try his skills. On Sunday afternoon, March 31st, 1901, Layne put the voiceless curiosity into a state of deep hypnosis and began what was to become one of the most extraordinary careers of mystical and medical history.

Essentially, Cayce actually put himself into trance, under Layne's supervision. Suddenly he cleared his throat and spoke out in a clear and unafflicted voice.

"Yes," he began, "we can see the body." He continued, pointing out that when in a non-trance state the patient was unable to speak due to a partial paralysis of the vocal cords due to "nerve strain." A cure could be achieved, he diagnosed, by increasing the circulation in that part of the body while the subject was still unconscious. His father, who stood by, loosened his collar and the surrounding area turned pink, then scarlet, with the self-induced rush of blood. Presently, the color returned to normal. Layne brought him completely out of the hypnotic state and he awoke. His vocal powers had totally returned. He was cured.

Cayce, his parents, and Layne, discussed the remarkable occurrence. The time Edgar had prescribed for the injury he received while playing baseball was recalled. His father brought up his ability to memorize books while sleeping on them. One after another the strange aspects of Cayce's career and personality were reviewed. The conclusion was that he had been given some unexplained power by some unknown source. It was agreed that he would try his power of curing on Layne, who had been suffering from various infirmities for many years—disorders that left him a weak and frail little man. Cayce lay down upon a couch and went into his trance state. Quickly and clearly he began to diagnose Layne's disorders, but this time in strange and technical language. He referred to various parts of the body by their purely medical names; he spoke of motor responses, body functions, organic parts, and physical disorders in words and phrases which one could only find in a doctor's dictionary. Only Layne, who had read considerably on medical subjects and who had studied osteopathy and "suggestive therapy," understood all that Edgar said; but to him it all made clear and practical sense. He explained to the others that Edgar had spoken as a physician.

"How do I do it?" asked the young man.

"You are psychic," replied Layne. "You are a clairvoyant."

And thus was begun the amazing professional career of "Edgar Cayce, Psychic Diagnostician." During the next twenty years, the ever-more-famous sleeping doctor treated, or, more accurately, his subconscious treated, some fifteen thousand patients. According to those who worked with the mystic, he always spoke from a hypnotic trance. The state was always self-induced, but never without the assistance of an "operator." His language was invariably lucid, his vocabulary technical, medically knowledgeable, and accurate, and infinitely beyond what anyone could possibly expect, considering his limited education. And, most unbelievable, his followers claimed that he never erred. It's pretty obvious that his percentage of success was astronomically high if you read the reports, articles, books, and pamphlets issued about him. Many thousands of "attested cures" are on record at the Cayce Institute at Virginia Beach.

To Edgar's severe regret, Layne did not always live up to what Cayce felt was the responsibility of their enterprise. Eventually they came to a parting of the paths. He then formed an alliance of sorts with a John Blackburn, with whom he seemed to have gotten along quite well.

Toward the beginning of the Cayce-Blackburn relationship, the medium suffered another of the weird physical afflictions which dropped down upon him so often during his lifetime.

Cayce was demonstrating his powers to several visitors when he fell into an unusually deep trance. All efforts to communicate with him failed and the observers became very concerned. Shortly, Blackburn was summoned with the ominous hint that his friend had died in his auto-hypnotic condition. When he arrived, he discovered that several doctors had been administering to Cayce. They had pumped him full of morphine injections, strychnine, and who knows what. Hot bricks, wrapped in towels, had been applied to his body—hot metal to his feet. No signs of life resulted. Apparently Edgar Cayce was dead.

Slowly, John Blackburn began to talk to the inert form of his associate. Over and over, he asked the medium to increase his pulse and normalize the circulation of the blood. Finally the sleeping doctor awoke and told his friend that he would have to go back into trance so that Blackburn could talk him back to health. Suffering from the original disorder and from the disastrous medications of the physicians, all of whom had now gone, Edgar had a pretty bad time of it for most of the night. But finally the poisons were rejected, the body was normalized, and the medium fell into a natural rest. When he eventually awoke, he was almost his old self again.

Time went by, and in spite of his ill-health and see-sawing

103

fortunes, Edgar Cayce continued his health and "life" readings. Then, around 1920, he decided to establish a hospital for the more severe of his cases. Of course, up to this point he almost never saw his patients personally. In nearly every instance his power was employed in long-range relationships, sometimes involving distances of hundreds of miles. Now, Cayce figured his efforts could be concentrated and increased if he was able to establish a hospital. A number of sponsors came forward, there were discussions, some dropped out, others joined, more left, changes and problems followed difficulties and revisions. One site was suggested, then another. And so it went. Although Cayce's psychic readings indicated that the place should be Virginia Beach, Virginia.

The plans did not fare well. There were a number of false starts, and people who put money into the plans lost it. Cayce was no better off than he'd ever been, and that had never been good. Finally a man named Morton Blumenthal, a former patient, became interested; and through him a house was acquired in the forecast community. True, it was a pretty rundown and shabby house, and the nearest stores were a long way away, but it was a house. And it was Cayce's.

"The Association of National Investigators" was incorporated on May 6th, 1927, in Virginia. Its purpose was "to engage in general psychic research, and to provide for the practical application of any knowledge obtained through the medium of psychic phenomena." Actually, it was wholly based upon Edgar's so-called power, and its objective was to establish an official Cayce hospital.

Two types of readings were to be the axles upon which this wagon would roll. The regular health-therapy readings and the life readings. The first diagnosed illnesses and treated them, but the second reviewed the entire present life existence of an individual, *plus* a review of his other lives, his lives of the past. A strong promoter of reincarnation, Cayce was able to bring out of his subconscious trance state the picture of what a person had been before. These, naturally, were tremendously popular since, amazing as it might seem, the people are more interested in believing that they were once a little slave girl of the Nile who was freed by an adoring and wealthy young Egyptian, than in curing their physical disorders and regaining good health.

At last the hospital was built and the Association took on a physical existence. The building was a thirty-bed affair, with a lecture hall, library, vault, offices, living room, screened porch, large garage, servants' area, tennis courts, landscaped lawns and terraces—in short, it was quite an operation. Morton, the financing wizard, had sunk close to a quarter of a million dollars in the effort. Everything went along wonderfully. The place was filled to the roof constantly. Each moment of the medium's time was taken up with readings. And then Blumenthal, and his brother, began disagreeing with Cayce. The budget was unbalanced. The hospital was losing money every month. Morton was losing money in the market. Besides which, he had split his resources right down the middle by starting a university as well, and it had cost him over a hundred thousand dollars and was still loaded with debts. And then, claiming that he was the only one the depression hadn't bothered, Blumenthal went under financially. The hospital was closed. Edgar Cayce left with his records. It was the end of February, 1931. Things were bad all over.

About four months later, Cayce gathered about him some of his more faithful followers and asked them whether a new organization should be begun to promote his work. The response was all in favor of starting up once more. The new group was called "The Association for Research and Enlightenment." However, it wasn't until 1940 that a new building was erected, and this was much more modest than the original. Yet, it was here that Edgar Cayce continued his work, readings and research. And, finally, "the miracle man of Virginia Beach," "the sleeping doctor," "the psychic diagnostician," lay down on his bed for his final earthly sleep, dying in the early evening of January 3rd, 1945.

But we might remember that, no matter what we think of the powers he was supposed to possess, he was a remarkable man. His great reputation and wide fame never gained him anything for himself, his family, or his friends. But he was a living saint to thousands of people. The Bible was beside him all his life, yet he was never bound by orthodoxy. He accepted all things as being possible, including reincarnation and spiritualism. Among the innumerable powers accredited to him by his disciples were psychic diagnosis, psychic and faith healing, clairvoyance, clairaudience, psychometry, levitation, prophecy, astral projection, the ability to contact spirit voices and spirit life, and general mediumship. Hundreds came to prove that he was a charlatan and stayed to believe, even preach, his doctrine. Even if only one-tenth of all that was said about him was true, it still leaves mysteries for which science has no explanation.

"The Association for Research and Enlightenment" continues its investigations and research under the direction of Edgar's son, Hugh Lynn Cayce. The father has almost been elevated to sainthood and the cause goes on. As with all the other things discussed, I don't buy any of the powers Cayce was supposed to have. I don't believe in what he did, I don't believe anyone ever did what he's supposed to have done. But I must admit that I believe that he was a devout and sincere man; and I'll never know what it was all those people saw that convinced him of something that I consider absolutely impossible.

Unfortunately, not all healers are quite so sincere as Edgar Cayce, because no matter how much I think his bit was all in his own mind I can't argue that he believed in all he said. But an entirely different case was the greatest of all the pseudo-medical men ever to arise in this country. His name was Dr. John R. Brinkley, and he was fantastic.

Brinkley's beginnings are somewhat vague, since he himself claimed, at one time or another, that he was born in Tennessee, Virginia, North Carolina, Kentucky, and Florida. But wherever he happened to decide it had been, at the moment he was describing the great occurrence, the event always took place in a log cabin. Before he was twenty, he had developed a driving ambition to be a doctor—any kind of doctor—so long as he could lay claim to a pew in the exalted church of medicine. He did a little elixir pitching here and there, and then he got hold of twenty-five dollars and entered the Bennet Medical College. Eventually he dropped out of this esteemed institution for want of money for fees. At one time or another, the charlatan claimed to have attended several schools and/or universities, but all indications are that his education was mostly self-acquired.

By 1913, the good healer had acquired a wife and produced three children, all of whom he left in Chattanooga. Not long after he married again, the daughter of a legitimate physician, and took in as a partner one James E. Crawford, who later ended up in the penitentiary for car theft. These two gentlemen opened offices in South Carolina, calling themselves "Electro Medic Doctors." The entire treatment, which was one that was supposed to increase sexual power, was a hypo shot of colored water. The charge for this: $25.00. After a few profitable weeks of this, the operation skipped out—leaving a pile of unpaid bills behind. The partners went in opposite directions.

Over the years Crawford and Brinkley met from time to

time, once being when they were housed in the same jail. But they never hit it off together again. Actually, Brinkley never needed the less talented man's aid again.

By 1915, John R. had a diploma to practice medicine (at least in eight states), from a diploma mill called the "Eclectic Medical University." The Professor Alexander who operated this gaff dealt out similar credentials to soda jerks, salesmen, chauffeurs, photographers, and just about anyone else who came wandering by with a hot little buck in his hayseedy little hand.

In 1916, this same professor of medicine, so-called, assisted Brinkley in getting a license to practice in Kansas and Arkansas. Soon after, the slippery pseudo-physician was accredited to conduct his operations legally in Texas, Tennessee, Missouri, and Connecticut, too. It was not long before the doctor went to work for a famous meatpacking concern, handling minor cuts and bruises. It was at this time that the great healer had an opportunity to discover extraordinary and mysterious truths about the glands of animals. It was here that he began putting together the theories that were later to make him a fortune and the possessor of considerable personal power.

Then came The First Great War, and our hero leaped into the medical corps as fast as he could, getting first looie's bars to sport about. Although it was Brinkley's claim that he was practically worked to death, dealing with the physical problems of over two thousand rookies at a camp in Texas, the real facts seem to indicate that he was only in active medical service for one month. Also, for all but three days of his duty time he himself was too physically ill to perform any functions. He soon was out of the army and settled in a rather shabby little town called Milford, Kansas, where he set up an equally shabby little practice.

Plodding along, Brinkley attended the usual general sicknesses until the great plan came to him. A patient came in with the complaint of having lost his sexual prowess. The doctor didn't have much to suggest, but remarked that it was unfortunate that he couldn't give the patient the vigor of the ram and goats he recalled from the meat-packing company days. When the patient asked why he couldn't perform such an operation, the opened-to-almost-anything-minded scientist began to wonder about that himself. Although he had always been taught that there could be no medical traffic between lower animals and human beings, he didn't remember that his professor had said—

positively. After some book, but very little soul, searching, he agreed to perform the transplant on the gentleman in question. The operation took place in the beat-up back room of his office. Two weeks later the patient, the doctor always told listeners, had an almost complete return of his lazy libido. A year later, Brinkley would top off the tale, his wife gave birth to a ten-pound baby boy. Of course, all this proves is that the patient trusted both his doctor and his wife, and there was plenty of room to doubt the integrity of his doctor.

And that was the start of the most fabulous of all the quack careers to flourish in the history of this nation. Of course, he had picked a tremendous symbol psychologically. The goat. The animal which, throughout history, has been thought of as the classic symbol of over-sexuality. The money began to roll in with the usual charge being about $750, sometimes even up to a couple of thousand dollars. Brinkley added the charming little touch of letting the subjects pick their own goats, and also there was the added advantage of an operation which took only a few minutes.

The pitch prospered, even boomed, as he invaded other territories, including Chicago, Los Angeles, Shanghai, Singapore, and other remote places. This was a big-time, round-the-world operator, by now.

Everything continued to grow, and in 1923 the Brinkley hospital in Kansas established a radio station with the call letters KFKB, the "home of gland transplantation." The power was 1,000 watts in a day when the biggest stations used only 500. Its signal could be heard for a couple of thousand miles. And the amazingly transparent bubble continued to grow. His public relations were phenomenally successful, but opposition was beginning to shape up. There were those who saw the great fake as just that. But more money than ever was pouring in and he had not a worry in the world that it would continue. He had found an almost perfect gimmick.

But he wasn't satisfied with the tens of thousands he was grossing each month—he wanted more. More money, and from it, more power. And so he began to zing his own bit to a special very wealthy mailing list, asking why they should have the operation and become half goats. Instead, it was offered, these selected millionaires should not receive the glands of a young goat, but those of a young and virile man. Sexy boy-glands that Brinkley was prepared to produce and install. Naturally, since he would have to relieve one human being of them so that they would be available to his special patients, they would be extremely expensive. The price would range between $5,000 and $10,000—but then the patient could look forward to being not only all man, but all human.

As things progressed, the master took over complete charge of the radio operation, programming himself as the star. And to his audience, he was far and away the star. Not only of that show, but of most of radio. However, the gentleman had not reached his peak of audacity. In September of 1930, Dr. John R. Brinkley announced that he was a candidate for the office of governor of the state of Kansas.

At first the professional politicians paid no real attention to him, but as the campaign moved along both the Democrat and the Republican (he claimed he was neither) began to take another look. It became obvious that he was more than just an issue—he was a serious candidate. At first it was thought that he might pull in about twenty-five thousands votes in the entire state. Soon this was upped to 50,000, and then to 75,000 votes. Then his opponents began to worry. To block him, and insure that one of the two legitimate (?) office-seekers would win, the state election law was to be rigidly enforced. This meant that all ballots for the pseudo-scientist *had* to be marked exactly: "J. R. Brinkley," and an "X" in the box that followed the name. *Any* variation, such as "John R.," or adding a "Dr." before, or a "MD" after, disqualified the vote. Brinkley conducted a tremendous campaign, using his radio station, KFKB, to great advantage. With all the professional politicians in the state on the other side, the result was pretty inevitable. The Democrat received 217,171 votes, his Republican opponent 257 less, and Brinkley got 183,278. The doctor and his followers always insisted that if all the votes that had been written in the wrong places or in a technically incorrect way had been counted he would have received just under 240,000 votes; and he would have won almost by a landslide. Almost no professional participant or observer denied, privately, that he would have won easily if his name had been printed on the ballot with his two competitors. But all of his write-in votes, and that, along with the "throw-outs," killed his chances and kept him from becoming governor—or more.

With the loss of the election, he began to lose power otherwise, and by 1932 it was obvious to him that he could no longer get away with practicing medicine in Kansas, or even with running his radio station. But as he withdrew from his adopted state he moved into a Mexican town, just across the border, where he bought the second most powerful radio station in the world—one with 75,000 watts.

Brinkley was not yet ready to give up the political ghost. In 1932 he ran again as an independent for the governor's mansion in Kansas. During the campaign he wore a bullet-proof vest. He seemed to think that it was a question of ballots or bullets. Although he polled 244,000-odd votes, Alf Landon won handily. He tried again in '34, but with even worse luck. There was no doubt about it. John R. Brinkley's political career had sunk into a permanent oblivion. He had a small revival in a couple of later contests, but they were even less than token in value.

His final glory was in his return to radio. The Mexican station, XER, which he had bought, had been given special permission by the federal government to boost its power enormously. When Brinkley got through, he had a nearly incredible 500,000 watts.

But, as was inescapable, the whole operation began to disintegrate. Brinkley began to sue, the government came after a half-million dollars in back taxes, then about a dozen suits were instigated against the doctor . . . back and forth it went. Back and forth went money, but far more was going forth than was coming back. Brinkley got involved with a number of very unsavory people in an attempt to save his failing fortunes, many of them professing and pitching strong racist and hate philosophies. Then came the back-breaking blow. His magnificent radio station was torn down by a demolition team of the Mexican army, while he was away. He became quite ill when he heard the news. And that was the end of his radio career once and for all.

After that everything just dwindled away, leaving behind only a shadowy memory of the man who was the greatest charlatan doctor America ever produced.

CHAPTER 8

"He who would distinguish the true from the false must have an adequate idea of what is true and false." — *Ethics*
Benedict Spinoza

THE HEALERS AND PHILOSOPHERS

VARIOUS KINDS of people claim to have the power to heal, and they claim it in various ways. However, considering only the unorthodox of the breed, one sees that they tend to fall into two major categories operating with either of two general approaches. Those who fall into the first group seem to be really convinced of their "power," those of the second class are obviously simply using their "power of the pitch" to promote and sell their services and products for whatever they can get for them.

Another place where the "healers" separate is in their approach. Some offer to cure all of the ills of man through the flesh with potions, salves and machines. Some through the mind with psychologies, mysticisms and rites. Many have all techniques available to the paying client, others specialize in only the "most effective methods" of restoring or elevating the body, mind or soul to its "natural state of well being." It's among these subtle distinctions that you might find the line that divides the "healers" from others who might more accurately be called "philosophers." Generally speaking, the latter are content with dabbling with the health of the mind, while the competition is promising dangerously absurd cures for cancer and brain tumors. I don't have to point out that there are millions of people who believe in this kind of nonsense.

I say it's all ridiculous—operators roaming the country offering health, happiness and eternal good fortune where regular doctors, psychologists and business instincts have failed. Naturally, it's possible that I'm wrong, possible that everyone mentioned in this book is a great whatever-he-claims-to-be. However, unfortunately, it's more likely that I'm not.

Appropriately, or at least not unexpectedly, one of the powerful health movements of our time was the invention of an imaginative science fiction writer by the name of L. Ron Hubbard (Lafayette Ronald Hubbard). His supposed new science of the mind went under the name of "Dianetics."

It more or less began when the founder brought out his first book on the subject in 1950, although it was his claim that he had originally discovered the basic principles of his "science" twelve years before. This is a claim that has been doubted by a good number of people involved with the bit; these take the position that it got under way in 1948.

When first writing on the subject, it was Hubbard's modest estimate that Dianetics was one of the greatest discoveries in the history of mankind, ranking right beside the invention of the wheel and the use of fire. He further took the positive position that his mental panacea would "invariably" cure the patient. Not once in a while, or often, but always. The reason for this, Hubbard insisted, was that Dianetics was an "exact science" based upon simple engineering principles, operating in the same manner as pure math. Therefore it was never wrong. It could not make a mistake.

Somehow it comes as no great surprise that one of Hubbard's first patients and promoters was John Campbell, Jr., the science fiction editor who was so helpful in introducing the miraculous Hieronymous Machine to the not-ready-for-it public. But exactly what was it Hubbard and Campbell were trying to sell?

The fundamental Dianetical approach assumes that all psychological problems are based upon one, or more, of the following three conditions. First, a great physical pain. Second, great

112

danger—either real or imagined. Third, "a non-analytic state of the brain." This last condition creates what Hubbard calls an "Impediment." By this he means that there's a block in the mind. A blank. An area where the conscious mind doesn't function properly, doesn't include something. Dianetics is designed, among other things, to fill in the blank, eliminate the block, make the thought sequence of the mind continuous in the area where the problem is.

Hubbard calls these aberrations "engrams." He calls the conscious mind "analytical," and the unconscious mind "reactive." The unconscious mind has no power to evaluate, according to him; it merely, but exactly, records all sensory perceptions—but only when the conscious mind is not functioning. It's the disorders registered by the reactive, or unconscious, mind—which he calls engrams—that cause all the mental problems in the world. Neuroses, psychoses, common colds, maybe even cancer, are caused by these troublesome engrams. And Dianetics is the cure-all and the all-cured. Remember, it works for everyone.

Hubbard has taken the position, in print, that psychiatrists are "the extant mental charlatans," and that psychologists are "the professional dabblers in abilities." This unqualified contempt for these two areas of evaluation and therapy led him to believe in the need for, and proceed to create, an operator called an "auditor." If you want to know what an auditor is, it appears that it's someone who has read Hubbard's books and can answer questions later. Providing they're about Ron Hubbard's books, and not about psychology, psychiatry, psychoanalysis, or the human mind.

It's the contention of Dianetics that "life" is fundamentally divided into "ability" and "mechanics." If you go a little further, you discover that "ability is demonstrated by the handling of matter, energy, space, and time" and put all those things together and they spell "mechanics." Things, like motors and mountains, are made up of matter, energy, space and time, and are affectionately called "MEST." As a matter of fact, neighbors, the entire subject is pretty MEST up.

Now, when you understand things like this, you realize that only "life" can "create." However, when it gets started, "life" really pulls out the stops. Take for example a process Hubbard calls "the remedy of havingness"; this bit is "capable of increasing a man's weight by thirty-five pounds—without changing the diet, or way of living. Fortunately, if you go overboard with the action you can do a reverse process called "perfect duplication." Easy come, easy go.

However, to go back to the basis for all the mental problems of the world, "engrams," the reader should be aware that these go far, far back in the subconscious memory—that is, in the "reactive" mind. Not in childhood, not in infancy, but before birth. Possibly even before the fertilization.

As the system goes, anything—or possibly it should be everything—has a profound effect upon the unborn babe. If Daddy yells at Mommy, it produces an "engram"; if Mommy had a stomach ache it produces an "engram"; if little brother-to-be bounces up and down on the bed Mommy is lying on, it produces an "engram"; if Mommy listens to syncopated music it produces an "engram"; if Mommy goes to the bathroom, it produces an "engram." But worst of all, if Mommy and/or Daddy try to abort the baby it produces an "engram."

One of the great difficulties for the unborn is the terrible way Daddy may treat Mommy. He may beat her, punch her, slap her, yell at her, curse her, and all this has a decidedly negative effect upon the baby of tomorrow. Unfortunately, Hubbard seems to feel that this is the normal relationship between Mother and Father, or at least the usual one. Once old wives and young mothers believed that the great danger lay in looking too long at a pumpkin, or being caught in the rain. Such things would cause a future offspring to be fat or tearful. Today, however, the fear is in the unkind word or slug in the head. These are liable to produce "engrams"! Things seem to have slipped from bad to not very much better.

After being born and growing up with all of these horribly unpleasant things floating about in the "reactive mind," the lucky individual takes a crack at Dianetics, putting himself into the hands of an "auditor." The "auditor" then proceeds to put the subject into "reverie." In this state, an attempt is made to delve into the unconscious—possibly into even the birth experience itself—and root out the "impediments." One by two and three they're removed, that is if the "auditor" is successful. And, of course, they always are—since Dianetics always is. As the problems become fewer the person becomes "pre-clear"; eventually the subject is a "clear." This means that he is "the equivalent" of a very superior person who can catch colds and all like that.

To try to sum up the subject briefly, probably the best definition would be from the founder himself. It's "a system of the analysis, control and development of human thought evolved from a set of coordinated axioms which also provide techniques for the treatment of a wide range of mental disorders and organic diseases."

Dianetics made L. Ron Hubbard famous, but that wasn't enough. With one planet wheeling happily about the occult-therapy sky, he decided to give it a sun to go around. He built such a sun, intended to dominate the many worlds of healing. He called it "Scientology."

Now arises the question: what is Scientology? The "official" description, to be found in Hubbard's publications, runs as follows: "Scientology is a system of organized axioms resolving problems of life and thought, developed through the application of the methodology of the exact sciences to the humanities by L. Ron Hubbard, American engineer and philosopher." In equally vague, but somewhat different, terms, it's classified as a branch of psychology, which is pretty interesting since its author displays an obvious contempt for psychology and psychologists in other areas of his writing. At least, however, Hubbard admits that it is another version, or an "extension," of Dianetics. Among the sacred writings it is pointed out that this mechanical occultism is to be "used by the trained and untrained person" to improve "the health, intelligence, ability, behaviour, skill and appearance of people." Naturally, like its forerunner, it's a "precise and exact science." ♦

Like Dianetics, Hubbard's second pitch employs an "auditor" (now described as a "Scientology practitioner," instead of a "Dianetics practitioner"). But now the auditor, who used to work with individuals, has expanded the operation. Imitating the competition, they now have group therapy. The advantages of this are pretty obvious, since this way an auditor can take care of many times as many patients as before.

In some of the Scientology literature, and there's an awful lot of it, it's claimed that the method is successful in curing about 70% of human illness. In an earlier Dianetic text the assertion was made that Dianetics could cure any patient of anything. Hubbard's explanation of why he makes such high claims for his new "science" is that it's the most completely and thoroughly "tested" subject on earth, except for physics and chemistry.

Although most of the claims for Scientology are pretty strong, some people are really jarred when they discover that the Scientologists also claim that their bit will cure illnesses diagnosed as incurable, measurably increase intelligence, and alleviate burns received from "Atomic Bombs." Or, to quote directly from one pamphlet, "Scientology is the only specific (cure) for radiation (atomic bomb) burns."

Scientology, which began as Dianetics as a fairly localized, kind of far-out bit for in-siders, reached a great number of people. This was no accident, but came about because Hubbard extended it into every field of operation. The religious, the psychological, the academic, the sociological, the mystical, and so on. On a piece of stationery with a letterhead reading "Scientology, United States," and below "The Congress of Scientologists," the left hand margin lists a number of "scientological" organizations and/or enterprises. The following are listed.

Founding Church of Scientology of Washington; Founding Church of Scientology, New York; Church of American Science; The Academy of Scientology; Society of Consulting Ministers; Hubbard Assn. of Scientologists, International; Hubbard Guidance Center; Scientology Consultants, Inc.; Congress of Scientologists; Hubbard Dianetic Research Foundation; Hubbard Research Foundation; American Society for Disaster Relief; Scientology Consultants to Industrial Efficiency; Committee of Examination, Certification and Services; Hubbard Communications Office; ABILITY Publications; and Distribution Center, Inc.

Unfortunately, the descriptions of the buildings and offices of each and all of these organizations were not immediately available, nor was very much other information about them to be found. But the impression is that they're all very much inter-related and that many may only exist primarily, if not exclusively, on the tops of stationery.

At least one exception to the last thought is the little eight- and sometimes twelve-page publication titled "Ability." This pamphlet, which has reached over 125 issues, is very cheaply produced and is filled with puffs (praise pieces) for Hubbard and his various enterprises, announcements of lectures and Hubbard lecture tapes for sale, occasional case histories, a few truisms, and very little else.

"A Brief Biography of L. Ron Hubbard," covering some eight small pages, including one full-page photograph, presents to the faithful a highly "copywritten" publicity-conscious, legend-making picture of the great bright father of Dientology, that is, Scientetics, . . . it makes a pretty good pitch no matter how you spell it. The most interesting thing in the entire brochure is the part that tells how Hubbard has been immortalized in modern literature. It states that Hubbard was the character of "Mister Roberts," famous hero of book, stage and screen, and that that story of his war experiences had been fictionalized without his permission. It also refers to several other fictional personalities who were, in reality, L. Ron Hubbard.

The scientological philosopher claims that $2,000,000 has been spent trying to destroy his creations, scientology and dianetics; he doesn't mention how much has been spent by the customers *on* them. Whatever the amount, it's up in the many figures. Few offbeat ideas of our times have been so patently successful as these. They've scientifically drawn in and measured out thousands of people; but, unfortunately, unlike this writer, they didn't say: "I don't buy it."

* * * * *

When the pendulum swings all the way in the other direction of modern off-beat theories of therapy, it crashes right into one of the weirdest bits in the history of "healeology." It's the thousand and one cures of Eli Greifer. This odd gentleman, who asserts that he's a practicing pharmacist and attorney, is unique among pseudo-medical practitioners. He's the author of "Poems for What Ails You," "Remedy-Rhyme for What Ails You," "Philosophic Duels with the Master Poets," "Psychologic Duels with the Master Poets," "Greifer's Quizzer on the Law of Evidence," and, the topper, "How I Cured My Incurable Ailments."

In his "Alphabetic Contents for Curability," to be found in the last of these books, Greifer notes a great number of disorders with his suggested cures for said problems. For "acidity" he recommends "friedfoodtherapy." For "age and rejuvenation" he offers "lovetherapy," and weighs the effect of "jobtherapy" on "hobbyosis." And as you wade forth into the deeper waters of Greiferisms, you encounter things like sleeptherapy, nightowltherapy and nightowlosis, potatofrytherapy, cafeteriatherapy, egomagnificationtherapy, frownosis, goodism and walkawayosis.

"How I Cured My Incurable Ailments" is a highly biographical volume describing in considerable and vivid detail the apparently endless and complicated disorders of the author, and hundreds of diagnoses and cures for such difficulties. One gets the impression that Greifer has spent his entire life being ill, but here he's offering himself as the only man with the true knowledge of how one can return to health. His style takes two main

117

forms: First person singular diary-type writing, and verses. Little "poems" pop in and out of the pages like symptoms. Much of what he says and suggests is completely sensible and reasonable, such as his passages on "nightowltherapy," "nightowlosis," and other nightowlogical subjects. The main point of this section merely points out that some people by their basic natures are "night people" and others, the majority, are "day people." He argues that it's very unwise and completely pointless for a person to take a "poisonous overdoseage of barbiturates to force a conventional-houred sleep rather than yield to instinctual shifts to nightowlism." Greifer believes that many people who haven't recognized their "natural" pattern become sick insomniacs or bums (because they can't keep jobs) simply because they should be working and living at night and resting during the day hours.

Like almost all amateur, or at least unorthodox, therapists, Eli Greifer seems to assume that there are no illnesses, disorders, or diseases which are too complicated or difficult for him to offer curative opinions on. For example, one line from the Greifertext-therapy runs as follows: "One of my earliest successes as a poemtherapist was the case of a psychopathic personality. . . ." If you've forgotten, the author of that reminiscence is, by his own definition, a pharmacist and attorney. One of the implied excuses for his venturing into the field of mental therapy, for which he hasn't been trained, is that there are "4,000 psychiatrists against 72,000 dentists." The technique employed by Greifer in dealing with the psychologically disoriented include "poemtherapy," during which patient and therapist read and create poems to and for each other; "musictherapy," which is about the same when he uses it as it is when most other therapists use it; "coddle-cudgel-therapy," having to do with the contrasting harsh and affectionate treatment of patients.

Eli Greifer's "medical writings" are a fantastic combination of obvious common sense and apparent madness. A mixture of fairly deep thoughts expressed in pretty poor poetry. A concoction of old and new wives' tales and esoteric references. Among the many allusions to be found in his texts are ones from top medical and scientific journals, and quotes from many historical and contemporary figures.

There can be little doubt that Greifer is an intelligent man, and when you speak with him you're almost forced to agree that he's sincere about his extravagant assertions. And yet, they're just a little too wild. Undoubtedly, many new discoveries have come from men with ideas that seemed pretty curious at the time, but this time they're just a foot or two beyond my reach. Which may explain why I don't buy the Greifer bit.

* * * * *

Sometimes, as in the case of Nikola Tesla, who's mentioned early in this book, a great creative or scientific mind achieves considerable heights—only to slowly, or suddenly, seem to "flip" completely. These thinkers, after having been rational, zoom off in some totally illogical direction. A perfect, or imperfect, example of this was the internationally eminent psychoanalyst and onetime friend of Sigmund Freud, Wilhelm Reich.

Reich, who loomed as one of the giants of psychoanalysis, was associated with Dr. Freud for some years. Later the two had a permanent disagreement. Going off in his own direction, he built his reputation higher and higher, along with others who had independent ideas about mental therapy, like Carl Jung and Theodore Reik.

An Austrian who turned to Communism in the early Thirties, the analyst brought out a book titled *The Function of the Orgasm*. This very widely-read volume took the position that the only thing wrong with neurotics was a "lack of full and repeated sexual satisfaction." None too wise politically, he found that his works were completely rejected by the Party as nonsense.

Proving even less popular with the Nazis than he was with the Communists, Reich fled from Germany to Denmark shortly thereafter. He wasn't well received there, and he moved on to other Scandinavian countries—finally ending up in the capitol of Norway. In Oslo, he lived for a while and continued his works, but with an almost unfailing talent he made himself loathed there also, and was driven from that liberal little country. As was the case with so many European intellectuals, Wilhelm Reich finally landed in the United States. Soon after his arrival, he created and presented to a small specialized public his "Orgone Institute," which he referred to as an experimental effort. He also started a private publishing operation to translate and publish the works of "Wilhelm Reich."

During this period several important psychoanalytic books became available to the American reader: *The Function of the Orgasm, The Mass Psychology of Fascism and Character Analysis.*

After having established the healthy sex life as being the

very foundation of a happy social and political culture, Reich began the development of his second dominant theory—the theory of orgone energy. This was a really far-out biophysical idea which might be related to "the ether" which was so widely discussed at one time—even to the point where it was considered the essence of nature. There was also a German named von Reichenbach who devoted many years of his life during the last century to the investigation of what he called the "odic force." This "energy" was supposed to be very fundamental and also to have great healing power. The Baron's theories bore a close relationship to the latter offerings of Reich. (All claims of partially reincarnated names will be rejected.) But back to the orgone theory.

Reich claimed that his orgone energy resembled "static electricity," and originated from the sun. It was the essential life force, and had the power to heal and put humans into their proper living rhythm. Orgone energy is reportedly sort of blue, which is pretty nice, you have to admit, and is more or less a natural electricity. It's related to all living organisms, and being the real life force, everything dies if it's removed. It's all over the place, and it gets into the system through the lungs and drinking water. This is obvious, since it's in all air and water—getting into them through the rays of the sun.

The way to health, according to the late off-beat psychoanalyst, was to have a free movement, to and fro through the body, of the orgone energy. Unfortunately, it seems that Reich found that the air and water didn't have enough concentrated orgone force, and so he decided that it was necessary to discover a way of providing a concentrated supplement of the stuff. To achieve this end, he invented and designed a thing he called an "accumulator," which I mentioned earlier. This curious compartment looked like an upright telephone booth, and it was composed of several layers of different materials. This multiple construction was supposed to "accumulate" orgone in the box. The theory was that if you have alternate layers of organic and inorganic material you established a controlled area where the orgone energy is collected from the atmosphere. In other words, although what goes up must come down, according to Reich, what goes in apparently doesn't have to come out. And so, depending on how many layers were used to build the "accumulater," various amounts of the mystical life force stuff was concentrated in the enclosure and the patient simply had to go inside and sit for a while to benefit from its glorious effects. A great many of these boxes were constructed and rented by the Reichian organization, all across the country.

Of course, the size of the boxes made them impractical to some people, like those who lived in small quarters or were on the move frequently, and so another version of Accumulator was devised—the orgone blanket. Such blankets were often made at home by the patients themselves, since the basic construction was relatively uncomplicated. All you had to do to have one of your very own was lay one layer of organic material, such as most animal-originated fabrics, on a layer of inorganic material like metal mesh. You do this over again, two or three times; or you add other alternating levels; and then you sew the thing all around the sides, and if you want to keep everything in place sew criss-cross back and forth several times in each direction. This is an orgone blanket. Lie underneath it for an hour or so and it will help what ails you, if your powers of auto-suggestion are strong enough.

But what is this stuff Reich raves about? What is orgone? Besides being a mystical, indescribable, all-, or at least semi-, powerful force? Well, as I mentioned before, it's blue and is found in all air and water—which obviously explains why the sky is blue and the ocean is blue. "Heat" that rises from the swamps, or deserts, or sun-pounded roadways, is not heat, but orgone. Static on your radio, or interference on your television set, or sun spots, or erratically functioning electric razors, or electrical storms, or streaked photographic film, and sometimes even so-called "spirit photos" are all caused by orgone. Will-o-the-wisps may be orgone, and fox-fire, and "ghosts." As a matter of fact, almost anything can be, since it is, according to Reich, like God, everywhere.

In the human being, it flows back and forth through his body, reaching every cell and corpuscle. It's the entire basis of sexual energy, and during intercourse it is attracted toward the genital regions; at the orgasm it concentrates in the sexual organs. After the orgasm, it slowly flows back to every portion of the body once more.

But that wasn't the total of the Reich pitch. He also goes into the cancer cure bit, and, as a matter of fact, there were few healing hopes he didn't play on. Almost all reputable psychoanalysts and psychiatrists had rejected him and his later theories long before, and now he was being attacked by most of the sciences, with medicine in the lead. Social and ethical groups condemned him. Eventually, his claims became so wild and his printed works so extravagant that the government stepped into his act. He was brought into court under the Pure Food and Drug Act, but he denied the court had any jurisdiction over him. He claimed that no one had the power to interfere with his "research" or prevent his spreading his particular brand of dangerous gospel. He went to jail for contempt of court, many of his books were destroyed, and his image was severely damaged in the eyes of the public. Of course, many of his more avid followers took the position that he had been martyred. When he died in prison, these disciples almost canonized him. However, the general public usually has a short memory and he passed out of common conversation fairly soon. Today, his works are still read by anyone interested in psychoanalysis, but the later writings stand as little more than curiosities to the serious student.

Whether one feels that Wilhelm Reich was a brilliant mind who deteriorated, or a man a hundred years ahead of his time, or a charlatan, it no longer really matters. No one can deny that he made a great impression in his own time, and that for years to come his name will arise when people discuss the peculiarities of the human mind. He may well have been the most fascinating patient he ever had.

* * * * *

As we have seen a number of times during this book, many of these stories divide into two, or more phases, and this is particularly true of the adventures and successes of Thurman Fleet. In the beginning, his "philosophy" of healing and health for the body, mind and soul, was independent of other specific bits. It was introduced as a thing and a thought in itself, later it became almost interwoven with chiropractic, at least a good part of it. In 1950, Fleet brought out a blue-bound, gold-lettered volume presenting his "laws of the body," "laws of the mind," and "laws of the soul." It was sort of a combination diet and hygiene, psychoanalysis and etiquette, religion and social philosophy, text. None of it very deep, none of it very original.

The portion dealing with the body was divided into four general categories: the law of nourishment, the law of movement, the law of recuperation, the law of sanitation. The first section was little more than a very fundamental "health food" pitch, with a few suggested menus tacked on the end of the advice. Part two was an early version of the power of positive thinking approach. Fleet took a strong position against "worry." Once you let worry begin, it grows and grows until it really gets out of hand. Therefore he wrote a "law that governs worry," which requires that one discover the cause of the worry, that he eliminate it by intelligent action. If this isn't possible he must accept the problem and stop worrying. Which, you have to admit, is a pretty wild way of preventing gray hairs. Fleet also adds that you shouldn't create worries. And how do you argue with that? It is, as must be obvious, a very, profound book.

The profound thinker also had "laws" against "anger," which may take the form of indignation, rage, or fury. In this category he also warns against desire, ambition, selfishness, pride, irritability, and such things. As you follow through his preachings, you note that he takes a dim view of jealousy, criticism, condemnation, gossip and slander. He disapproves of vanity, deceit, hypocrisy, prejudice, intolerance, and self-destruction. He is also against hate and sin. He wholly approves of moral aspirations, generosity, patience, and faith, hope and charity. Of course, these last are properly found in his "laws of the soul." If all of this has a faint ring of familiarity, it's understandable. You have heard it before. Everywhere.

As the years went by, attractive mailing pieces went out, executed in appealing colors with audience-wise copy. "Live a Life More Abundantly—Concept-Therapy Teaches You How!" "How to Get Well and Stay Well." "The Secrets of Living." ". . . essentials for obtaining health, happiness, and financial success." In short, the strong pitch continued, telling how Concept-Therapy teaches a philosophy of life which coordinates the basic truths of religion and philosophy—but is not a religion— and embraces the evolution of consciousness both human and Divine, making them more comprehensible. How about that!

The circulars go on to assure the reader that with Fleet's all-purpose panacea they'll find out that Man is a composite personality that must be considered in its entirety. You discover that the brain is like a broadcasting station, that negative thought is bad and positive thought is good, that man can control both kinds if he reads Mr. Fleet's books, and takes his courses. And oodles of other deep, thinky things. But that's just the beginning. When you've been taken through the entire Concept-Therapy bit, you're then offered the opportunity to wade into the additional books and courses where you realize that maybe Concept-

Therapy wasn't so great after all, since now they feel you require the gloriously revealing—"Conceptology."

Now, it was mentioned a little earlier that many of these gaffs are divided up into two, or more, phases. This is true of Concept-Therapy. While you may go through considerable material by Fleet and never come across the idea, or word, "chiropractic," there is one arm of the operation which is tightly tied-in with that particular area of "therapy." Without going into the subject itself, it might be pointed out that chiropractic and its practitioners are licensed in some states and not in others; at least such is the case as this is written. The system itself is based upon the idea that disease and disorders are cured by manipulation and adjustment of the spinal column, or segments of it. It's not surprising that one might wonder what a "philosophy" which announces: "If you are a layman, Concept-Therapy will end your quest for 'What Is Truth?'" has to do with a system of physical therapy.

The answer is not complicated. Fleet has what has been estimated as a half-million-dollar "National Home" for his "On the Beam" Club headquarters near San Antonio, Texas. Named "AUM-SAT-TAT RANCH," it also serves as a school for the instruction of Concept-Therapy, particularly of "doctors." In one of Fleet's pamphlets, it's highly recommended and introduced to the reader by the "Pres. Texas Chiropractic College." The good gentleman's name appears right above his title, but beyond "Jas R . . ." the scrawl is unreadable. Here, in addition to all of the other universal teachings of Concept-Therapy, chiropractic, itself, is taught. The best and most scientific and all like that. But more interesting is the "complete course in "How to Sell Chiropractic Service." And if you really want to get a clear and brutal picture of the entire pitch, you naturally would want to take the "Business Building Plan"; which is "considered the best in the field by well-known doctors." If you don't get the point yet, you look a little further and you find out that it's a "complete instruction as to how to secure patients." After that, what need be added?

*　*　*　*　*

However, don't believe that the list of such operations is short. Some are more subtle, some are less, but many activities fall into this self-same category. Take, for instance, "Humanetics." This is the "philosophy" of Richard W. Wetherill.

124

"Humanetics is the science of perfective thinking. It is an exact science. It develops unused faculties. It releases brainpower. It cures sickness. It ends a wide variety of troubles for men, women and children in every walk of life." So writes Wetherill, and if you think that he intends to leave any possible customer for his new philosophy out, you haven't yet begun to get the picture of these operations.

Protecting itself with the occasional statement that it isn't sponsored by any group, which is easy to believe, at least, it sometimes claims that it doesn't need support. But, of course, its publications aren't all free and neither are the lectures given by its originator. It also takes the position that it's in no way a religious organization or crusade. Its only purpose is that it opposes "illogical thinking."

Like all of its friendly (one group rarely says anything to discredit another) competitors, "Humanetics" claims to be a "formula that would end all human afflictions." And how does it go about accomplishing all of these marvels? Well, it seems to go something like this. According to the good Mr. Wetherill, there's a single cause of human afflictions, and that is "wrong thinking." That is, "illogical thinking . . . thinking which leads to illogical action." Of course, you undoubtedly realize that this means action which "causes trouble."

In one of Wetherill's pamphlets, he observes that "the average man goes to bed when he would rather stay up. Next morning he gets up when he would rather stay in bed." He points out that this creates emotional distress and illogical thinking. If this sounds at all like an echo, go back and re-read the part about Eli Greifer's "Nightowltherapy."

Humanetics views the mind as an electronic computer, thinking being accomplished by the making and breaking of nerve connections in the brain. Each thought establishes a connection, an "illogical concept establishes an illogical nerve connection." That is, illogical "commands" repeated are liable to become fixed; and this can cause permanent trouble. This leads you into the paths of "negative thinking," and everybody knows how bad that can be. In other words, you really have to keep your ears open and your nerves shut to "command phrases."

Now, the problem everyone has is to eliminate these "command phrases" from the brain. And the way to achieve this end is to put yourself into the swing of Humanetics. Echoing psychoanalysis, Wetherill tells his followers that it's necessary to raise the illogical thought from the subconscious to the conscious levels, making it possible for the patient to view the command phrase without "negative emotion," which apparently means, clearly. In that moment of illuminating truth, the problem is recognized and erased. Employing this method, according to Wetherill, one can eliminate, cure, and in general relieve the problems of all mental, emotional, spiritual and physical sicknesses, illnesses and disorders.

As is the case with almost all of the healer and health merchants, Wetherill has lectured extensively, has innumerable pamphlets and a couple of books available for the faithful, and is happy to get any and all publicity he can. As far as I am concerned, there's little to choose between one physical, spiritual or psychological medicine man and another.

* * * * *

The Reverend James W. Welgos is another of the prophets with a different flag in each hand. Operating out of a small community in Alabama, he's the promoter of a thing he calls "Nexology." In this "metaphysics," the claims are even more dramatic and ridiculous. They include the powers of telepathy, mind-reading, telekinesis (moving physical objects with thought), teleportation (moving physical objects, including one's body, over a considerable distance), levitation (raising physical things), and healing. In other words, "Nexology" is the "science that explains all things." It's a pitch that's woven completely through with religiosity and mysticism. Welgos has a pamphlet which quotes satisfied customers, or anyway followers, who assure the reader that they have learned how to redistribute the weight on their bodies without diet or change of poundage, to make and stop rain, to dissipate clouds, to force actions with the power of thought, to control the mind and the flight of a fly, to make money without talent, to read Braille in two hours, and other equally exaggerated and improbable claims.

Apparently another, or interlocking name, for "Nexology," is the "Living Faith," both of which seemed to be produced by an organization called "Human Engineering, Inc." The last of these three gives the impression of being the mother and dominant of the enterprises. Naturally, all were created, and are operated by, the Rev. James W. Welgos.

Unlike many of his counterparts, Welgos tends to keep himself in the background—that is, as a personality—and concentrates on pushing his pitches. Often the materials coming out from his group, and, one assumes, written by him—are unsigned. A second point he builds into his "philosophy" is levels of achievement. You begin by being completely on the outside. Then you become a student called a "neophyte." The second degree makes you a "disciple," and when you've completed your studies you're a "master."

"Human Engineering" offered many outlets for your energies and interests, among them: "Lessons in Living," which were twice-a-week instructions for personal adjustment; many monographs and pamphlets; a bi-weekly magazine; group meetings and counseling; personal counseling on a daily basis; a several-month summer training course; special meditation circles; and more.

Among the basic points of the Welgosian philosophy are the division of all mankind into two categories: "those who wish to change themselves, and those who wish to change their environment." Since almost all students begin in the second group, the major problem is to raise them into the first. After that, they have to work for the real "integration"—they must rise above both classes.

The "tools" for achieving the powers of Human Engineering are eight in number. "Verbal Realness," "Own Actions," "Actions of Others," and so on. If it appears that there are areas of duplication, it's because they often repeat themselves, and you can't say a good thing too often.

There are, says Welgos, various levels that the would-be humanistic engineer can work on to improve his lot. One is the "Social Level," where he can indulge in reverse "command phrases,"—although, of course, he doesn't actually use Wetherill's words. In this effort, the student tries to "build a new reality" by building commands into the conscious, and by extension subconscious, mind. An example would be: "I will not gamble." Repeated over and over again, it's the contention of the good Reverend that the habit will be eliminated. Word association is offered as an effective way of locating a problem so that it can be cured. And there are a number of other techniques on the "Social Level."

Another category is "The Action Level," where poise, physical culture, sports, dancing, yoga, and massage are considered important. The third area of effort is the "Sensory Level," which includes dieting, medical attention, Gestalt psychology, dianetics, hypnotism, gas therapy, electrical therapy, light therapy, music therapy and sound therapy. The music therapy reminds one of Greifer, and his bows toward L. Ron Hubbard are several. "The Awareness Level" is the final and most glorified of all, being attained through much subtler methods.

The "light therapy" reminds one for a moment of another wild gaff which might be called "color therapy." It's the "Color and Personality" theory of a woman named Audrey Kargere. She suggests that a would-be patient lie on a bed and cover his face with a piece of green cellophane. Now he stares at an electric light. The result of this bit of nonsense will be that "the pituitary gland, which is the master gland governing all other glands of the body, will be stimulated." The power of color is relatively unlimited when she gets her "Philosophy" onto it. Red helps to cure lagging appetite, hiccough, colic, smallpox and superficial pain. Blue is good for inflammation of the iris, difficulty in breathing, and convulsions. Other colors are equally valuable for other disorders.

Dr. Rolf Alexander is a gentleman of a humanist attitude and an interesting approach to life, and while I don't put him into the same grouping as I do most of the preceding I still feel that I should mention his theory of cloud dispersal. He's sort of a rain-maker turned inside out. That is, he believes—and even believes that he can demonstrate——that he can stare at a cloud and make it disappear. Dr. Alexander also speaks of some kind of psychic anthropology which has attracted the attention of a number of people interested in the off-beat.

And then there is Dr. Banik, who tried to stimulate interest in "Hunzaland" where people live to be considerably more than one hundred, and the advocates of "H-3," which is reputed to rejuvenate the aging and increase the life span.

It isn't necessary to point out that simple health food fadists number in the tens of thousands in this country, and the various pitches appealing to this form of enthusiasm are way up in the hundreds.

Someone is always seeking health, many seek super-health, and the allied areas of spiritual and mental well-being have even greater attraction. From these natural wishes and wants spring literally millions of potential customers, who have no problem finding people who are anxious to tell and sell them something . . . anything. There's always a new pitch, even if it is very much like most of the old ones. Pseudo-scientific, pseudo-religious, pseudo-metaphysical, pseudo this, that and the third thing. Add them all together and they spell most of the philosophies, so-called, referred to in the last few pages. But that's the story of this kind of bit.

CHAPTER 9

"By night an atheist
half believes in a God."
                    —Edward Young

DEROS, DEVILS, AND SNOWMEN

THE EXTRAORDINARY creature, the sub-and super human being, the other worlder, is as old as the imagination of man. In prehistoric times he was always bodiless—a spirit of the forest, waterfall, or cave. Even though he was pictured that way, he had a tremendous influence over primitive man—to the degree of actually directing all of the more important functions of his life. As the ages went by, the advancing mind of ancient man peeled away a thin veneer of its gullibility; and so the tribal leaders began materializing the demons right out of the night. Giving them animal and half-animal bodies, horrible faces, unhuman voices,—all the while, of course, retaining their extranatural powers.

Then, as the prehistoric superstitions started to change into the slightly more sophisticated primitive religions, the descriptions of these mystical creatures began to be translated into crude drawings, carvings, and eventually idols.

By the time man had reached ancient China and Egypt, the other worlders had become a vast and complicated society of their own. And this society was peopled by good, in between, and bad citizens—most of whom could be contacted to perform special services by people of the normal world who were "on the inside."

Down through the history of Europe one can find dozens of such creatures, a great many of which were common to, and lived in, a particular region or country. The trolls of Scandinavia, the little people of Ireland, the dwarfs of Germany, the elves of England, and so on—although of course there were many others, and often a term common in one country was almost equally popular in another.

Diabolical as some of these creatures were described to be, they shouldn't be confused with the specifically satanic familiars, devils, and demons of the several-hundred-year period of actual witchcraft hysteria that took place in these and other countries.

Obviously one might fill up books, investigating the thousands of types of strange "things" that populate the shadows and the night in the various countries of the earth, but we're concerned with the myths, half-myths, and— who knows? —maybe even realities of our own time. Of course, the following will be stories of the comparably unbelievable legends of this age; we won't be concerned with dredging up a few of the fragment tales about the old-time dwarfs, elves, and gnomes who still "appear" from time to time in the Twentieth Century.

In March of 1945, *Amazing Stories* published a piece called "I Remember Lemuria." The author was identified as Richard Shaver. Although the publication was a science fiction magazine, the implication was strongly present that the material was an actual "report," and that, if not all fact, it certainly had its basis in fact. According to the editor of *Amazing Stories,* Ray Palmer, the immediate response was astounding. First, thousands of letters, then tens of thousands, poured in—all reflecting a reaction to the Shaver tale. The normal monthly mail was some fifty pieces. Sales of that particular issue had zoomed more than 50,000 extra copies. Dealers were demanding more. The "Shaver Mystery," as it came to be known, was an over-month sensation.

As described by Ray Palmer, the background to this affair was a little off-beat, but not unique in itself. He had received a letter from Shaver detailing an ancient alphabet which "should not be lost." Admitting the alphabet to be a strange one, the writer anticipated rational argument by stating blankly that language experts would have no chance of understanding it, since they operated on incorrect principles.

The first point one should learn is that English is the original and universal language, it is the tongue employed throughout the entire cosmos. It is also the communication technique used by angels, according to Shaver. Of course, in its original dialect it was called "Mantong."

To say that Mantong alphabet is mildly imaginative would be a fair appraisal, but it's certainly not a brilliantly creative effort, no matter who dreamt it up. Conveniently, it has twenty-six letters; as a matter of fact they're the same twenty-six letters as we have in the alphabet we use, the Phoenician. And this is pretty clever of it, since according to scholars two of our letters are quite modern additions. Another claim Shaver makes for his original language and alphabet is that all the languages of the world are descended from it. If the philologists can't find much of a connection between it and the old and younger tongues of Sanskrit, Chinese and Egyptian, he shouldn't worry; since the man who brought Mantong to light doesn't think they know very much anyway.

The alphabet itself is comparatively simple, if kind of arbitrary and irrational.

THE MANTONG ALPHABET

A—Animal.   (Used AN for short).
B—Be.   To exist. (Often used as a "command").
C—Con.   To see. (C-on; to understand).
D—De.   Detrimental, disintegrant energy. (The second important symbol in the alphabet).
E—Energy.   (An all-pervading concept including the idea of motion).
F—Fecund.   (Used "fe," as in fe-male—fecund man).
G—Generate.   (Used "gen").
H—Human.   (A very metaphysical concept here, not fully understood, but used in the sense "H-you-man": a human is an H-Man).
I—Self. Ego.   (Same as our English I).
J—Generate.   (A duplication of G, but with a delicate difference in shade of meaning. Actually Ja, in contrast to Ge, is a very important distinction. G is the generating energy, while J is animal generation per se).

132

K—Kinetic.	(The force of motion).
L—Life.	
M—Man.	
N—Seed.	Spore. (Child, as "ninny").
O—Orifice.	(A source concept).
P—Power.	
Q—Quest.	(As "quest-ion").
R—Horror.	Danger. (Used AR, symbol of a dangerous quantity of disintegrant force in the object.)
S—Sun.	(Used "sis"; an important symbol, always referring to a "sun" whose energy is given off through atomic disintegration).
T—Integration, Growth.	(Used TE; the most important symbol of the alphabet; the true origin of the cross symbol. It signifies the integrative force of growth; as all matter is growing—the intake of gravity is the cause. The force is T. TIC means the science of growth. Integration-I-Con (understand)).
V—Vital.	
U—You.	(Used as VI; the stuff Mesmer called "animal magnetism").
W—Will.	
X—Conflict.	(Force lines crossing each other).
Y—Why.	
Z—Zero.	Nothing. Neutralization. (A quantity of energy of T neutralized by an equal quantity of D. Futility.)

But, neighbors, if that seems wild to you, it's nothing compared to Shaver's explanation. Just starting at the top and taking the letter "A" we find that "when Adam named the animals, he was using the basic, unchanging meaning of the sounds (letters), and he named correctly . . . When Adam said "Ape" . . . did he say "A-pe"? Shaver thinks he did. He feels that we have lost the vital accent "e." And what is the importance of that final vowel? Well, according to the mystic alphabetized, this is the way it goes. The initial letter "A" indicated that the subject was an animal. The second letter "p" represented *power*, therefore Adam added that to the "A". Now he has an *animal of power*. Now, the only way for the animal to express this power was via movement, or motion, which was an expression of *energy*. The letter for energy was, of course, "e". And so, to describe an *animal* whose *power* was expressed in *energy*, he naturally put down the letters "A-p-e." And that, I guess, is how you make a monkey out of someone.

However, to get back to the general picture of the "Shaver Mystery," after Ray Palmer had printed the alphabet and its accompanying letter, a number of people wanted to know more about the bit. In answer to a request for more information, Shaver replied with the ten-thousand-word letter that Palmer turned into the manuscript called "I Remember Lemuria!". As a matter of fact, the editor often admitted that while he assures us that the original material comes from Shaver, he has edited most of it prior to its publication.

Mr. Shaver has made many mad and fantastic claims regarding the inner Earth and what goes on there. According to him, the outer crust of the Earth is honey-combed with great caverns. In fact, these caves are so tremendous they cover more area than the entire surface of this planet. The fact that this idea is in complete conflict with accepted scientific ones regarding the structure of the Earth, the increase of temperature as one descends into it, and the like, doesn't bother him at all.

As his revelations continue, and he has frequently asserted in print that this is all fact, he tells about the "abandonderos" who live down there. According to Shaver, these "deros" (to use his abbreviated name for them) are what is left over from a very ancient race who lived on this planet about 12,000 years ago. At that time certain radiation of the sun had made it impossible for the people to remain on the Earth. These rays were radioactive, and they were penetrating into the bodies, saturating the water, infecting the food, contaminating the air, and, in general, giving old mankind a pretty rough time of it. The solution that was being shot around at the time was that the inhabitants of the Earth would have to drop everything and go to live on another nearby planet, or possibly on one with no sun at all. Some thinkers took the position that everyone would end up living out in what they called "dark space." These people, by the way, were named "Titans," or "Atlans."

After several unsuccessful attempts to escape, the "Titans" began moving down into the natural caverns of the Earth, and setting up cave-keeping.

Unfortunately, although they were used to living for many thousands of years, now that their systems were polluted with this radiation their life span was cut down to a meagre half-century, or so. As the centuries went by, these abandoned people, these "abandonderos," or, rather "deros," were not only protected from the deadly sun rays, but they also lost the benefit of the healthy sun rays. As a result, they couldn't win either way, and they began to degenerate in all of their aspects. Finally they became, as they are today, distorted, midget idiots, whose complete personality is evil. Whose main drives and desires are morbidly sadistic. In other words, they have become most unattractive devils. And if you want more information take the word "dero" and match it up with "Mantong Alphabet."

Yet, in spite of all this degeneracy right here under our feet, there is another group in this lower region. They are called "teros." This was a much smaller clique who, by the use of chemicals, machines, and beneficial rays, were able to prevent their own deterioration. Although they too die in a matter of fifty years, they have been able to maintain a high degree of intellectuality. However, Mr. Shaver is sad to report that they are so few, and the deros are so many, that they are almost powerless to prevent the war of evil the little monsters wage.

Although he never explains how such mentally degenerate people were able to maintain and operate such amazing and advanced ancient machines, Shaver reports that these evil undergrounders have some extraordinary devices at their disposal. They have a vision apparatus which penetrates hundreds of miles of solid rock; with this they can pick up scenes from all over the world. They have mental machines which can produce three-dimensional, apparently concrete illusions, which are used to confound and deceive surface inhabitants. They have short and long range death rays, interplanetary space craft and rockets. As a matter of fact, even before Kenneth Arnold had his experience, which led to the coining of the term "flying saucers," the Shaver stories described, in considerable detail, the kind of ships that seemed to become so plentiful later.

Another of the dero devices which aroused considerable interest was the "stim machine." This instrument's sole purpose was to revitalize the sexual power and desire of the users. Shaver makes it quite obvious in his stories that this is the most popular of all their inventions since, according to him, the majority of their time is spent in orgies. As a matter of fact, he pictures these sexual marathons as being so violent as to horribly deform many of the participants. Fortunately, for them, they also have what they call "ben" rays, which revive and restore the body when it is over-exhausted and crippled by the bizarre activities of the deros.

The surface people, Palmer and Shaver tell us, are descendants of the original Earthians who didn't get down into the network of subterranean caverns. This part of the human race was reduced to a state that produced the Neanderthal man. Most of these died off, but enough remained to develop into the present day man.

Of course, Shaver insists, the deros not only still exist below, but they are responsible for almost all of our troubles. War, transportation accidents, homicides (incited with destructive rays), suicides, and even nightmares.

Although, through Ray Palmer, Shaver introduced deros to the world, and was the sole authority on them for some years, in more recent times other gentlemen have offered reports on the same subjects. Among such are included Dominick Luchesi, Augie Roberts and Curtis Gibson.

Dr. George Marlo, referred to earlier in this book in one of the chapters on flying saucers, also advances the idea, which he calls fact, that something strange is going on "down there." This particular prophet of the off-beat claims the earth is hollow, and that it's filled with birds, animals and people. He points out that the great mastodons didn't die, they went to live inside the earth.

And so the legends of the deros and dero-like creatures goes and grows.

Off in an entirely different direction is the fantastic story of mysterious Ceylon, as told by Aung Lin, an ex-Buddhist monk.

During the time he was in holy orders on the other side of the world, Aung Lin found himself in residence in a monastery just outside a small village. Around these two islands of humanity the Asian jungle spread out for hundreds of miles. After a short time, Aung Lin became aware of dark and curious stories that were told by the other monks, and by the village people, about a renegade monk who lived by himself on the edge of the steaming forest. He soon realized that everyone in the vicinity was very fearful of the twisted, evil-looking little man.

One day, as he was walking along the dry and dusty road toward his monastery, with several of his spiritual brothers, they encountered the ancient recluse coming from the other direction. Without warning, Aung Lin's companions fled off the opposite way. He, lacking the ingrained fear, and also being extremely curious, stood his ground and spoke a greeting to the monk. In return, he was invited to the hut of the monk, and he accepted.

As they proceeded along the road, Aung Lin noted that his new acquaintance was extremely dirty, and that his robes were shredded and filthy. Arriving at his "home," he discovered that it was even less appealing than the old man who lived there, if that was possible.

Later, seated opposite one another in the dank hovel, they conversed—although the monk actually said very little. When he did make an observation or ask a question, he almost always repeated it.

"So you are from the United States. Ah, so you are from the United States."

The face of the man was the most interesting thing about his appearance. It looked as though he had been immersed in evil for so long that it had had its effect upon his face, which was gross and very coarse. Aung Lin could begin to understand why the native population so feared "the monk that practices magic."

The weirdest of all the tales told about the old monk was that he kept a mummified, or as Aung Lin prefers to call it, a "preserved", child in his home. An incredible little creature who did all of his evil bidding.

Apparently the renegade monk had, some time earlier, excavated the cadaver of a two-year-old child from its grave and taken it home. He then proceeded to "tan" the dead thing, "much as you would leather." From that point on he was able, with mystical rites and forbidden incantations, to raise and activate this preserved child by calling forth spirits of the darker worlds and projecting them into the little dried-up body. Now, filled with the evil animation, the leather doll-like thing became a miniature monster, doing the will of the ancient witch—robbery, assault, even to murder, killing his enemies as they slept.

When the horrid deed was finished, the half-living thing returned to its master and the diabolical spirits were withdrawn and the "child" became inanimate once more. The old monk then lifted it up and put it on a shelf, pausing only to dust it once in a while, until he needed its evilness again.

Of course, although intrigued by the legend, Aung Lin hardly accepted the tales as fact. That is, until one night some time after his original meeting with the devil-monk. He was taking an evening stroll along the road from his order's retreat. The moon was high and silver. The hills rolled away into the shadows on either side of him. The tall thick grass moved silently in the gentle breeze. And then, suddenly, he saw it. A small, leathery figure, not more than a dozen feet away, moving swiftly through the grasses, with a slender, shining, thin-bladed knife in its hand, the moonlight catching it up for a moment as though in a spotlight. The mummy child!

From that moment on, Aung Lin believed. When he speaks of it today, he's almost matter-of-fact about it. Speaking in the way one does when they've told an obvious story many times, he often concludes: ". . . and that is all there was to it." All I can say, neighbors, is that I'm glad there wasn't any more.

However, if you toss aside the deros and the mummy child, as being too unbelievable, remember that all of the stories about the strange unhuman creatures on this earth aren't quite so easy to reject. One example of this are the reports of the so-called "Abominable Snowman." Stories about this strange creature have been filtering back from the Orient for over half a century, many going back to the days when Westerners had to disguise themselves to get into Tibet where the original semi-men were supposed to come from.

Although the first word of the snowmen precedes the '90's, it wasn't until thirty years later that the "evidence" supporting the existence of the things began to gain strength. At that time a company of climbers trying to conquer Mount Everest reported that they had observed at some distance a group of upright living creatures far above them in the peaks. Later, at around 25,000 feet, they discovered footprints of enormous size, three or four times as large as a human being's. The leader of the expedition decided that they were the tracks of a giant wolf, but all of the native guides insisted that they were the marks of the *metch kangmi* or "the abominable snowman."

The early descriptions of these upper elevation animal-men were pretty far out as well as far up. They were supposed to be enormously large semi-human creatures who lived in the highest caves of the mountain ranges. The faces were white, but the bodies were entirely covered with thick dark hair. These monster-like things were very wild and dangerous, living on the meat of yaks, and occasionally of humans, and even each other.

Tales of the snowman have come from hundreds of places thousands of miles apart, ranging all the way from Burma to Western India and up to Mongolia. But it should be pointed out that the snowman exists more than just in the minds of little- or un-educated natives. An Englishman named Knight claimed to have seen one of these creatures many years ago, and to have seen one carrying bow and arrows! In 1925, a Fellow of the Royal Geographical Society reported and described in considerable detail the snowman. Among the things his observations pointed out was the "fact" that the *metch kangmi* were ten to twelve feet tall.

Over the years many reputable Westerners, a number of them supposedly practical-minded Englishmen, saw the prints left by these creatures, or so they felt. In many of these cases the descriptions of the footprints have been remarkably detailed, and in a number of instances photographs of the tracks have been brought back to the civilized world for closer examination. All through the Twenties, the Thirties, and the Forties, the material poured into the files of the researchers interested in the mysterious monster of the Himalayas. By the Fifties the fascination with the subject, far from diminishing, had increased; the conviction as to the truth of the claims had not weakened, it had strengthened.

In 1951, Eric Shipton photographed footprints of "the abominable snowman" in the snow. Dr. Wyss-Dumant's expedition discovered similar tracks in 1952. In the following year, Sir John Hunt was told by Tibetian monks that they saw the snowmen occasionally, the last time being four years before. One of the foremost lamas of Tibet, Tsultung Zanbu, met a snowman face to face, who passed by without incident.

The *yeti*, which is the popular name for the creature in Tibet, was seen in a mummified state by Chemed Rigdzin Dorje Lopu, a noted lama—or so he firmly claims. His description was that they (he saw two) were very monkey-like, about eight feet tall, with thick flat skulls, and dark brown hair covering the entire body.

In 1954, Charles Stonor found more *yeti* trails which were somewhat smaller than most of the earlier reports. During the following twelve months Abbe P. Bordet, geologist, photographed more tracks, and a couple of months after that British Wing-Commander A. J. M. Smyth spotted others. In 1956 there were reports that head-hunters had killed and eaten a snowman on the Chinese border.

Tom Slick, well-known American oilman, led an expedition into the Himalayan mountains in search of the creature in the spring of 1957. He seems to have been thoroughly convinced of the existence of the *yetis* from the data he dug up. His information indicated that they are large, ape-like things, with pointed heads who walk upright. It seems that it's strong enough to kill a yak, but it doesn't eat them, preferring small field animals and roots and herbs. His conclusion regarding the *yeti* are most fascinating regarding the "types." It's his conviction that there are two species. One with reddish or auburn hair about man-sized, the other almost eight feet high with coal black hair. Other size distinctions are pretty common. One set tells that there are not two, but three types. The first about fifteen feet high, one about eight, and the last man-size.

And so the stories grew and changed, developed and twisted, always finding supporters, and always finding sceptics. In the late Fifties the noted zoologist and explorer of unquestioned background and integrity, Ivan Sanderson, stepped to the forefront of the snowmen investigators. Then the world-famous conqueror of Mount Everest, Sir Edmund Hillary, turned his attention to the mystery. He led an expedition into the Himalayas to establish once and for all if there was or wasn't such a thing as an abominable snowman.

Beginning with a definite scepticism, Hillary spent four months trying to track down the truth, or find evidence to support his doubts—I don't really know which. Although he himself had found what his guide had called a tuft of real *yeti* hair on a trip in 1952, he tended to disagree with the many explorers and scientists who suspected, or were sure, that there was something to the legends.

Again the subject of how many and what kind comes up, and according to Hillary the Sherpas, the fabulous mountain guides of the Himalayas, claimed that there were three. The first he refers to as the "clutch." It's supposed to be sandy and black haired, about eight feet tall, a vegetarian, and not unfriendly unless annoyed. The second type he calls the "mitch"; it's about four-and-a-half feet tall, with a high pointed head, and the feet are said to be backwards. This variety is reported to be very dangerous, and likely to eat any humans who come his way. The final of the trio is referred to as the "thelma." He's quite small, about eighteen inches high, and, unlike his mountain brothers, lives in the jungles. He's rather human in appearance.

Hillary heard that there was a *yeti* skin in one of the villages the expedition passed through and decided to trace it down so that he could examine it. After much investigation and a number of rupees it was uncovered. But, to the disappointment of all, the group agreed that the hide was nothing more than a fine specimen of a rare Tibetan blue bear skin.

As the days passed, the expedition pushed further on in their search for the *yeti*. After a couple of weeks had passed, they came upon tracks which their Sherpa guides insisted were authentic *yeti* footprints. However, Hillary claims that later the group found prints of a wild fox, and that this animal, when running very fast, produced "clusters" of pawprints which were very close together. When the sun melted these a little, the effect was "as fine a *yeti* track as one could wish." This "evidence" the noted explorer offers as disproof of all the previously seen, and photographed tracks of abominable snowmen.

Progressing through other Himalayan villages and talking with the natives, Hillary assures the outside world that he not only never found anyone who had actually seen a *yeti*, he had never even found anyone, including two ancient lamas, who had ever heard of anyone who had seen one. All of this is in complete disagreement, of course, with many other notable reports on and by the inhabitants of this region of the world.

Among other evidence found by his company were *yeti* "scalps." These were like pointed hats with reddish and black hair, and seemed extremely ancient. Upon careful examination, Hillary and his associates could find no indication of seams, or stitching, or, in general, that they had been tampered with. However, apparently they all quickly agreed that it *might* have been the molded skin of some other animal. They attempted to duplicate this "possible process" and were satisfied that the results showed that such a manufactured scalp of a *yeti* was feasible.

Upon having both the skins and the scalps examined by zoologists and anthropologists selected by him, Hillary tells us that they came up with the conclusion that the skin was definitely the blue bear and the scalp was a piece of molded goat-antelope hide. And so the sum total of Hillary's expedition seems to have been to prove what he seemed to have been pretty sure of in the first place, and that is that there—ain't no such animal.

That, you might think, pretty well completes the story, at least the superficial story, of the abominable snowman. But it's only half of the tale.

Quite probably the leading authority on these amazing myths is the famous zoologist, animal collector, explorer, author and personality extraordinary, Ivan Sanderson. Having spent years investigating the legends and reports, he is firmly convinced that there is more than "something" to them. That is, he believes that there not only are snowmen, but several kinds. Different ones in different parts of the world. But possibly the most unbelievable Sanderson opinion is that we have *yeti*-type creatures right here in our own country. Abominable snowmen in California!

It started, more or less, back in August of 1958, when a man named Gerald Crew was out driving along a desolate and barren section of California countryside. Crew, a level-headed, tee-totalling church-goer, was crossing a section of the state whose total area was over 100,000 square miles, but which had almost no human living in its tremendous space. It was here that Crew discovered a number of naked-footprints, human in shape, and 16 inches long! Measuring the stride, he found that it varied from 45 to 60 inches. Twice his own.

The highway construction crew, with which he was working at the time, was divided between those who thought it was a hoax and those who didn't. But it gave them all something to think about at night. Several weeks passed and nothing else happened to add to the original tracks. Then one morning fresh tracks appeared near the camp. After that, the prints would sometimes show up for several mornings in a row, then there wouldn't be any for a few days, and then they would come back.

It was around this time that Sanderson was told about "Bigfoot," as they had begun to call him, through a letter from another zoologist. He discounted the whole report because he thought that the location had been mistaken, or misprinted. Sanderson knew there were strange things in the Himalayas, and in Mozambique, but not California.

The second series of happenings which caused a good deal more commotion was the moving of heavy objects from one place to another. Objects so heavy that one would think that a strong man might have considerable difficulty with them. But a full 55-gallon fuel drum was apparently thrown through the air, as was a 250-pound length of steel pipe.

One night one of the workers and a hunter decided to go out and see if they could find any fresh trace of the "thing" that was causing all the trouble. As they drove along the isolated and deserted road their headlights suddenly exploded upon a giant figure that seemed to be human, or, at least, humanoid. It appeared to be both ape and man, or something in between, and covered with brown hair or fur. Leaping from their car they saw the creature disappear into the underbrush. Immediately they sent the dogs they had brought with them after the "Bigfoot." And that was all for the evening, since they heard nothing more from it or the hounds. However, one story goes that a few days later the dogs were found dead, looking like a sack of shattered bones.

When Sanderson got into his personal investigation he discovered all sorts of remarkable things. A report of a husband and wife who had seen the "Bigfoot" below them as they flew low over the territory in their private plane. Another statement he came across was of two doctors who had met such "snowmen" in 1958. Another report was of a woman and daughter who saw them feeding on a hillside. The same lady claimed that she had seen the things since her childhood, in the Hoopa Valley of California. An old Indian of the area merely commented: "Oh, have the white men finally gotten around to them." And so the stories piled up, many dating almost a hundred years back.

In August of 1959, more tracks of the creatures were discovered, as well as many dark hairs up to 10 inches long found on the trunks of trees, 6½ feet off the ground.

So read the highlights of the California "snowman," called the "Bigfoot." Ivan Sanderson suggests that three explanations are possible. That the entire series of events were caused by an abnormal human being, by an animal, or by something in between man and animal. If it were a human he would have to have feet over 16 inches long, take strides of up to five feet wide, and weigh in the neighborhood of 750 pounds, plus being extremely agile and fast. These added to other restrictions seem to eliminate that as a possibility. The second, that it's an animal, is out of the question logically and scientifically. The third, that it's a humanoid, is, to quote Sanderson, "unthinkable." But when we're made aware of the discoveries of anthropologists like the 8 to 12-foot prehistoric human-like ape-man called *Gigantopithocus* of southern China, we wonder. Which explanation do you prefer? What do you think of the stories, the legends, the reports, Hillary's opinion, Sanderson's opinion—what do you think about the "Bigfoot," the *yeti,* and/or the Abominable Snowman?

The world is still filled with millions of square miles which are dark, dangerous, and unknown. The depths of the Amazon, beyond the Himalayas, and even in our own mountains, plains and swamps. Who knows who, or what, may live there? Who can guess who shares this still only half-known earth with you and me? Who and what?

CHAPTER 10

"I am listening for the voices
Which I heard in days of old."
—Caroline Norton,
Lady Maxwell

HAPPY MEDIUMS AND THEIR NOT-SO-HAPPY CLIENTS

ALTHOUGH THE gullible have been buying the spiritualism and life on other planets bit for as long as mankind can remember, no one seriously began checking up on the occult operators until the end of the last century. At that time, around 1882, a group of men in London founded the British Psychical Research Society. Some very big names were tied in with the organization. Two world-famous scientists, Sir William Crookes and Sir Oliver Lodge, had a piece of the action, and so did Henri Bergson, possibly the leading philosopher of his time. These great thinkers had made up their minds to settle the question of mediumship and spiritualism once and for all.

The Society investigated and tested one medium after another, and one after another was awarded the uncoveted "Faker 1st Class Medallion" for his demonstration of "communication with the dead." The one exception might be called the founder of modern spiritualism. He was one of the few to convince highly intelligent people from all over the world that he was an authentic medium. His name was Daniel D. Home (pronounced *Hoom*).

The claims for Home were, and still are, so fantastic that it's hard to believe any rational person could accept them, but it must be admitted that all attempts to discredit him proved unsuccessful. He convinced hundreds of the best minds of his time that his powers were genuine, and he alone, among all of the mediums who were tested, was never condemned as a fraud. A record that remained clean even though he submitted to the Society's investigations over and over again.

One really amazing incident is reported to have occurred in 1868, during an afternoon seance. Home is supposed to have risen from his chair, walked across a second floor parlor room, and stepped out of a window onto—nothing! No balcony. No ledge. Suspended some twenty or thirty feet over the thoroughfare below, he floated along beside the wall of the house and around a corner of the building. Moments later he re-entered the parlor, floating in through another window.

The Earl of Crawford, other celebrities with titles, some military men, and a few plain people watched this happen. Or so the story goes. Lord Adere, who was supposed to have witnessed the entire bit, claimed to have seen Home do many other fantastic things like burying his hand in a flaming bed of coals or putting his face into the fire—all with no ill effects. Anything any other medium ever did, he seemed to have been able to do better, but most of the time what he did no one else could do at all. Then, or to this day. He was the king.

On one occasion Home walked into a house he had never seen before to conduct a seance in the broadest daylight. The climax of this particular performance was the medium's causing a full-size concert grand piano to elevate to the ceiling, hang for several moments and gently return to the floor. As usual, a large audience is supposed to have seen it all happen.

Many, many writers have tried to offer explanations for his "phenomena," saying he might have done this, or that, or the third thing. Often the complaint is made that he was not investigated by magicians, that they would have exposed him. But the truth is that almost every approach was used to prove that D. D. Home was a fake. Scientists, philosophers, magicians, doctors, soldiers and police—all kinds of people tried to show up

Home for what he was. Maybe they did, maybe they didn't. It all depends on just what he was.

Two other famous mediums of the turn of the century were Anna Eva Fay, who was another favorite of the scientist Sir William Crookes, and the great Italian wonder worker, Palladino.

Then, in the Twenties, the United States came up with the sensational "Marjory." The prominent wife of a Boston surgeon, she was supposed to do just about anything occult—automatic writing in languages she didn't know, apports—that is, the sudden appearance of physical objects, often living ones such as birds. She demonstrated her power to levitate tables, conjur up visions, receive spirit messages, and materialize spirit forms. In other words, Marjory went all the way; she did the whole bit.

However, being an across-the-board operator wasn't her only virtue. She was also very shrewd in the publicity department. With this two-way combination going for her, it's no surprise that she was a national figure in a couple of years. Then the perfect opportunity came along for her to top herself. The *Scientific American* magazine offered a considerable amount of loot for any medium who could pass all of the tests imposed by a group of investigators selected by them. Marjory jumped at the chance, sailed through the tests with colors flying, and came out with the big numbered check in her hot little ectoplasmic hand. The headlines of the time announced that at last a medium had been proven authentic, and she was Marjory.

That began one of the most famous spiritualism, if not spiritual, battles of all time. Out of his own brilliant limelight into hers came the greatest escape artist who ever lived, master magician, and by far the foremost debunker of mediums of his time, Harry Houdini. He claimed that no one really had the ability to judge the talents of the blonde from Boston, that only a master of trickery, such as himself, was able to tell whether tricks were being performed or not. He, Houdini, personally offered a forfeit of a thousand dollars if he couldn't prove that Marjory was an out-and-out fake.

The contest was arranged, the seance to be held in Boston with Marjory conducting, Houdini debunking, and a group from the *Scientific American* refereeing. The results were conclusive. Of course it depended on where you stood as to what was concluded. Houdini, and a large body of people, agreed that the great magician had proven positively that all of the medium's effects were achieved by extreme cleverness and misdirection, that she was a fascinating illusionist, but no contactor of the

147

spirits of the dead. On the other hand, Marjory and her faithful followers contended that Houdini was so anxious to prove fraud against her that he, himself, was guilty of deception and trickery. They claimed that he had faked evidence!

Today, when you look back on the great controversy, there seems to be little doubt that Marjory was far more clever than psychic. Of course, just why the wealthy and prominent wife of a famous surgeon left herself wide open to charges of fraud and exposure to ridicule no one ever explained. The whole action was pretty weird, and I certainly can't give you an explanation to it where all the experts failed.

A very well-known medium of our own time, Arthur Ford, once claimed to have made spirit contact with Houdini. It is even said that the great magician's wife OK'd the contact. However, it's also said that she didn't, and frankly the whole bit was so spiritual I never really made any sense out of it.

One of the strangest men I ever met was Frank Decker. This mysterious medium lived in a high walled and shadowy house on a dark side street of Greenwich Village in New York. The famous and wealthy from all over the world came to consult him and obtain his services for seances. Before I actually met Decker I heard absolutely fantastic reports about his psychic abilities. Telekinesis, levitation, materialism and not only double, but *triple* simultaneous voices! Almost every time I had a medium on the show I'd get calls and letters telling me that my guest had proved nothing (with which I must admit I usually agreed), compared to the amazing Frank Decker. Finally one night I had a "great psychic" on the show, but his act wasn't going so well. As my panelists were sort of toying around with the operator I got a call on the "beeper phone" from Decker, who said that the guy was making his profession look ridiculous and giving it a bad name. Immediately I jumped at the chance to invite the famous medium up to the studio to conduct a complete seance on the air. I even offered to let him set up his own conditions, within reason. Decker made a counter offer that he would show me a completely successful seance, with the whole routine, if I'd like to attend one of his performances at his studio. I told him that that wouldn't give me much of a radio show, but suggested again that he accept my offer to stage his entire bit in my studio at WOR. Unfortunately, Decker declined, and that was as close as I ever came to seeing the psychic wonder work. However, I can't deny that I have met thirty or forty people who saw him perform, and they all claim

148

he was really amazing. If a copy of this book comes to Frank's attention in that spirit world he lives in now, I hope he'll reconsider and visit me on a show some early morning. Let's face it, if my regular guest happened to be a so-called medium it might scare him out of his quick wits, but, neighbors, it would make for a sensational show.

As a matter of fact, I have had a number of seances on radio, and on one of them Jack London, famous stage pickpocket and magician, demonstrated several of the simpler psychic tricks. During this program he exposed one of the most common gaffs used by phony spiritualists. It's called the "one ahead." In this operation, the good and psychic reverend gets up on the platform and, after giving his opening pitch, he calls for written questions from the marks. These are scribbled on cards or small sheets of paper, put into envelopes, given to the reader's assistant, and brought up to the platform. Any of several devices are used to reveal to the "psychic" one of the questions. Sometimes the assistant has gotten one open and left it face up in the basket for the operator to see. On other occasions the "reverend" holds the first message up to his forehead and meditates deeply. Finally, after much concentration, he announces that "the contents of this message are of a personal—I might even say sexual —nature, and therefore cannot be answered tastefully in the presence of a mixed audience."

He then begins to toss the message into the discard pile, when he stops for a moment, saying: "I will check the contents, just to make certain the messages are coming through clearly today." He opens the envelope and reads the question. "Just as I saw it, friends, this could not possibly have been answered with these dear ladies present."

Now, for the next one. Here, the spiritual pitchman picks up the next envelope and holds it to his head. Concentrating, he begins to get the word. "This poor soul asks for her long-lost brother, who left home twenty-three years ago . . ." And so he goes on, answering one after another of the gullibles questions. Of course, neighbors, the real truth about the whole pitch is that there never was any first indelicate message. The opening bit was a complete fake. What the con man was actually doing was setting himself for all the questions to follow. When he concentrated on, and answered the message in the "second" sealed envelope, he was really answering the contents of the first one. The one he had opened to check that it was not fit for a mixed group. But, since it never occurred to the suckers that the good reverend was a fraud, they never noticed how simple a deception it would be.

Another example of a skillful debunker at work was the television show I did with the greatest living escapologist, successor to Houdini, and master magician as my guest: an amazing gentleman named "The Amazing Randi." On this occasion, Randi really had my other guests and the studio audience flipping. After explaining some of the less complicated techniques of the fast buck spirit contacting promoters, he actually performed several of the mystical bits. Except they weren't so mysterious when he got through.

Selecting a bright young lady from the audience, "The Amazing Randi" requested that she sit opposite him at a bridge table in the center of the stage. He then handed her two children's slates, asking her to give them a careful examination. This she did, holding up both sides of both slates so that the television audience could see that all four faces were completely clean. Randi then had the subject place one of the slates on the table and he handed her a small piece of white chalk.

"If you would just place this little piece of chalk on the slate you have there on the table. Thank you. Now, would you please place the other blank slate exactly over the first one, so that the chalk is firmly caught between the two slates."

Listening carefully, the young lady did as Randi requested.

"I will ask you to hold the slates together firmly," he continued, "and take this roll of masking tape. Wrap a full strip of the tape around from one side to another until it meets itself. Now turn the slates in the other direction and do the same thing. Would you show the television audience."

The slates were held up by the girl so that the "plus" strips of tape were seen on both sides of the slates, which were now sealed face to face at four separate points. Randi then explained that he wished her to hold the slates on her lap and concentrate on them as hard as she could. Then, when he said the one word "Now," she would pass them under the table to him, and he would immediately pass them on across the table to her.

All of this happened according to schedule, and a couple of moments later she was holding the slates again.

"Open them, please," he requested, "and tell us if there have been any changes."

The guest pulled off the tape in one direction, and then she removed the tape that ran in the other direction, and she pulled the slates apart. With a surprised gasp of breath and a

150

laugh, she held the inside surfaces of the slates up to the cameras.

"*NDH 25d*," read one, and "*VITAMINS*," read the other.

I immediately asked the youg lady if the "messages" had any personal meaning to her, and she admitted that they did. She then gave the following explanation.

"*N D H* are the initials of a psychic I go to, and the *25d* must stand for the fact that she charges twenty-five dollars for a 'life reading.' The word *VITAMINS* must refer to the fact that my husband opened up a vitamin department in his store this morning."

Well, let's face it, friends, you have to admit that that is a pretty good psychic phenomenon. The gal volunteered, along with several others, from the audience, and Randi comes up with writing on absolutely blank slates and a completely personal message. Naturally, when I explain the gimmick to you it will just be "a pretty obvious trick," but people pay millions of dollars a year because no one ever explained that pretty obvious trick to them and they weren't shrewd enough to figure it out for themselves.

The actual bit went something like this. The card table was in the center of the stage from left to right, but it was very near the rear curtain. When the girl handed the slates, taped together, under the table to Randi, an assistant instantly substituted an entirely different set of taped slates, which were identical in appearance. The first set was taken from the girl by the assistant and the second set was handed to Randi at the very same moment—all under the table. Neither the young lady, nor the TV audience, nor the studio crew saw anything. Of course, the substituted set had the message all prepared on them, and were ready to be read when opened up.

As for the accuracy of the personal message, the assistant had been planted out in the audience before the program and had overheard the information as the guest conversed with a friend. You're right—just another "pretty obvious trick." But they're all that kind when some one writes them out.

Seances, where mediums do most of their work, vary enormously from place to place, medium to medium, and time to time. However, the same large catalogue of effects is employed by the vast majority of wonder workers. The floating trumpet, the moving luminescent cross, the voice, or the two voices overlapping; or objects suddenly appearing on a table, or things flying through the air, or ectoplasmic manifestations of unknown personalities, or direct contact with relatives and friends who have "passed on." All of these are in a catalogue of gaffs available to the professional medium. Of course, some spiritualism workers specialize in particular powers.

Another extremely popular form of spirit phenomenon is the "rap." The rap is heard at almost all seances. Supposedly indicating replies from those who have "passed over," they come once for "yes," twice for "no," and three times for "maybe." Now, since the medium's hands are secured by persons on either side of her or him, in a properly-produced seance, the raps obviously have to come from spirit sources. That is, unless the Electric Spirit Rapper device has been purchased from the previously-mentioned supply house for twenty-five dollars. A non-mechanical version, which is really only for amateurs, is available for three or four dollars.

As the years have gone by, the mediums' clients have become more sophisticated, and therefore more demanding. By sophisticated I don't mean less gullible, but merely that they're no longer satisfied with the simpler effects such as "rappings." Today taps in the darkness are only good as introductory bits. Wilder and more powerful gaffs are the order of the modern seance. The slate effect described earlier is often employed in the second stage of a session, but to keep the customer really going you have to come up with a strong "levitation." If you're making an all-the-way hard sell, then you'll have to produce "spirit voices," which drift in through the floating trumpet, or, always the absolute topper, you do an ectoplasmic manifestation —you give the mark a "genuine physical spirit."

The trumpet from which come most of the "voices" heard in the seance room is usually a silver metal cone ranging from twelve to thirty-six inches in length. This gimmick, which rises and floats about the room, is available for a reasonable price; but if you want to create a really good effect the trumpet must "speak," must "talk," and this is somewhat more expensive. The most powerful of all, of course, is ectoplasm. This is where the "spirit" actually comes to life before the very eyes of the amazed marks. Such effects vary enormously. For less than twenty skins you can get a fairly good ghost. Naturally, if you want to spring for the deluxe, skeleton-type ghost, this may run you up to two yards a clatter. But take my word for it, the effect is the wildest.

If you're beginning to wonder just where you have to go to find these strange people and their off-beat operations, I can tell you that you won't have to go far. There are more cons of this type than you can count, and most of them are getting plenty of action. The smallest town has at least one such pitch, the large city has thousands. Often, the front for the setup is a straight religious, philosophic or mystical bit. For instance, many of the leading major cities' newspapers carry notices of such services on Sundays, and often on weekday evenings. It might be the Exhultant Temple of the Seventh Spirit, or the Divine Church for Universal Enlightenment through Spiritualistic Insight; but whatever they call themselves, they're there.

For many years, there have been about a hundred so-called camps where mediums congregate in what might be roughly compared to summer resorts or schools, or a combination of both, with a little of the carnival thrown in. Here, sometimes housed in one large structure, or often operating from independent cottages, you'll find the specialists who offer all forms of psychic phenomena. If your desire is a specialist in voice contact, you'll find him. If you dig the spirit writing bit, you'll find that. If you want prophecy, you just consult the camp directory. If you simply want to know that all's well in the other world, well, they'll all tell you that. Three of the largest such camps, although there are many others, are Camp Chesterfield, the spiritualist camp in Chesterfield, Indiana; Lilydale, and Silverbell.

Camp Chesterfield has long been one of the most popular operations, calling itself the hub of the spirit world. It's featured many leading mediums, and people from all over the country have come to consult them. Then, suddenly, the explosion came —one of the most interesting and spirit-world shaking things to happen in the medium camps for many, many years. This was the great exposé by Tom O'Neil, editor of the *Psychic Observer*. Tom O'Neil for years has been a major figure in the mediumistic field, an investigator of considerable reputation and a publisher of one of the leading papers on the subject. On this particular occasion, he had gone to visit Chesterfield with the intention of doing a story on the remarkable powers of some of their very well-known mediums. However, it was going to be more than merely a written report, for he had received permission from the Chesterfieldian authorities to take motion pictures, filmed with infra-red lighting, during a seance.

Apparently the powers that be at this particular spiritualist camp knew very little about photography, because when the films were developed and run off, to Mr. O'Neil's amazement, where he thought he'd seen authentic spiritualistic manifestations of contact with life beyond, what he actually saw were figures—all too human—fluttering in and out from behind drifting curtains, and much hanky-panky going on by associates of the medium, while the medium, sitting in the blackened room, was supposedly helplessly inactive—except, of course, for his great spiritual powers.

To say that Mr. O'Neil was shocked at his unintentional revelation would be an understatement. He had spent much of his adult life conducting serious investigations, presenting to the public his conviction that there was no doubt as to the authenticity of some of the phenomena he witnessed. And now one of the major camps in the entire country proved to be harboring mediums, so-called, who were nothing more than out-and-out frauds, charlatans deceiving the hopeless, the unhappy-hearted, the poor in spirit, the pathetic.

Had he been the sole exposer, it's possible that the more fervent believers might have had some doubt as to the genuineness of the incident. However, apart from his personal integrity, he was accompanied in his investigations by the noted psychic researcher, Dr. Andrija Puharich. This well-known gentleman in the field of parapsychological investigation supported Tom O'Neil's position to the letter, and wrote lengthily on the "frauds, fakes and phantasies of the Chesterfield Spiritualist Camp"!

It's pretty obvious to anyone who has examined the "stills" clipped from the movie film taken at the Chesterfield seance that there's a striking, even an identifiable, resemblance between the "spirits" and several of the resident mediums at the camp. Only a fool or a blind man in a dark room could fail to recognize the fact that the entire session was totally gaffed.

After the news and photos of the exposé were published far and wide, particularly in the "exclusive" carried by the mediums' monthly mag, O'Neil's own *Psychic Observer*, the great controversy got under way. On one side were the supporters of Tom O'Neil and Dr. Puharich; on the other the exposed mediums and their die-hardest friends who even accused the exposers of faking the exposé. (Remember the same charges were made against Houdini.) It was often obvious that the decision as to which side to go on depended on who the medium or psychic thought would come out on top. All in all, however, there isn't much doubt that for the moment the high cards were being held by the two investigators. Yet, in spite of the dark cloud that hung over the now unhappy mediums, regardless of the obvious fakery, the suspicion and the doubt cast over the entire spiritual field, the expose actually did very little to discourage the tens of thousands of wonder-wishers who flock into the perfumed parlors to get messages from Aunt Minnie, or Uncle George, or Abraham Lincoln, or just to hear the pinched-faced pseudo-parson speak his chair and call it "contact with the great beyond."

Of course, regardless of the fact that I just don't buy any of the kooky off-beat bits, particularly mediumship, occasionally something happens and I have no explanation for it. An example of such an extraordinary instance featured an interview I had with a singularly curious man named William Daut. This particularly "doubtful psychic experience" happened in the following way.

William Daut, medium and spiritualist, was invited to appear on my radio program one evening. He arrived punctually just prior to midnight, and we began the show. For several hours, the panelists and I questioned him about spiritualism, spirit reading, spirit writing, and allied subjects. His answers were direct and prompt to every question—which, I must admit, immediately moved him up in my book. I've had many, many people request an appearance on the show, only to find them extremely evasive after they arrived.

It had been an unusually interesting program, and around four o'clock in the morning one of my boys asked if he had ever turned his mediumship to extra-sensory perception. Daut answered "Yes." I interrupted to ask, without much feeling of confidence, "Would you like to demonstrate your ability?" To my surprise, Daut said, "Why, yes. Why not?"

Now, the reason I was surprised was that on past occasions, mediums and so-called mediums (and I'm not certain there's any difference) had always come up with one excuse or another to show why it was impossible for them to demonstrate their great powers. Powers which, of course, they demonstrated at the drop of a dollar bill anywhere else.

The color of the studio was not right for the proper mood.

"There are too many sceptics present."

"I just had my dinner before coming here, and it's difficult to practice on a full stomach."

"E.S.P. is not something you can use any old time."

But William Daut unhesitatingly accepted the idea that an experiment was perfectly in order.

"I usually need a period in which to concentrate my thoughts, entirely without sound and without interruption. If I might have thirty seconds or so to achieve this, I should be glad to try to produce some results," Daut said.

I got a wave from my engineer, who called me on our intercom.

"Ask him to read off the number on my Social Security card."

I thought this was a very good test, although a rather tough one.

"Mr. Daut," I said, "My engineer, inside the control booth there, behind the glass panel, is holding up his Social Security card with the numbers concealed. Can you tell me the number?"

I should add at this point that Daut was not facing the control booth, nor had he met my engineer. Nor did I know the number on the card.

"I'll try it," said Daut.

He appeared to concentrate for about twenty-five or thirty seconds. He closed his eyes and his brows wrinkled. On the other side of the table, the panelists smiled; one of them winked at me. And I must confess, too, I was certain that nothing of great interest would happen.

"I see the number 104 . . . I see a 2 . . . and a 6 . . . and something like a dash . . I need a moment to concentrate." Daut went on. "10426 and 914."

In the control room my engineer was waving furiously. He picked up the phone and said, "It's unbelievable. He was off only one number. It is 104 26 954—not 914."

Daut smiled when I told him.

"I don't know why you're so surprised. Actually, this was not a tough test since the card in question was only a matter of thirty feet away. I have sometimes been successful at much greater distances."

"How about ten miles? Would you care to make a test at that distance?" I asked.

"Why not?" Daut replied.

At that moment, fortunately and coincidentally, my producer entered the studio from the control room, where our teleprinter is. A telegram had arrived which suited our purposes admirably. It read:

"LONG JOHN. WUX. NEW YORK. MY CAR IS PARKED IN FRONT OF MY HOUSE IN NEWARK, NEW JERSEY. (and here an address was given). CAN MR. DAUT TELL ME WHAT THE NUMBERS ON

THE LICENSE PLATE ARE AND WHAT KIND OF CAR IT IS?"

It was signed by a listener from whom we had received telegrams regularly, and who owned and operated a well-known tavern in our neighboring state.

This was the kind of test I liked. Here was a case where no one knew any of the answers—but it was a difficult one. I could understand if Daut ducked this one.

"This will take a little longer," was his only observation. "And I make no guarantees. I just ask for absolute silence."

In about three minutes, he began speaking a little slower than his normal pace, but not haltingly.

"I see a black—no, a black and white car. It has white wall tires . . . no, only three . . . one tire is black. It has a New Jersey license plate. HL . . . HL . . . 312 . . . HL 31254. I also see a a copy of (and he mentioned a prominent newspaper) on the front seat, folded, with half the headline showing."

Adding the make, year and model, he short of slumped back.

Meanwhile, my producer had the sender of the wire on the phone, listening to the description over his radio. The report came in. The result was amazing. The car was black and cream, not black and white. All four tires were actually white walls, but one, the right rear, was rubbed almost black. There was a newspaper on the seat. The license plate number was entirely correct, and the make, year and model of the car was accurate. When asked if he had any explanation of his powers, Mr. Daut merely suggested that having them was enough; he would leave the explanations to other people. I must admit, to this day I've never dreamed up an answer for that one. I know all the tricks and all the gimmicks and all the gaffs. I know all the devices and the machines and the instruments—I know all the swindles. But this time not only didn't I buy it, I didn't even understand it.

Of course, not all so-called psychics perform like Bill Daut, whose technique might be classified as the non-mystical, or parapsychological. Some are really far out, almost eerie.

I remember one night I had a lady on who called herself Pauline. She claimed to have various kinds of psychic powers and each one was a little wilder than the last. To begin with, she was responsible for some of the most amazing paintings I've ever seen. They were brilliant oil color pictures which sometimes seemed to have faces or eyes or half-hidden figures peeking out from behind great swirls of paint, others appeared to be highly sexual in their meaning, a few were completely too gaffed for me to read. According to Pauline, they all had very special meanings and messages which came from "The Elders."

Her second bit was as fascinating as the first. These were her masks. And take my word for it, neighbors, you never saw masks like these before. Some covered her entire face, others only half of it, a few were just for the eyes. They came in thirty or forty different shapes. One was fringed all across the bottom, a second sprouted antenna-like things all across the top, a third flew off into wings on both sides, and on they went in greens, blacks, scarlets, golds, silvers, with beads, chips of mica, spangles, feathers, embroidery . . . believe me if it was something a fantastic imagination could think of, she had turned it into a mask. And almost every one was really beautiful. Of course, I don't mean to imply that they were all designed at random; that would be untrue. Each mask was the face, or expression, or something, of a genuine, one hundred percent "Elder."

But to get on with the interview. After all of these remarkable works of mystical art had been described and discussed over the air (and shown when I had the lady on television) she prepared to go into trance. I had the studio darkened and only the dim light from the engineer's booth was visible. I could just make out the face of my guest about three feet away across the table. It was completely quiet.

"Are you ready to go into trance, Pauline?" I asked.

There was no answer, but I got the impression her eyes were closed.

"Are you ready now?" I tried again.

There was no reply. Instead the medium began to sway from side to side. I had a kind of weird feeling that one of us was out of touch, and I was beginning to have my doubts as to which one it was. Then it happened.

"OOOOOoooooooeeeeeeeEEEEEEEEEEEooooooooaaaaaaaaaaA AAAAeeeeeeeeeeuuuuuuuuuu!"

Square count, friends, I must have cleared my chair by a good six inches. The siren-sounding moaning-modulated wailing whine came out loud enough to be heard three studios away, and they're soundproof to begin with. Like, man, I was really shook! During the deathly silence that followed, it took me about five minutes to calm down. I spent this time trying to describe Pauline's swaying and quiet mumbles, expecting the message to come through. Unfortunately, I had miscalculated the entire bit. I was totally unprepared when it screamed out again.

"AAAAAAARRRRRggggggggggaaaaaarrrrrroooooooEEEEEEE
EEEKKKKuuuuuuuueeeeeeeeEEEEEEEEKKK!"

Over went the microphone, which hit a glass of water—and
that went over, too. The engineer, who had almost had a heart
attack the first time, was now in a state of hysterical convulsions. I could hear his roars of laughter through the heavy glass
between his booth and the studio. But there was no time to
worry about any of these things. Now the message was beginning
to sing-song "through" in a ghostly chant.

"We are the spirit forces, Pauline. We have answered your
call," she howled.

"Pauline," I asked, "are we in contact with 'The Elders'?"

"We speak for the great ones," came the reply.

"Can you tell us just who 'The Elders' are?"

" 'The Elders' are the super-spirits, the Masters; they rule all."

"Where do they come from?," was my next question.

"They always were, they always will be. They were before
mankind and will be here when it is long gone."

As the trance interview continued, I learned that "The
Elders" were an invisible race of giants who existed on a
parallel time stream. They occasionally condescend to interfere
with the lives of human beings, but not too often. One of the
more interesting things about them is that they're all female. It
seems that males were a later development in history. The result
of some sort of goof. Actually, we're all really mutants. As a
matter of fact, when you hear the whole story you realize that
Pauline probably has material here that Freud never heard of.
But eventually everything will work out, she promises, because
one day "The Elders" will take over again and straighten out
the store. That's one of the most original parts of her pitch,
she doesn't particularly deal with those who've "passed over."
Her contacts always were "over." That is, they aren't dead
people, they're live spirits. Well, I suppose she understands
what I'm talking about.

Falling into a somewhat different category, although having
a similar interest in prehistoric races, is Mark Probert. Mr.
Probert has established contact with a control named "Yada,"
who speaks in the language of "Yu." As I recall, both are from
civilizations which existed some fifty thousand years ago. "Yada"
speaks in a strange, musical tone, which is untranslateable except by Mr. Probert's charming wife and himself. However,
fortunately, Mr. Probert can often induce "Yada" to translate

159

and speak in English. At which time he reveals many curious and interesting facts about his native land and time zone.

And so it goes. A few raps, a few taps, and a message on a slate. Semi-pros up through the levitation mediums, the voice mediums, skeleton mediums, partial materialization mediums, and complete ectoplasmic materialization mediums. Then, jumping across the bridge to the other stream, the off-beat among the off-beat: clairvoyant mediums, the mediums who contact the invisible races that roam between us, above us, and beside us, who were here before we came, and who will be here after we're gone. Some are dull. Some are interesting. Some are fascinating. Some are successful, like Florence of New Jersey who, because of a reputed service to the phone company in locating some stolen goods, has been listed in the phone book as "Florence—Psychic." She's the only one listed in the Manhattan phone book this way, and, as far as I know, the only one in the country. Each one has his own bit, each has his own pitch. The ones like Daut, and Pauline, Florence and Probert, are intriguing. Even if you don't believe a word they're saying, they're fascinating. And they're not dangerous. However, that doesn't change the viciousness of some operators, the swindlers who clip the few hard-earned dollars of the gullible little old lady who would give up her very life to talk once more to her son, who was killed in the war. Sometimes it's entertainment; sometimes it's religion. Sometimes it's business. Sometimes it's just pure, unadulterated, sadistic con.

CHAPTER 11

"Only the dream will last."
—Anderson M. Scruggs

TALES OF MAGIC AND THE OCCULT—
SOME WITHOUT ENDINGS

I SAW HIM disappear. To this day, I say that without hesitation. But let me tell you the whole story.

Several years ago, although the New York Paramount Theatre had discontinued its stage presentation policy, a couple of times a year they would revert to some live entertainment on their stage, such as a show featuring top names in the rock-and-roll field, a ghost show, and on one particular occasion they booked Dr. William Neff, great stage illusionist, a real friend—and a great guy.

Bill, from time to time, had appeared on my show discussing witchcraft, voodoo, and some of the other controversial mystical subjects. He had been in touch with me and told me that he would be appearing during the then current week at the Paramount Theatre. During that week, on Thursday morning, after I wrapped up the radio bit, instead of going over to Carnegie Delicatessen and Restaurant to enjoy my hearty breakfast, I decided to hit the pad early so I could make the afternoon performance at the Paramount.

The movie for that week was a horror movie—and let me again emphasize the fact that it was a real horror. Not being a sportsman I actually don't know what happens at Yankee Stadium on a snowy afternoon with the temperature at two below zero. But I have an idea that it's possibly about as populated as the Paramount Theatre was on that eventful afternoon that I witnessed the disappearance of Dr. William Neff. In a theatre built to seat approximately three thousand people, I noted that I had approximately a hundred and fifty companions of the cultural arts scattered far and wide. And for some three or four minutes, during the time that all the house lights are on after the feature has ended and just prior to the live entertainment, the traveler curtain is closed and this is considered intermission—whatever that means. I have an idea that it's a period of time when the ushers walk up and down the aisle taking an inventory of the number of seats that have been stolen during the last performance, how many large cuts have been made in the upholstery, and of minor smoldering fires in unused sections of the theatre. This keeps management on their toes so, in the event that a large crowd shows up for the evening performance, if there's a need they can quickly get additional seats to replace those stolen by the patrons of the fine arts who have attended the symposium of the afternoon.

You know, I just thought I'd mention this in passing. When I first came to New York—and I know what you're thinking, that it was at the turn of the century; actually, it was around 1930 —I was employed as an usher in the New York Paramount Theatre. And in those days they were employing young men who had either completed their college education or were in the process of acquiring it. How I could do it? Well, that's a book in itself. And if you'll write the editors at Prentice-Hall, Englewood Cliffs, New Jersey, and ask them to publish L. J.'s next book, "How I Got My Job at the New York Paramount with a Public School Education," who knows? maybe they'll publish it. With no reflection on the present management of the New York Paramount Theatre, that afternoon I realized that there was a vast difference in the quality of the audience. I didn't have time to do any research into the current qualifications for usher material. So I will not comment. But as I looked around during those few minutes when all the house lights were on I wasn't sure whether this was the annual meeting of the kid gang chiefs

162

from the various parts of the country and a handful of pick-pockets, muggers, and to season this melange, a handful of derelicts thrown in. How Neff had the courage to work to that house has always been one of nature's greatest phenomena.

All right, I've digressed a little from the story. And in case you're wondering, I heard the word "digress" from one of my guests one morning, and I liked it so I added it to my vocabulary. So I now have 803 words—and mispronounce about 772 of them.

Now that I had checked the other members of the tip that I was a part of to witness the good doctor's performance, the lights gradually dimmed and music emanated from the public address speakers around the theatre. And naturally it was obvious to me that this was not really a low budget show; it was budget-less. There were no live musicians in the pit, under the stage, overhead, underhead, or any place for that matter. And if I'm mistaken, in other words if this music was being played by live musicians, I sincerely hope that a member of that aggregation will read this apology and certainly this accolade. These guys were so sensational that they were even able to create sound effects that would make the average guy think he was listening to a record that had originally been poorly recorded, and had been used thousands of times, and for that particular performance somebody had possibly taken out the diamond stylus from the cartridge and had replaced it—not with a zircon, but with a sliver from a broken Coca Cola bottle. Again I repeat—this was a show that was budget-less. Bear in mind, however, that this had nothing to do with the tremendous talent, know-how, knowledge, superb dexterity and ability that Dr. William Neff is endowed with.

After some technical electronic genius backstage, who no doubt considered himself to be a top sound engineer, gradually pulled the pot down—which means to lower the volume of the music—we heard a voice that came from the great beyond (at least beyond the proscenium arch). This voice alerted all of us —those who had been honing the blades of their switch-bladed knives to keener surgical cutting edges, others who had been nervously switching the weight of their bodies from the left cushion of their derrieres to the right cushion, and a handful who had reached the point of slumber that strange noises were emanating from them, having no definite tonal quality except that which is commonly known as snoring—to become ready for the mysteries of the east, the E.S.P. of Duke University, the

163

witchcraft and demonology and the general enchantment of a William Lindsay Gresham book. Minutes later, after this announcement, we all witnessed the appearance of the great one, Dr. William Neff.

All of the activities being practiced by our little group of searchers for the cultural things of life were discontinued. Hones and knives were put back in pockets for later hours of unlicensed dark-street surgical work; the nervousness of those shifting from the left to the right cushion, as they became intensely aware that it would start in a moment, they straightened themselves into a position that possibly they considered a demonstration of welcomeness for the purveyor of mysticism; and the sound of the snoring gradually faded away to such an extent that even the finest decibel meter would fail to register. I can't honestly say that there was a tremendous ovation. It would be unfair to say that the applause was deafening to welcome the great man. Possibly the applause was unanimous. It could possibly be described in this manner: No doubt every fortunate individual that afternoon genuinely wanted to be a part of this tremendous ovation. But to applaud requires the use of the left and the right hands, and these two extremities must come in direct contact, and after they have reached a contact, by some reflex action they are separated again and again and again. In other words, this activity is repeated many times. The sound that this creates is known to people of the theatre as applause, and to many a nutrient. That's why I'm puzzled. I think if it had been possible to have talked to these people as a group prior to the performance we could have learned that many of them would have been happy to use their right hand in combination with the left hand of their neighbors to have created the same sound effect. But to use all of this energy by using both of their own appendages no doubt to some seemed a trifle unnecessary, and certainly it was not a part of the assumed contractual agreement that was made with the management of the theatre upon purchase of the ticket.

My reason for taking up so much space with the past material is based on the personal desire to let one and all know that Dr. William Neff was working under the most adverse conditions that I think any performer has ever been forced to endure. Let's get to the story.

Gradually the house lights darkened, the footlights became less and less distinct, lights around the proscenium arch faded, and we now see a pink spotlight focused on the split in the traveler curtain. There isn't a sound for some twenty or thirty seconds. And then we see the traveler curtain being manually separated by the appearance of Dr. William Neff, elegantly attired in tails that would make the Prince of Wales, when he was looked upon as the standard of sartorial elegance, feel extremely envious.

Neff is a tall, slender man in his early fifties. Luxurious, closely-cropped gray hair, finely chiseled features make up his face, and in general there is no doubt in my mind that had Dr. William Neff decided to enter the theatre as an actor rather than a prestidigitator he would have no doubt found the going rather rough as he would leave the theatre at the end of any given performance, because of the tremendous number of women fans who would be waiting for autographs or just a glimpse of this charming debonair gentleman, who would, no doubt, be the main character in the dreams of many of these ladies.

In a voice quality that's hard to describe, but certainly all would agree that at least this one simple adjective could be employed—interesting—he welcomed the audience and told them in a few well-chosen words what they would be witnessing during the next sixty sensational, mystical minutes.

To this very day I am still extremely puzzled. For the life of me I can't tell you what caused it, of whether it was just a good illusion. But this I'll say without fear of contradiction—it happened.

As Neff was making his opening pitch, the area illuminated by the spot gradually became larger and larger as the technician controlled its diameter. And then the footlights were gradually coming up from a faint glow to a rather modified . . . possibly better described as a subtle different amount of illumination to add mystery and yet sufficient light for those fortunate few to witness the many effects that were to be presented by the master illusionist, Dr. William Neff. As I watched and listened, for a moment I lost confidence in what I thought my eyes were seeing and yet my heart could not believe. I tried to rationalize this phenomenon in the seconds that I know I saw it happen. It seemed that Neff's body was becoming minutely translucent.

I felt that his clothed body was turning to frosted glass or some form of plastic that was not transparent, but would permit light areas to be seen through it. It gave me an uncanny—or should I say unreal—feeling that something was happening that afternoon that possibly many members of the audience had not yet become aware of. And as the seconds ticked away—and they actually didn't seem to be seconds, they were possibly hours, maybe even days—I lost complete track of time. Because the body was now undergoing a complete change. It now appeared that it was no longer translucent, but completely transparent. The black tails were not made of translucent black plastic. The white dress shirt was not milky glass. The small area of human skin—the hands, the head—were not made of flesh-toned translucent plastic. All of the material that made up this body was now gradually becoming transparent. The black, the white, the flesh-toned areas, could all be seen through clearly. You could see the traveler curtain clearly behind this transparent figure. And now it seemed that it was taking a very, very long time. Yes, slowly it was no longer transparent; it was disappearing completely.

Again let me emphasize the point that I saw this with my own eyes. The voice of William Neff continued to be audible. It was coming through the speakers connected with the public address system. The stand that supported the microphone that Dr. William Neff was speaking his opening remarks into continued to remain in its material state. Even the wire that dangled from the microphone until it touched the floor and gradually snaked its way under the traveler curtain until it presumably was connected to the theatre's public address system remained. At no time did it become translucent and then transparent and then disappear. Although Neff had disappeared, I know that his larynx and other organs that make up the auditory, physical equipment of the human being were still functioning.

Gradually a rather faint outline, like a very fine pencil sketch of Neff, appeared again. And then, as if after the artist had made his outline he quickly replaced the pencil with charcoal and filled in the dark areas that formed the evening attire. And yet it was not a dense black at that moment. It had a translucent, and at times transparent, quality. And then, as if our artist were a lightning sketch artist, with bold strokes he added more charcoal to this gray area so that it became a dense black solid material again—and all of a sudden our imaginary artist added the flesh tones to this quick sketch and we had appear before us a fine, realistic, full-length in all of its dimensions, a portrait of William Neff—life size. And then, as if our imaginary artist was even a superior magician to the great Dr. Neff, with some mystical movement he was able to take away the canvas-like portrait quality of this life-size portrait and to replace it with a sort of reality. And then it appeared to have all the quality of a fine piece of Arnold Bergiere sculpture, and then I realized that this was not a stone-like substance, but once again I was seeing the real, live, activated body of Dr. William Neff.

If you've ever listened to me on radio or if you've ever seen me on television, you know I have a favorite expression that has now become a cliché: I don't buy it. I'm considered by many to be one of the most sceptical men in the business. Many of my former guests have even used obscenities to describe my ignorance and closed-mindedness. But I'm giving you a square count —I know this actually happened. I saw it with my own eyes.

I could go into great details at this time to tell you how I rushed backstage afterwards to talk with Bill about this. But I'm going to be brief and to the point. I spoke to Bill; he told me that if I actually witnessed what I claimed, he was unaware of its happening. It is not an illusion that's a part of his performance. In fact, when I pressed him to discuss it with me at greater length he became slightly perturbed.

I wrote a report of this occurrence for *Fate Magazine* and, about a year later, for the *Psychic Observer*. And both times I received considerable mail from readers. I'm going to take paragraphs from certain letters that I received to give you an idea of the interpretation and analysis given to this, and I think we should put the word in quotes, "phenomenon"—by a metaphysician, a radiesthesiast, a student of the occult, and a nonbeliever:

H. V. L., a student of the occult from Honolulu, Hawaii, wrote:

"I believe that I have an answer as to how he did it. Mr. Neff, in my opinion, should pass his knowledge of this to the scientific research. Mr. Neff is able to harmonize his body and mind simultaneously to meet the elements of the air. This is a form of Yogi meditation and this fact is known to Father Pio of Rome.

"I sincerely believe that Mr. Neff is afraid of his knowledge and of what he performed on that said date.

"If this act has not been repeated by Mr. Neff, I am of the opinion that it is purely fear on his part."

And from a well-known New York radiesthesiast, Dr. H. B. M,. I received a letter that read, in part:

"... *Mr. William Neff is a Spiritualist medium for physical phenomena, whether he admits it or even knows it himself; and the unusual things that happen because of, or around him, are the doings of his band of Spirit Helpers, consciously or even unconsciously directed by him. ...*

"... *a person becoming invisible ... (is) well recognized by psychic science. This phenomenon is called Dematerialization, and it is accomplished by Spirit Entities around the medium, who speed up all the vibrations in every cell of his body until the rate is so high as to render them invisible. But the person's Etheric Body remains intact, and when the Spirits slow down the vibrations again the cells rematerialize in their original positions, and the person's physical body is whole once more. This is what happened to Mr. Neff on the stage.*"

The following excerpt from a letter sent by H. W. G. of San Francisco, a gentleman who claims to be a metaphysician, is spelled, punctuated and capitalized exactly—and I do mean exactly—as we received it:

"*So You Been Playing Araund in Several Branches Of Mratphysics Including Hypnotissm Eh, Have You Got Any Idea What Youre Playing Araund With, Plenty People Read Something Abaut Such Mybe Successful Experiments An Think Thy Know All Abaut It And Start Experimenting, An A Lot End In The Nuthause, Jes My Dear Sir, Metaphysics Means, Manipulation And Application Of Natural Laws, ...*

"... *Another Thing, If Your Paal Jeff Should Praktice His Disapearing Ackt Openly On The Stages, I Bet, He'LL Get Some Nice Blackcoated Longfacet Gentlemen Visitors Tonsuret Or And Others, An Thy'll Verry Kindly Sugesting Th Him To Please Cease An Resist From Farther Demonstration Of His Trik, OR ELSE, An Believe Me There Are And Have Been Quite A Few Who Choose To Ignore Thet Or Else An Mow Wish Thy Had, The Nuthouses Ore Good Storagebins, An Justtyy To Get Aut, Of Course, if Your Friend Jeff Has By That Time Fully Developet His Pover To Dematerialize His Body An Transport It At Will At The Instant, He Could Make A Laughing stok Of The Whole Caboddle, An Believe Me Something Similar To That Is Likely To Happen Repeatedly Not So Faar Ahead, Jeff Is Not The Only Student of E,S,P,*"

Of course, we also got letters from "non-believers," like S.M. of Darlington, Wisconsin:

"It just seems to me that Neff did not do anything, and that if this happened at all it happened to you, not to Neff. Your friend seeing it would not alter this anymore than the seeing of a collective hallucination would mean that two people seeing what they claim is the same phenomena would alter the fact that others would not see it."

In writing a book, you don't sit down and do it all in one night. Since I last sat in front of this typewriter, I've been in touch with Dr. Neff by phone, and I told him that I'd come to the point in my book where I'd described in minute detail his appearance at the Paramount Theatre, and that I'd also taken excerpts from the letters I had received after the two published reports I'd written on his disappearance at the Paramount Theatre.

I said, "Bill, this happened a few years ago, and you may not remember it, but I think you got a little hot under the collar in your dressing room that afternoon when I pushed you a little bit to try to get more information about that disappearance. Can you add anything to it at this point . . . in other words, is it a gaff? And if it is I won't hesitate to admit to you that I don't want to know it. And . . . after all, you'll admit that when you're sawing a girl in half it's a trick—and you admit it's a trick, although you don't tell how it's done. Bill, what happened at the Paramount Theatre that afternoon?"

Bill's reply to my questions—and may I add that my questions and his answers during that telephone conversation that afternoon a couple of days ago are recorded so I'm giving it to you verbatim—

"John, I don't know what you hope to gain by rehashing that. When you first came backstage that afternoon I was a little hot under the collar. A situation almost identical to what happened at the Paramount Theatre happened to me about three years prior to that Paramount date, when I was playing in Chicago. And since then I've always been a trifle concerned."

"Well, Bill, are you saying that people saw you disappear in Chicago a few years ago?"

"John, let me answer you this way. I don't remember all of the details because, frankly, if there ever was anything that I wanted to erase from my memory it was the stories that I heard after my fourth day at a theatre in Chicago.

"The other day, Evelyn was sitting watching TV in our apartment (Evelyn is Mrs. William Neff) and I was sitting in a rather comfortable over-stuffed chair, reading Robbins' book on

169

witchcraft and demonology. Evelyn started to say something to me, but evidently she was continuing to watch the TV fare for that particular time, and all of a sudden she screamed. And I looked at her. I became very concerned. She looked to me like a woman in a trance. She stared at me. A moment later tears started to flow from her eyes. She said, 'Bill, where are you?'

"John, I was in that chair! I closed the book, I got out of the chair. I went over to her. When I touched her to offer her some form of consolation she let out a piercing scream and said, 'Who's touching me?' "

"Bill, I'm sorry to interrupt, but I've got to get this straight. You were actually sitting in that chair? You didn't leave the room or anything?"

"John, it's just the way I told you. Evelyn was watching TV. For the life of me I don't know what she said, or anything, because I was interested in what I was reading in Robbins' book . . ."

"Bill, let me ask you this. Assuming that you disappeared, as far as Evelyn was concerned. She screamed. And then you left your chair, to go over and touch her. Did you then reappear? Or maybe I'm assuming something, but . . . well . . . at least, do you feel that you were invisible, or visible, at that time?"

"John, I guess that's the best way to explain it. I walked away from her to go to the bathroom, to get her a glass of water. All of a sudden she jumped up. She threw her arms around me . . . and I quickly unlaced her fingers and quickly turned around so that I'd be facing her, and again she put her arms around me. I don't remember what she said—I mean her exact words or anything—but she said something about, I think she said, 'Oh, Bill, I was so frightened. I couldn't see you for a few minutes.' "

"I guess this is a stupid question, Bill, because man, you've told a fantastic story—but, is there any more to it?"

"John, I guess that's about all there was to it."

"Bill, I know you're always in favor of publicity, but I know your great reluctance to have anything in print about your family or your personal life, but would you permit your number one fan—yours truly, L. J.—to use this in my book? No doubt you've heard the beeps, because I've been recording this call."

"John, in answer to your request, I'll do it under this one condition: that any mail that you receive about this I want you to promise me that you will not send it to me, and if Evelyn

170

comes over to your studio one night you'll not show her any of it."

"Bill, that's a deal. I'm not going to ask you why, because I think I know the answer myself. Give my best to Ev, and maybe in a week or so we can get together and break a little bread."

"Thanks for calling, John."

"See you around, Bill."

And that, neighbors, I think will bring you up to date. I saw him disappear. To this day I say that without hesitation. Yes, I saw him disappear. And now, you too know the whole story.

Actually, when I look back over the years, it's amazing how many strange, almost unbelievable things have happened during the show. Unfortunately, it seems that the most interesting ones had no ending—that is, explanation—at least, not for me. One that comes to my mind at the moment is an experiment in astral projection conducted by the well-known hypnotist John Kolisch.

To be accurate, this one didn't actually happen in the studio. It took place in an apartment I had for a number of years in midtown Manhattan. John Kolisch had been on my half-hour show two or three times. This show preceded the long all-night show that I'm doing at the present time. It was on from 11:30 to 12:00 for about a year and a half. John Kolisch contacted me by phone and told me that he had an excellent hypnotic subject, a young man around 17 years of age. And Kolisch wanted to know whether I'd be interested in witnessing an experiment in astral projection. Kolisch had a theory that a person in a deep hypnotic state could be given a suggestion to permit the psychic body to separate from the physical body . . . well, wait a moment. I'm getting a little too far into the story.

I told Kolisch on the phone that day that he could come up the following Thursday night. He arrived and introduced me to the young man—and for the sake of losing all identity I'll refer to this young man as "Tommy."

Tommy was attending a parochial school. His parents, I was told, were under the impression that these experiments in "astral projection" were possibly sacrilegious and no doubt would not be condoned by the hierarchy of the Catholic Church. Evidently John was not only a good hypnotist, but a rather persuasive individual, because he was able—at least John told me—to get Tommy's parents to agree to continue the experiments providing he would not regress the boy to a pre-natal period. You think that's wild? Wait'll you hear this story.

171

My apartment was located on the sixth floor of a 32-story building on Manhattan's east side. The windows of my apartment faced the rear windows of the apartment on the next street. I think this is important to point out because there's a possibility that some readers may feel that a view of the street below may have been of value to the hypnotist and his subject in reference to this experiment.

Kolisch is a very smooth and competent hypnotist. He's not a bellowing, theatrical type. In giving the induction phrases he almost whispers the words into the ear of the subject. Standing a distance of three or four feet away, it's virtually impossible to hear the phrases. Of course, Tommy had been hypnotized many times, so it required no great effort on the part of Kolisch to get him into what's known in the hypnotic field as a deep, deep hypnotic state. After Tommy was in this hypnotic state, John Kolisch made the necessary tests to make certain that this was not a light, surface hypnotic condition. And he proceeded to give the boy instructions and then to ask him questions in a regression experiment where the boy was regressed from his then current age of seventeen down to twelve, ten, seven. . . . and then at the age of five we could notice a definite change in the voice quality and the range.

Oh, and let me add something at this point. Prior to regressing the boy, but at the point where he was already hypnotized, Kolisch asked him to write a sentence and to sign his name—which the boy did with the pen and pad given to him. Now, at the age of "five," Kolisch gave him the pad and pen again and asked him to write his name. In a sort of childish combination of writing and printing, he was able to write "Tommy"—but with little legibility. Upon questioning, he described some of his toys; a favorite one was a teddy bear.

And then Kolisch regressed him to three . . . to two . . . to one . . . and I don't think it's my business to be critical, but I was wondering whether or not Kolisch was not going a little beyond the agreement he had made with Tommy's parents when he regressed him to the embryonic period in the womb. And upon the suggestion that he was now living in some place prior to birth, the boy seemed to automatically curl up and assume the fetal position.

I don't think it's necessary in this book to relate Tommy's impressions of the place he was in during this purported embryonic period. At this point I said to Kolisch, "Bring him out of it, and let's sit down for a moment and have a drink." He proceeded to give the boy instructions that he was now three years of age . . . five years . . . seven . . . twelve . . . and at this point he proceeded to ask him questions such as the name of the student who sat next to him in school today, etc., . . . and then he brought him up to his present age of seventeen. And then, as hypnotists do, he asked him how he felt; and Tommy said "fine." It was as if nothing had happened to him. He looked around the room at my recording equipment that was up against one wall, and saw my record collection. He spotted a Louis Armstrong record and asked if he could listen for a minute while I went to the kitchen to prepare drinks and get a Coke for Tommy. I put on the record, and while he was listening to the Louis Armstrong record Tommy was snapping his fingers to the rhythm of the music and doing a few steps that evidently were steps of tomorrow, because as an ex-hoofer I was unfamiliar with them, and during the time that I was preparing for my doctorate from Roseland I had never used them.

The point I'm trying to make is that Tommy was completely unaware of anything that had transpired during experiment number one that evening. However, experiment number two was the one that made me wonder whether my closed-mindedness was really a manifestation of ignorance.

At this point, after enjoying our liquid refreshments, we permitted Mr. Armstrong and his talented group to relax, and the switch controlling the activity of the turnable was put in the off position. And Tommy once more was put into a deep, deep, *deep* hypnotic state.

Kolisch sat down on a small cocktail table facing the subject, who was seated in a canvas-backed deck chair. Kolisch informed me that he hoped to be able to prove to me that good hypnotic subjects become great psychics. Many people become clairvoyant, a handful telepathic, and, through personal experience conducting thousands of experiments, he had found one or two who were definitely able to control things telekinetically.

At this point he told Tommy (who was still in the hypnotic state) that his astral body was going to go to the ground level of this building and then his astral body would walk out of the double set of doors and stand under the marquee.

There was silence for possibly some fifteen or twenty seconds.

And now Kolisch told the boy that he was leaving the apartment.

"Tommy, go through the door. Tommy, don't stand at the door there waiting for it to be opened or waiting for somebody to open it for you. Go right through the door, Tommy. Tommy, you're going through the door now. Tommy, you're now in the hallway. Turn to your right. That's it, now, turn to your right. Walk forward. Wait a moment . . . you've gone a little too far, Tommy. Turn around. That's it, turn around. Go back till you see that other section of hallway . . . that's it. Turn to your right. As you go a little further, you'll see that there's an extension of the hallway . . . that's it. Turn to your right, Tommy . . . that's it. You're now at the elevator.

"Tommy, don't press the button. Tommy, you don't have to press the elevator button. Listen for the elevator. It's coming down, Tommy. It's on the ninth floor now. Somebody is getting out of the elevator on the ninth floor. Now it's coming down again . . . it's on the eighth floor . . . the seventh . . . Tommy, I don't know if it will stop on this floor or not, but even if it doesn't you'll be able to go right in as it passes . . . you'll just go right through the doors, through the gate, and you'll be in the elevator, Tommy. It's still on the seventh floor. Someone has gone in. The doors are closing now . . . it's coming down again. Tommy, it's stopping. The elevator is going to stop on this floor, Tommy. It's stopping now—the doors are opening. Tommy, step aside a moment. Let the people out of the elevator. Now go in. It doesn't matter if its crowded, Tommy. You won't take up any space. That's it, Tommy.

"Now you're going down, Tommy. Fifth floor . . . fourth . . . third . . . second . . . you're on the ground floor. The gate is opening, the doors are opening, and with your astral body you can walk out and through the double doors. Tommy, even though the doors are closed you don't have to open them. Walk right through the double doorway. You're in the street now. Feel that breath of fresh air, Tommy, as you're standing under the marquee of the building? Tommy, do you hear me? Tommy, answer me . . . do you feel the breath of fresh air? Your astral body is under the marquee . . . you're standing in front of this building on East 42nd Street."

Please bear in mind that up to this point our subject, Tommy, has not said a word. He was first informed by Kolisch while he was in the hypnotic state what was going to happen. And then Kolisch proceeded to guide the astral body, which separated itself from the physical body, through the door, into the hallway, down the elevator, and out into the street.

In a rather weak voice, in a halting style, with a lack of accurate continuity, Tommy answered the first question in the affirmative.

At this point Kolisch asked me if I could help him by telling him if there were on the curb or a part of the building—which had an approximate hundred-foot frontage—any landmarks. It dawned on me that there was a fire hydrant adjacent to one of the supporting poles of the marquee. This meant that no law-abiding citizen would be parked in front of the marquee or west of it for at least twenty feet.

During our conversation—that is, Kolisch and I talking together—we did not speak in subdued tones. And it was certainly obvious to me that the hypnotized subject was unaware of our conversation.

I suggested to John, because of the hour in the evening, that the odds were that there would be a car twenty feet from that fire hydrant and that he should suggest to Tommy's astral body to walk over to the car and describe it as to brand name, 2- or 4-door, color, and any other outstanding characteristics. The suggestion was accepted by Kolisch, and he proceeded to tell Tommy to walk over to this car and to describe it.

I had a legal pad of paper handy, and I made notes as to the description. I then suggested to Kolisch to ask the astral body to feel the hood of the car to see if it was warm or cold; Kolisch hastened to explain to me that an astral body cannot differentiate between hot and cold. I then requested Kolisch to get the license number, and after this had been ascertained I told Kolisch to get the astral body back into the apartment, and I'd go down and check.

Once again Tommy was brought out of the hypnotic state, given an additional bottle of Coke as a reward, and the opportunity of hearing the other side of the Louis Armstrong album to keep him occupied while I proceeded to take my physical body—not through the closed door, but stopping a moment to open it— and to go to the ground level of the building.

As soon as I saw the car I realized that his description was extremely accurate, with one minor discrepancy—he said the car was bluish; actually it was greenish. When I first saw it, I thought it was blue—and then I realized that the street light had a tendency to make it appear bluish.

I put my hand on the hood of the car, because, being a sceptic, it dawned on me that this car could have been a plant that had been quickly brought over—a car that Tommy knew the description of, and Tommy got a break in possibly being able to park it at this particular location. And of course, as a reader, you're beginning to wonder how Tommy and the hypnotist could enlighten their outside confederate—if there was one—as to where to park the car. This is quite simple. The confederate could have been standing outside of my apartment door during the entire experiment, listening to the place that we had decided to look for a car to describe.

When I went downstairs, I put my hand on the hood of the car, and it was cold. It was obvious to me that this car had been parked there for at least an hour or so—certainly prior to our experiment.

Tommy was inaccurate, however, in one digit in the license number. Or I should say he had the numbers reversed. Instead of being 897468, it should have been 894768.

Can I explain it? Honestly I can't.

It was weird, wild, and I give you no answers. Don't mistake me. Things like this are extremely confusing. They beat me completely. But my attitude is still the same: I just don't buy it.

As I'm writing this, I'm just beginning to wonder if my editor John Gudmundsen will come to the conclusion that possibly this experiment in astral projection will not be interesting enough; so we'd better cut it. I've got a lot of confidence in John, and if he says it has to be cut that's what we're going to do. So I'd better protect myself by relating one more story, which even he wouldn't delete. In fact, maybe I'll get a break and they'll leave both stories in.

This happened in Studio 6, which we usually refer to as the Martha Deane Studio. And please don't construe this as a commercial, but if you live in New York you're mighty lucky because if you can get near a radio at 10:15 any morning between a Monday and a Friday you'll hear 45 minutes of the greatest interviewing in the field of communications. This very charming, articulate and knowledgeable lady, Martha Deane, has no peers. I'm honored, lucky, and, I might add, very proud to be able to use the Martha Deane Studio facilities some 36 hours each and every week until 5:00, and sometimes 5:30, in the morning.

In order to be able to form a mental picture of what took place it's necessary for me to take a moment to describe the physical set-up of two studios on the 24th floor of 1440 Broadway.

Studio 6 and 7 are identical studios with the front of each studio facing the other. If you were coming in from the hallway, you would come in the door and then you would be standing in a small area, a maximum of 125 square feet. To your left would be Studio 7, and to your right would be Studio 6. If you'd open the door of Studio 6, you'd find that it was a very heavy sound-proof door that you'd be activating. Inside, to the right would be the engineer's booth, and to the left would be what's known as the sponsor's booth. You'd see another soundproof door directly ahead of you, and if you'd go through this door you'd go down two steps and you'd be in a very large room—approximately 30 feet long by 20 feet wide—having a rear door in the right-hand corner of the studio proper.

Going back for a moment to this original little areaway that separates 6 and 7, if you'd go instead to your left it would be Studio 7 that you would enter, and the physical description would be the reverse as that of Studio 6.

In each of the studios there is a very heavy oak table, padded on the top in the event that a guest became slightly nervous and tapped his pencil or started to fiddle with a paper clip—so that the noise of this activity would not prove to be irritating to the listeners at home. On these tables, microphones are placed in the number that are necessary for guests participating in a discussion. However, when a studio is not in action—the term used in the profession is "not hot"—these tables are clear of any encumbrances, such as ash trays, microphones, etc.

On the morning when this experiment in teleportation took place, I had four guests, plus two or three other people sitting in the studio watching the proceedings. It was about 2:15 in the morning. I had just returned to my chair after ordering food from Carnegie Delicatessen and Restaurant for our coffee break. Evidently, during the eight or ten minutes that were required to place the order for the food to be consumed during the coffee break, a hassle had started between the guests.

Dr. William Neff was relating an experiment that he had conducted in teleportation. Three of the other guests pooh-poohed the whole idea. At this point I participated in the discussion by challenging Neff to conduct an experiment in teleportation. And now the details.

We removed everything from our talk table with the exception of the five microphones—four for the guests and one used by me.

We always supply our guests with small sheets of note paper, approximately 5 x 7 in size, so that during the time that they're participating in one of our talk sessions they can doodle, make notes, etc.

Bill suggested for all of us to take out of our pockets two, three, or four single dollar bills. Among the four of us, we tossed to the center of the table a total of fourteen dollars. Some putting in four singles, one person I remember had only one single with him, and the others possibly two or three. The total amount I remember—as clearly as if it happened yesterday morning—was fourteen dollars.

Neff requested a lady seated in the studio—a non-participant —to come over to the table and select at random one of the bills from the group. The lady, incidentally, had not even been introduced to Dr. Neff—had not even heard of him before—but no doubt she has never forgotten him since she witnessed that experiment. She was the wife of one of our engineers.

The bill having now been selected, it gave everyone the opportunity of retrieving his original contribution to the experiment—with the exception, of course, of one individual whose bill was being used.

At this point the only thing on the table with the exception of the microphones is a single dollar bill that has now been inspected—for what I'll never know—by all of the participants.

Dr. Neff now requested four sheets of the note paper described a few paragraphs ago. Everyone, with the exception of me, went as a group from Studio 6, through the little areaway that separates 6 and 7, and then proceeded to go into Studio 7.

Dr. Neff carried with him two of the sheets of paper.

The lights in 7 were turned on, and there, again, an almost exact duplication of the furnishings and fixtures one would see in 6 included the old reliable oak table—completely void of anything. Just a blank—or should I say empty—table.

Bill Neff carefully took the two sheets of paper, I'm told—because at this time I was doing a commercial in Studio 6 for my sponsor, Hudson Vitamin Products, followed by one for General Tire and Rubber Company—and he lined up these two sheets together. As he told those in Studio 7, he felt that one sheet would not be sufficiently opaque because of the thinness of the paper, so he thought it would be better to have two sheets. He placed these two sheets in dead center of the table, after lining them up together, with such accuracy that if you were to come into the studio and touch the two sheets you would not think there were two sheets—it would appear to be just a single sheet of paper.

The lights were left on, and all the participants came back to Studio 6.

Please also bear in mind that the rear door of Studio 6 or 7 cannot be entered by anyone from the outside hall unless someone on the inside opens it.

Everyone was now seated around the table once again, and Neff brought me up to date as to what had transpired in Studio 7. He now asked each individual to either make a mental note or to write down the serial number on the dollar bill that had been selected by the engineer's wife. He then placed the dollar bill on the table, face down. On top of this bill he placed the two additional sheets of paper left over from the four sheets he had originally requested. Possibly I could describe it in this manner: The sheets of paper acted as a blanket for the bill, making it impossible for anyone to suspect that anything was underneath this ostensibly single sheet of paper—which, actually, was two sheets combined to create additional opaqueness.

A last-minute request on the part of Bill Neff was for someone to bring a cardioid microphone that was not being used at the present time, but was standing on a shelf in the rear of the studio, to him. I'd say this microphone weighs approximately twelve to fifteen pounds. He set the microphone on top of the paper.

Think about this for a moment. It would be virtually impossible for anyone to remove this bill from under the paper without lifting the microphone off the paper.

Now everything is set.

And he requested the engineer's wife to come over to the table again.

Bear in mind that during this entire experiment people at home are listening to this entire conversation.

Bill told the lady to lift up the microphone, lift up the pieces of paper, . . . and there was the dollar bill, face down. He then asked her to pick up the dollar bill and to read the serial number—which she did. And we all checked and found it was the same bill that he had placed there a few minutes ago.

I know. You thought there'd be a different bill . . . and to be honest with you, so did I. How it could be accomplished I had no idea. But I'll tell you I was disappointed. I thought that Neff blew the gaff. No doubt he noticed the look of dejection and disappointment on the faces of all concerned, and he said he merely had this very charming lady come over to the table to prove to us that no slight of hand was employed to remove the bill or to change it.

He then asked the lady to replace the bill face down on the

table, put the double sheet of paper on top of it, and put the microphone on top of that.

At that time my engineer attracted my attention and I picked up my phone, and he told me that the food had arrived from Carnegie Delicatessen. I then proceeded to tell my listeners that we were going to take a twenty-minute coffee break, and during the interim they would listen to music from Carteret, New Jersey. Just as I was about to identify the station, Neff interrupted me and said to me,

"John, I will now prove to you and to your guests that teleportation is a real phenomenon; and when we return from the coffee break you can tell your audience what had happened."

I identified the station, gave the verbal cue to my engineer by saying, "Let's hear the music."

Normally, at this point everybody jumps up to get at the sandwiches and the coffee because usually, after two and a half or three hours of talking, they're famished.

Not a person moved from his chair.

And, as I look in retrospect, I don't think an individual even moved in his chair.

The suspense was so great that all of us just waited there, almost reluctant to take a deep breath for fear that possibly we could cause some disturbance that could kill the possibility of witnessing the phenomenon of teleportation that each one of us, individually, down deep in our hearts, knew would never happen. But none of us could afford to gamble against the remote possibility that this was the M.O.M. of our lives—the Morning of Miracles.

We are now off the air, and Neff asked all of us to stand up—and he emphasized the fact that we should gradually, in a rather slow pace, move away from the table, and to sort of shape up in the center of the studio. He requested the handful of visitors who were in the studio also to become a part of this group standing in the center of the studio. He asked our engineers, Walter McDonough and Jack Keane, to also join the group standing in Studio 6.

And then, as a great general would possibly guide his troops to an island that's possibly just raised the white flag of truce, he marched us as a group from Studio 6, all following our leader, Dr. William Neff.

At no time did anyone go back to that table. But I must admit that we all, as we left Studio 6, sort of took that last look

180

at the center of that table where that heavy microphone was sitting on two sheets of paper, and we assumed underneath the paper, lying face down, was the dollar bill whose serial number we all knew.

We're now standing in the areaway that is the space between the doors of Studio 6 and Studio 7.

The General—in this case Dr. William Neff—took a quick head count and realized that his troops were all intact.

He asked Walter McDonough and Jack Keane to go first and open both doors leading into Studio 7. And I can honestly say that the closest thing to a group arriving simultaneously was certainly accomplished that morning.

We all stood to one side of the studio in positions that made it possible for all of us to view the oak table, which was clear of everything with the exception of a piece of paper.

Dr. Neff then requested that the three visitors—one the engineer's wife who had participated in a portion of the experiment, as I've related it—stand one on each of three sides of the table, and then he asked me to be the fourth witness. At all times the balance of the group was able to see every movement.

He then proceeded to tell us in beautiful, mystical phraseology that the bill in Studio 6 had left that studio during the time that the group was standing between 6 and 7. And he said the reason that he had to request the assistance of the two engineers, so that the double doors in Studio 7 would both be opened at the same time, was because he realized that the teleported bill for some reason which he could not explain had not sufficient mystical or teleportational power to go through the doors. And that's why he needed the assistance of both engineers. Although he admitted later that the bill, when it was in this state of limbo between its presence in 6 and 7, was not visible to him in a tangible way, his keen ability to do eyeless vision enabled him to sense, through other powers that are difficult to describe, an object that gets stuck during teleportation.

Let's get back to the studio—that is Studio 7 . . .

The four of us are now standing around the table, and Dr. William Neff instructs me to lift the paper from the table. And as I did so, it was the first time in my life that I have ever heard a simultaneous gasp of awe on the part of a group.

There was a dollar bill, face down.

And then Dr. Neff suggested for me to lift the dollar bill from the table and read the serial number—which I proceeded to do.

And as I read each digit, you could feel and hear the sense of mystification on the part of all those who participated in that teleportation experiment.

Do I have the answer? Believe me, I don't. But I've got about 184 additional questions that I would love answers to.

CHAPTER 12

"Everything that deceives
may be said to enchant."
————Plato

THE PROFESSIONAL ENCHANTERS

SOMETIMES I THINK that fifty million years ago one pre-man was standing on top of a rock saying:

"Friends, I'd appreciate it very much if you'd step in just a little closer. I can assure you that if you miss a single word of the brief lecture I'm going to give on the wonders of hide reading you'll shed tears as large as melons. Yes, I said, and I repeat, I'm going to show you this afternoon the wonders of hide reading. If any one of you within the hearing of my voice has a good skin—a dinosaur, a great bat, a python—I want you to bring it forward and let the master hide reader tell you what the future holds in store. Yes, my good friends, you'll learn what's going to happen tomorrow, you'll also learn more about the things that happened yesterday. Yes, all of this—and much more—is revealed in the lines and conformations of your favorite dried-out hide."

In the modern sense, it began with Friederich Anton Mesmer,

who was born in Germany in 1733. He went to the best medical school of his time and first made a name for himself by writing an important paper on the power of the planets over the bodies of men. According to him, the human being acted as a magnet with positive and negative sides. His theory was that disease and illness was caused by a "dislocation of the animal magnetism." This "animal magnetism" was a fluid in the body which could be controlled by the mind—if the powers of concentration were strong enough. At other times, however, the situation was goofed up, and you ended up feeling beat.

As a matter of fact, Mesmer's own magnetic fluid seems to have gotten kind of twisted around. When he was at the peak of his operation, the French government decided to appoint a commission to investigate the action he had going for him. The bit they called "Mesmerism," which was pretty much like our hypnotism of today.

This panel of scientific men, including the visiting American diplomat Ben Franklin, brought in a very negative report and killed Mesmer's whole pitch. He died twenty years later, broken and broke.

The top man in the hyp department today is Dr. George Estabrooks, head of the Department of Psychology at Colgate University. He has presented fascinating theories on it, covering many different fields of human activity. Hallucinations, pain killing, multiple personality, mental disease, allergy, obsessions, asthma, crime and its detection, politics, dictators, vocational guidance, and many other subjects.

Anyone not familiar with the inside gaffs of hypnotism usually has a stack of questions about this "mysterious art," and there are a lot of false impressions connected with it. Take for instance the old routine about not being able to put a subject "under" against his will. Actually, except for rare cases, this would be true; but it isn't also true that you have to have the subject's consent. In other words, if you've ever put someone into a trance state you can condition him to go under again, in a matter of seconds, without his knowing it. This is accomplished with a post-hypnotic suggestion. It would work like this.

You have a subject hypnotized. You tell him that in the future he'll always "go under" when you, and only you, say the words, *"I won't try to hypnotize you."* You repeat this until it's firmly implanted in the unconscious mind. You also suggest to the subject that he'll remember nothing of what happens during the trance when he awakens. Then he's brought out of the hypnotic state.

An hour, or a day, later, you can be speaking with the subject and say to him: *"I won't try to hypnotize you."* Without his consent, without his even knowing what has happened, he'll once more be in trance. That's how a man may be hypnotized without his consent.

Another fear you often hear about is that a subject will not wake up when he's told to. Dr. Estabrooks states he never had this happen to him in all his years of experience, but that if it did there would be nothing to worry about. The operator would just let the subject rest quietly. In a matter of time, he'd slip from the trance into a natural sleep from which he'd simply awaken.

As far as the bit about a person in the hypnotic state never doing anything against their moral code, there are a lot of "ifs" in this claim. The truth probably is that in almost every case the subject will not do something that is contrary to his sense of morality, but it's also true that a clever operator can disguise the action so that a person might do something he wouldn't do normally, without knowing what he was doing. An example of this would be if the hypnotist put a subject into a trance state and gave him a pistol. The operator might now tell the subject that he was nine years old playing cops-and-robbers with his friends. He would point out that the gun was a water pistol and then urge him to shoot it at someone. Under these conditions, it's quite possible that the subject would perform an act that would surprise, even horrify, him, when he came out of the trance.

Of course, such things are very unlikely, although I did hear at one time that the police had suspected that one of the infamous plane bombings, as well as occasional murders, might have been pulled off by a hyp gimmick.

In recent years, the medical profession has begun using hypnotism quite freely. Childbirth, dermatology, and hypnodontics have been areas in which hypnotism has been found to be helpful as an anesthesia, particularly where the patients were in physical conditions that made chemical types of anesthesias dangerous. The second area where it has been of considerable value, and where it seems to have a great future, is in psychiatry. In the treatment of neuroses, hysteria, phobias, obsessions, compulsions, and, in general, where the problem has a disturbed

185

emotion basis, it has been brought into play. Now the uses of hypnotism in the problems of alcoholism and drug addiction are being looked into, and the future in this department appears promising.

It's highly interesting to point out, however, that there are scientists who are spending a lot of time in the study of the powers of hypnotism, who are not medical men. A major example is Dr. Wallace Minto, famous nuclear physicist, whom I've mentioned before. On one of the many occasions when I've had the privilege of having him on my show, Dr. Minto offered to demonstrate the use of hypnotism in the field of parapsychology, specifically astral projection. I readily agreed, since this type of bit always makes for a great radio program.

After a brief discussion, it was decided that I'd suggest to the listeners that they send telegrams into the studio if they were interested in participating in the test. I then told my engineer to write down a number on a slip of paper, without telling me, or anyone, what it was. When that particular telegram came in (they're all numbered automatically in order of reception) it would be handed to Minto and he'd give the address of the sender to his subject. In this way, only the engineer knew what number telegram would be selected, and he'd have no idea who was going to send that particular wire. Minto, on the other hand, would have even less idea of what would come up, and the subject would have no idea at all. In effect, it seemed like just about a foolproof test.

Everything was arranged. Minto had the subject in trance. The selected telegram, number 34, came in (out of a total of 137). The address was noted. And the experiment began.

"You will now sink deeper and deeper into a calm, quiet sleep, and activate your astral self. The address is 348 West 14th Street. (This, of course, was not the actual address.) Visualize your astral body and direct it to project toward this address. 348 West 14th Street, here in the city." Minto's voice was even and firm. The subject said nothing, but his breathing could be heard over the microphone which hung about his neck.

You are approaching 14th Street," the doctor continued. "Now you have found the house. You are to go to the third floor, rear apartment, right side. A lady is wating there and you are to describe her apartment. Do you understand?"

."Yes," announced the subject in a startlingly strong voice.

"Are you in the apartment?" inquired Minto.

"Yes," snapped the subject again.

"Please describe it," asked the physicist.

"The room I'm in is about fifteen feet square. The walls are white and so is the ceiling. The floors are light and parquet. Two pictures hang opposite each other, and they are portraits in oil—one man, one woman. All of the furniture is quite old. The sofa is dark red plush. The two big stuffed chairs are dark green. Across one end of the room are two very high windows going down to the floor. In front of these is a huge black wood table with a lace cover. There are flowers and magazines on this table. Under the picture of the man is a wide marble fireplace, but it is covered with an iron plate. The opening, I mean. The carpet is red, green, gold and . . ."

The description of the room was in amazing detail, and the young man never hesitated. He seemed positive about everything he "saw." In a few minutes, when he had announced that he couldn't think of anything else to tell about, Dr. Minto woke him up and he went out into the sponsor's booth to watch the remainder of the program.

In about ten minutes, a telegram came in from the person whose original message had been selected as the key to the experiment. This lady stated that there was absolutely no connection between her apartment and the place the astral projectionist had described. It ran something like this:

"WU141 PD
  NEW YORK NY (Date) 2:21 A EST
LONG JOHN   WUX
WITH REGARD TO THE YOUNG MAN WHO, UNDER DR. MINTO'S HYPNOTIC INFLUENCE, ATTEMPTED TO ASTRALLY PROJECT TO MY HOME AND DESCRIBE IT AND ITS CONTENTS, LET ME SAY UNEQUIVOCALLY THAT HIS REPORT BORE ABSOLUTELY NO RESEMBLANCE TO MY STUDIO WHICH HAS ALL ORIENTAL MODERN FURNISHINGS AND ONLY FIVE ABSTRACT PAINTINGS ON THE WALLS. UNFORTUNATELY, I ALSO HAVE NO FIREPLACE, BUT I WOULD HAVE THOUGHT THAT HE MIGHT HAVE NOTICED MY GIANT, AND I DO MEAN GIANT, BLACK GREAT DANE, WHO WAS AND IS LYING IN THE MIDDLE OF MY SMALL FLOOR. SORRY, BUT I HOPE HE USUALLY PROJECTS MORE SUCCESSFULLY THAN HIS PERFORMANCE OF THIS EVENING."

Well, neighbors, I'll give you a square count. Although, naturally, I didn't expect any success, I had hoped it wouldn't bomb out this badly. Minto looked genuinely surprised for a moment and then observed:

"I would say that if one was to put an evaluation on this test that it would have to be classified as unsuccessful."

"I'll certainly buy that," I laughed, and the show continued along other lines for a while. About twenty minutes had passed when another telegram arrived, which really shook me up and even seemed to unnerve Minto a little. It reads as follows:

"WU143 PD
  NEW YORK NY (Date) 2:46A EST
LONG JOHN   WUX
I DON'T KNOW WHAT TO SAY OR HOW TO SAY IT. FRANKLY, I FEEL A LITTLE SICK ABOUT THE WHOLE SITUATION. BUT TO THE POINT, AND THIS IS IT. THE DESCRIPTION GIVEN BY DR. MINTO'S SUBJECT MATCHES, TO A "T", THE HOME I HAVE MAINTAINED AT THIS ADDRESS FOR OVER FORTY YEARS. THE PORTRAITS ARE OF MY FATHER AND MOTHER. THE GREAT TABLE BELONGED TO MY GREAT GREAT GRAND-FATHER WHO ONCE SAT AT IT WRITING RE-PORTS TO GENERAL WASHINGTON. I AM TOTALLY ASTONISHED. I HAVE NEVER BELIEVED IN THE OCCULT IN ALL OF MY SEVENTY YEARS, BUT NOW I JUST DON'T KNOW."

(Signed)

When we checked the message out, we discovered that the sender of the second telgram lived directly across the street from the sender of the first one. Both lived on the third floor.

"Apparently," speculated Dr. Minto, "the subject simply misread the street number, went up two flights, into the apartment, and began to describe the wrong place. I have no other explanation."

I could see no way for Minto or the subject to have "set-up" the original message, since they had no way of anticipating what number my engineer would select. As a matter of fact, I hadn't thought of the experiment until the show had been on the air for at least an hour. Even if the whole deal had been gaffed, they certainly would never have had their accomplices send in a denial of the whole bit, unless they had also set up the second wire. All for a greater dynamic effect. And such an involved procedure would have been too complicated to be practical, anyway. However, the most important thing is that I knew Dr. Minto was far above employing any kind of deception in a scientific experiment of this kind.

So, the old story was out in the open again. What is that? Why, that I didn't buy it; but, I've got to level with you, I certainly couldn't understand it either.

To wrap up the hypnotism bit, I will just mention that I recently received a book which promised to better your golf game through hypnotism, which was a new bit even for me, and I've heard most of the routines.

A gaff which is probably a lot older than calculated and conscious hypnotism is astrology. This bit, which is generally considered pretty kooky today, can easily be called the beginning of science in general and astronomy in particular. It's the occult art which is interested not in how to control others but in what controls us, and it dates back to the earliest recorded history—probably over ten thousand years ago. Apparently the gullibles always went for this kind of action since every civilization had a little astrology going for them. Of course, back in those days no one was sitting around writing notes on stone so the family tree is pretty vague, but the general opinion is that it all started in India, or maybe Babylonia.

Ptolemy, who sort of invented astronomy, was an astrologist; and so was Hippocrates, who holds the same slot in medicine. Even a couple of thousand years before either of them were on the scene, the stars were influencing the course of history in the ancient courts, military camps and bedrooms.

In 800 A.D., there was a school of astrology in Baghdad, in the 1400's a Polish University had a department devoted to these studies, and it was under the personal direction of the king. The great mathematician Keppler was looking into the field 150 years later, and Galileo found it a fascinating subject. Elizabeth I of England had her coronation date decided by her personal star-gazer John Dee, and today Mr. Adolph Menjou, the brilliant Hollywood actor, has stated in print that he makes no important decisions without checking with his astrologer.

I remember one of the first times I ever tried to interview a practitioner of this particular area of the occult. I was a little green in the horoscopic department at that time, and so I wasn't familiar with some of the proceedings used by a few of the astral (but not the same as projection) operators.

That evening I got to the studio a little before any of my staff checked in, and was on my way down the hall to my office. In this short journey it was necessary for me to pass the open rear door to Studio Six, where I broadcast from. Usually, this entrance is open, for airing, but the room is dark and empty— that is, until one of my gang begins setting up for the evening session. This time it was different.

The studio was completely lit, all the switches were in the "ON" position. Everything had been pushed back. Chairs, tables, standing mikes. Everything. There in the center of the floor was a red silk balloon. At least that's what it looked like. Actually it was a fat little woman, on her hands and knees, wrapped in a billowy, flowing scarlet robe. Shooting off from her in all directions was an enormous diagram. With several pieces of chalk, she had drawn circles within circles within circles. These various sized chalk donuts were cut up into squares, and these were full of numbers and far-out symbols. It was an insane mess.

"What on earth are you doing?" I asked, astonished.

The little woman looked up for the first time, and leapt to her feet.

"Oh, my dear man, you must be John, Long John Nebel, that is. How do you do. I'm your guest for the evening. What am I doing? Why, what I'm doing is a multiple reading. Stars, you know. Well, more the planets than the stars, but everyone thinks that it's the stars, so why upset them. Of course, the main point of the . . ."

"Hold it. Just one moment, please," I insisted. "Why have you messed up our floor? Who told you to do this?"

"Why, no one. It was my pleasure. You don't understand, though, do you. More's the pity. I will explain. On your floor you have the interlocking horoscope of you and your, if I may say so, your distinguished guest of the evening."

"Meaning you?" I guessed.

"Meaning me? Why yes, of course. After all, I was invited." She babbled. Positively babbled.

"But not to mess up the floor," I tried to point out.

"I wish you wouldn't keep saying that I've messed up your floor. This is a beautifully designed and executed chart. It is the interlocking . . ."

"I'm afraid that I'll have to cancel the show for tonight," I

190

decided. This was a really wild weird one. She could be very difficult if she got out of hand, and she was out of hand already. Square count, neighbors, it was almost impossible to get her to stop talking. It took some persuading, but eventually I was able to convince her that I was serious and that I wouldn't do an astrology program that evening. As she was departing our premises, she made a remark that I thought was kind of strange.

"I knew this would happen," she snapped, "it was all in the chart. It said I should just up and leave. Bad luck, that's what it showed."

"But if that's what the chart and your astrological knowledge told you, why didn't you leave?" I asked.

"Don't be ridiculous," she snorted and disappeared down the hall.

Of course, all people who are interested in the zodiacal have a slightly different point of view regarding it. Some consider it a form of religion, some a personal philosophy, some a parapsychological phenomenon, some even claim that it's a science.

Recently a young man appeared on the program to "prove that astrology was based on science." His specific pitch was that the orthodox (?) occult explanation was too direct, on one hand, and too vague, on the other. That is, it's too direct because it claims that the individual is influenced directly by the action of the planets; and that it's too vague because there's too much superstition involved. Now, if that's clear up to that point there's not too much anyone can do for you anyway. Actually, this young man had it all worked out. It all depended on the ions. Some were good ions and some were bad ions, and when you add them all together they make up a new version of astrology that makes the old styles seem simple.

To be honest, astrology is a pretty difficult thing to try to define. The word means the "study of the stars." The results of this study is usually a chart or a horoscope, which means "hour picture." That is, it's a diagram of the solar system at the moment of your birth. This picture consists of a circle divided into twelve wedges called "houses," and quarters called "quadrants." And then there's the "sign" under which you're born. And on it goes, getting more complicated by the moment, until the astrologer comes up with a reading which tells you nothing very definite. Of course, if you dig vague generalities, it's the greatest.

However, don't get the wrong impression. Although my scepticism "runneth over," millions of people buy this nonsense.

There are stacks of newspapers, magazines, and books which are dedicated to the bit of explaining and proving the accuracy of the star-gazing gaff. Of course, that involves only a quarter, or at most a few dollars. But if you want to spring for real loot, you can go for a fin or five hundred for a first-rate horoscope, depending upon how elaborately you want yours drawn, how fancy you expect your personal kookery to be. It's a fast-turnover, newspaper-columned, money-making business—so what else can I tell you?

Numerology is another long-time gaff that has been sold all the way from the gypsy tent to the royal court, and back again. It's not as organized a gaff as some of the other cons around, but it has its occasional tip, too. There are dozens of versions of the numbers game, but in general they function in similar ways. Basically, the numerologist believes that each numeral has a special value, and that this can be found by investigating the numbers in a person's name, address, and so forth. Problems of all kinds can be solved by consulting the numbers. ·

In one popular book on the numbers racket, we find that the number One is a "pioneer number." This means that the "creative lines," combined with "foresight, intuition and initiative" make Number Ones decisive. Among the professions of this type are included creative artists in music, opera, stage, radio, writing, illustrating, designing architecture; or they may be neurologists, psychiatrists, surgeons, diagnosticians, character analysts, lawyers, politicians, aviators—and there are others, many others. The writer points out that Alexander Graham Bell, Winston Churchill and Albert Schweitzer are all Number Ones in good—I might even say excellent—standing.

Actually, you'd be amazed at the influence these routines have on some people—even the guys who pitch them. I remember one character who wanted to be on the program, so he wrote a letter to my office. The first two pages told how great he was. It related his profound powers of numerology. It was a real strong bit. But the last page was the blow-off. It was a schedule we would have to follow if he was going to appear with me on the air. He wouldn't be able to arrive in the studio before midnight, since he must remain as physically inactive as possible between 11:26:12 and 12:26:11—both A.M. and P.M. Also, he wouldn't be able to do anything but nod(!) on the one-minute every quarter hour, and it would be necessary for him to leave before 4:38—here he didn't specify the seconds.

I was so skeptical about the entire pose that I decided to give the kook a call. After the operator had assured me that the time schedule was essential, I asked him if these were all of the conditions required for his gracing us with his presence. This was his reply:

"Well, Mr. Nebel, of course I couldn't appear with Al Lottman" (one of my regular guys).

"And just why is that?" I asked.

"I am assuming that his first name is Albert."

"So?"

"Well, that put him in the thirteen-fourteen series, with which I am completely at odds," he explained.

"What is the thirteen-fourteen series?" I inquired.

"Albert equals 58; five and eight are 13. Lottman equals 95; nine and five equal 14. And, what is almost as bad is that his inclusive phase is 27, which of course he is inescapably caught in the nine field."

"How's that?"—I followed into the trap. I was really fascinated by this nonsense.

"Two and seven are 9. Three nines are 27. That's four 9's, which are 36. Three and six are 9. I mean, Mr. Nebel, it's as plain as day. Poor Mr. Lottman is just all nined up. That's all there is to it. He's caught and there's nothing I can do."

After thanking him and saying that we might be in touch with him some time, I hung up and tried very hard to forget the whole thing. I haven't succeeded to this day.

Naturally, I don't mean to imply that all people who believe in numerology are quite this wild. As a matter of fact, one of America's greatest orchestra leaders is a very famous astrologer. His name is Vincent Lopez. This top musician has appeared very frequently on a show run by a fine gentleman—Hy Gardner, famous syndicated columnist for the *New York Herald-Tribune*—and on these sessions he has explained all of the intricacies of the numbers bit and made some amazing prophecies. According to Hy, whom I'm proud to call a friend, Vincent Lopez's forecasts have been very, very high in the accuracy department. Of course, by this I don't mean to say that Hy buys the bit—I don't know. But he obviously has been impressed with the results.

However, with all respect to Vincent, I can't help being convinced that the most important numbers to me are found on checks and chicks.

For many years palmistry—nowadays sometimes called chirology—was an active occult occupation. Although it's been passed down from hand to hand for a long time, it's probably much more recent than the cruder forms of hypnotism, astrology, or even numerology. Of course, along with card reading, it's always thought of as being a gypsy gaff, but a lot of other people have succeeded in having their palms crossed with a little silver for finding a little malarkey in someone else's hand.

Essentially, the sell is fairly simple. According to the spieler, the hand is a built-on life indicator. The life line, the heart line, plus many other heavy and light, definite and feathery markings on the palm, the sides and the back of the hand, are supposed to reveal to the handy man what has happened, what is happening, and what will happen in the months and years to come. Now this kind of turn can be pretty impressive, but the real con goes even further. He examines the various mounds, such as the one of Venus; he traces the shape of the fingers, the roundness or pointedness of the tips; he checks the pliability of the fingers and palm; he investigates the texture of the flesh, the lie of the down on the back of the hand; the wrist; and anything else he can conjure up, including the nails. If he operates strong, he goes through this entire kooky performance on each hand, because each one reveals different things. Finally, he adds up the sum total of his "observations" and gives a reading. The bite may be anywhere from a buck for a fast look to possibly twenty-five for the full treatment.

I remember one time everyone on the program was caught red-handed in a palmist pitch. I had invited a mitt camp operator up for a show, and we were well under way. Part of the gaff was for her to read my hand and the palms of all of my other guests. Unfortunately, she had dreamed up a new gimmick. Instead of merely looking at the mitt with the naked eye, she had a big pad of red ink, and another big pad of white paper. One by one, we all had to plant our hands down on the ink pad and transfer the scarlet impression to the blank paper. Of course, the palmist had made certain to have highly washable ink on her little red pad. After the impressions were all collected, one by one everyone went to wash his hands. Shortly everyone returned. The great tragedy had occurred. The mystic had made a mistake. The ink was indelible. For weeks each of us wandered about with closed fists, occasionally startling someone with a brilliant open palm greeting. Of course, eventually it wore off. But I always thought there was something kind of symbolic about the whole thing. But just what, I'm not sure.

Some branches of the occult have just about faded out. One

194

of these is called phrenology. But occasionally, on some dim side street of a city, or off on the edge of a small Southern or Mid-western village, you'll find an old crone still peddling this childishness. Some almost forgotten die-hard hanging on by a local head or two.

Phrenology was the art, or so-called science, of reading the bumps—I believe they called them "conformations"—of the skull. It was generally conducted in a dingy back parlor by a creepy old woman. Quite often this crone would also pitch a little astrology or card reading to keep things active in the loot department. Once in a while, some smoother operator would set up a pseudo-medical office and wear a white coat. In this type of action, all of the mysticism was dropped in favor of "clear cut cold science . . . statistical fact . . . the new discoveries of the mind . . . what Freud does on the inside we can tell from the outside . . ." and similar claptrap. Either way, the actual examination was about the same.

The phrenologist would run his fingers along the skull, under the hair, feeling the shape of the top and the sides and the back of the head. He would examine the temples and the frontal bones, the occipital bones, and whatever they call the rest of them. When he had completed his examination he was able, he assured the mark, to tell very informative things about the personality and the future of the patient. As a matter of fact, these phrenologists used to use a model of the human head to explain all of these wonders to their suckers, and some of these were really great gaffs—beautifully made, and all divided up with kooky labels. Square count, friends, I'd love to have one of these heads—they were really wild pieces of merchandise.

Eventually, as science moved forward, people began to realize how phoney the whole bit was. They were far more interested in what went on inside than what surface information could be discovered about the outside, and so this great field of investigation faltered and, by now, has just about failed. It's very rare to find anyone nowadays who buys the bit, let alone someone who actually tries to palm it—no, that's something else—who actually tries to get ahead (!) with this kind of con.

Tea leaf reading, to look in a different direction, still has its followers. In New York alone there are a great many "rooms" where you can have this service. Of course, it's exactly what it says, the reading of the arrangement of the tea leaves left at the bottom of a cup, and generally it's another of the off-beat bits which is strongly associated with the gypsies.

The locations where readings are available usually fall into one of two kinds of fronts. Ground floor stores with wide display windows, where brightly colored, if rather soiled, curtains hang, are one kind. Often there are artificial flowers in the window and a couple of chairs. Towards the rear is a curtained doorway, through which you sometimes have to go to get your fortune told. From time to time it's quite obvious that more than fortunes are available to the tired traveling man.

The other tea rooms are up one long, badly lit, flight of shaky, or at least slanted, stairs. These setups are often fairly large and actually have facilities for the customer to sit quietly and have a cup of tea. The tab is likely to run a little higher here, but it's also possible to name your own fortune in some of these operations. However, most of them cater to the slightly dopey or bored housewife who thinks that this sort of little "adventure into the unknown world of the occult" might brighten up a pretty dull day—or life.

The final touch in some tea rooms is the offer of "any three wishes" you want. This is a bonus. And, let's face it, you don't hardly get them kind of offers no more. I regret to say, however, the wishes are almost never guaranteed.

In a similar department to tea leaf reading, but more esoteric, is the occultism of the cards. Preferably tarot cards, although the bit is also sometimes done with ordinary playing pasteboards.

The tarot deck consists of seventy-eight cards which are divided into two sets called the "minor arcana" and the "major arcana." The first series is supposed to be the oldest version of our regular playing cards; the second is claimed to be "the leaves of the oldest book in the world"—which would be pretty difficult to disprove or prove, unless you employ the tarot cards, of course.

Miss Eden Gray, actress, author and proprietor of the well-known off-beat book store in New York called "Inspiration House," has been with me on the air close to a hundred times. On several of these occasions, we've talked about the mystery of the tarot—a subject in which she is a recognized expert and teacher. One of the experiences she relates concerns the time she was giving a reading to an elderly lady. As Eden commented on several revelations, the woman agreed as to the accuracy of the indications, when two particular cards turned up—the Four of Penacles and the Queen of Swords. The combination signified contention with a woman over money. Her guest denied any understanding of this reading, but shortly recalled that it did have meaning. An invalided woman friend whom she had been supporting had recently taken the money the benefactress had given her for her rent and opened a charge account in a prominent Fifth Avenue store. She then ran up a considerable bill her friend would have to pay. Miss Gray's guest had forgotten this affair for a moment, but it was in her subconscious mind.

As a matter of fact, Eden Gray attributes a great deal of the "magic of the cards" to the stimulation of "buried thoughts and emotions."

There have been many, many other forms of prophetic analysis. At one time, oriental-looking gentlemen could be found on carnival lots or in fortune-telling parlors, who sifted sand into a tray and read in the patterns that lay there your entire future life. But I imagine all of these are gone now. Of course there are many, many other versions of prophecy, of life reading, of offbeat sciences, arts, and what have you, but they're becoming more and more rare. However, this is not to mean there are not several million people at least—if not five or ten times that many—who still think there is basically something to one or more of these strange studies. Probably we'll always have one or another version of them with us. Certainly there are an enormous number of people who consider them perfectly natural beliefs of Americans today.

CHAPTER 13

"Worth seeing? yes; but
not worth going to see."
—Samuel Johnson

THE ON-BEAT RESEARCHERS
OF THE OFF-BEAT

SEATED AROUND the table were five of my "regulars." We had
been on the air for about half an hour and an experiment in
Extra Sensory Perception was under way. It was one of many
that had been conducted during the time I had been doing the
all-night, every-night show. "The Amazing Randi," world-
famous escapologist and magician; Sam Vandivert, well-known
photographer; Sergeant Morris Paley, police officer; and the
famous character actor Khigh Dheigh were discussing the "conditions" I should impose on the test.

"John, a couple of years ago I did a bit with a strong box,"
recalled Randi. "Do you remember just how that experiment
was arranged?"

"Yes, I bring it to mind quite clearly," I replied. "You
brought a locked metal box up here to the studio. No one had
any idea what was in it, including yours truly, L. J. We merely

told the people out in radioland—with apologies to Jean Shepard—that a strong box was sitting on the table, and that there was 'an object' in it."

"Right," agreed Randi. "Then I said I would concentrate on the object inside the metal box for a period of three full minutes. You had everyone remain absolutely silent."

"And during the dead air the listeners were supposed to attempt to guess or psychically receive an impression of what was inside the container," I explained to the other guests.

"What were the results?" asked Sgt. Paley.

"Kind of wild, as a matter of fact. I received about six hundred cards and letters on that one as I recall, and not one even came close. That is, only one came faintly close."

"It seems to me that about twenty percent, remembering that I specialized in escapes, thought that the box contained handcuffs," remarked Amazing. (We sometimes call him by his second name.)

"What was the mysterious object?" asked Vandivert.

"A folded silk American flag, in a manila envelope," I revealed.

"And," began Khigh Dheigh, just a little sceptically, "what was the 'almost' answer you received out of the six hundred replies?"

"The word 'Stars.' Nothing else. Just that one word on a card.

"But John," he continued, that's very good. Didn't it make you wonder at all?"

"Yes, I'll give you a square count. It did. Until about a day later when I remembered something. A month or so before the experiment took place I had been doing a commercial on a book for younger people on astronomy. To simplify matters for the listeners who wished to purchase the volume by mail, I had told them just to put the one word "astronomy" on a postal card, with their names and addresses, and the book would be sent to them. Unfortunately, what had happened was that this particular gentleman had forgotten and written the word "stars" instead of the word "astronomy." And that pretty well killed that experiment."

But to return to the ESP test we were trying to conduct that night. It was decided that a test pattern would be drawn by the panel with each person contributing one, or no more than two, lines to the diagram. The result would then be left on the table for a minute or two so we could all concentrate on it. During this time, any listeners who wished to participate could sketch the design at home. These attempts at reading our collective thoughts could then be mailed in and we would compare them against the "original test pattern."

On this occasion, even more replies came in than was usual for this kind of on-the-air experiment—about eleven hundred, I believe. The results from a psychic point of view, however, were much less encouraging. Only one letter in the entire response bore any resemblance to the test design at all, and this similarity was so vague that even the most open-minded people I showed it to had to admit that it was a totally negative result. But, of course, you can't always have them turn out like the William Daut bit.

I remember one night the prominent physicist Dr. Wallace Minto was my guest, along with the great doubter and cyberneticist Ben Isquith. Back and forth they battled for and against Extra Sensory Perception. At one point in the exchange, Minto suggested that he hypnotize a young lady, one of his regular hypno-psychic subjects, whom he had brought along with him that morning. While in the trance state, he challenged Ben, she would be able to demonstrate some parapsychological ability.

"Why does she have to be put in trance?" Isquith wanted to know.

"Very well," agreed Minto. "We'll do it without hypnosis, but I won't guarantee the results. Is that all right with you, Renée?"

The girl nodded and I had a chair brought over to the table for her. A neck mike was put on her, and I asked her how she would like to begin.

"If I may have something belonging to Mr. Isquith. A ring, a lucky piece, watch, photograph . . ."

"Here's my watch," offered Ben.

She sat back, with her eyes closed. About thirty seconds passed, and then she spoke.

"I sense that you have recently been in lower Manhattan, in Greenwich Village. I see you walking along Eighth Street. You are with a young lady . . . a lady . . . and you are going into a pottery shop. You are looking for something. Wandering through the store. You are looking at one piece, then another. Now you have made your choice—a bean-type pot. You are purchasing it. That is, actually you are charging it. It is a gift."

"Do you sense anything else?" I asked.

"Only one thing. It is a holiday. Just before East . . . No!

200

Christmas. It is the day before Christmas, and he had bought a pot as a holiday gift. That's all. Nothing more."

That was about it, except for the fact that Ben Isquith had to admit that the psychometric reading was accurate in every degree. I hasten to add that, like old L.J., he doesn't buy the smallest bit of the psychic bit. But he did concede that Renée was correct in all she said.

Of course, although I've conducted many such experiments on my radio show, or had other people on to conduct them, I have to be the first to admit that these efforts haven't been run under very severe test conditions. Also, I certainly wouldn't make any claim at being an investigator myself; but several people who have appeared on the program certainly have a right to such a title. Some of these would be Stewart Robb, Dr. Wallace Minto, and most of all Dr. J. B. Rhine.

For a great number of years, Rhine has been the top name among the psychic researchers. It's been the strong pitch he's made for ESP that's been largely responsible for the general public's becoming parapsychology conscious.

Unfortunately, the terms ESP, parapsychology, psychic power, or whatever other label you prefer, include an awful lot of things. To a real kook, they might mean anything from a table tap to a full-blown ghost. To legitimate researchers, to men like J. B. Rhine, they mean telepathy, clairvoyance, psycho- or telekinesis, and maybe just a little more. Often these conflicts of definition lead to considerable confusion.

One night a couple of years ago, I had invited a fairly well-known "legitimate" type ESP investigator on as my guest. To participate in the questioning, I had brought in a couple of complete sceptics; and, to support the guest, a man who called himself a "serious psychic researcher." I assumed that this would mean a sort of two for and two against setup, but almost before the show began this kind of exchange took place:

Legitimate Researcher #1: "Now, as we all know, and at least I'm sure my investigator friend will agree, the true psychic, that is the genuine master of ESP, has great mystical powers not found in other persons."

Legitimate Researcher #2: "Well, let's not put it quite that way. I think that we might say that they have extra normal responses. I don't think that I would use the word 'mystical.'"

L. R. #1: "What I mean by 'mystical' is that the power of, say, telepathy is essentially spiritual in nature."

L. R. #2: "I would have thought maybe that phrase 'electromagnetic,' or something like that, might have been better."

L. R. #1: "We must remember the light that guides the psychic will. We shouldn't forget the watchers of the other planes."

L. R. #2: "The light that does what? The whichers on the other wheres?"

L. R. #1: "The spirit guides, of course,"

L. R. #2: "What has that nonsense got to do with parapsychology?"

L. R. #1: "Why, everything. I'm afraid you don't know very much about ESP."

L. R. #2: "You, sir, obviously know nothing—about ESP or anything else."

L. R. #1: "Well, I can tell you this. If I'd known you were going to be on this program I'd have known enough not to show up."

L. R. #2: "That—I believe!"

And so ended the collaboration of those two gentlemen for the morning. But I must admit that the three-sided kookery turned out to be a better show than a regular two-on-each-side debate-type bit would have been. However, this sort of confusion is pretty common in the off-beat fields.

Now, getting back to Dr. Rhine and the really legit investigators. As early as 1930, J. B. Rhine, Professor of Psychology at Duke University, was conducting experiments with ESP cards. He used a deck of twenty-five bridge-size cards marked with five different symbols: a square, a circle, a star, a plus sign, and wavy lines. Five symbols, five cards each, twenty-five cards in all. When you had the deck, you had to dig up a couple of participants: one dealer and one clairvoyant. Sometimes they would sit at the same table with a high partition between them so they couldn't see each other; on other occasions they sat in different rooms, different houses, and in a few cases even different cities or states. Then, when everything was all arranged, the dealer would start turning the cards over one by one, with maybe a second or two interval. The receiver, the number two man on the psychic relay team, would then attempt to guess each card as it went by. If they were operating on a one-second schedule, the receiver would mark down one of the symbols on a piece of paper every second until the entire twenty-five had been guessed.

If the sender looked at the cards, concentrating, and tried to convey an impression of the right symbol to his partner, that was supposed to be a test in telepathy (although it could also indicate clairvoyant overtones). If the cards were gone through "blind" by the top man of the team—that is, if he went through the deck without looking at the cards—then that was considered a test in clairvoyance. If that seems a little confusing, for once it really isn't. Telepathy is the ability to send or receive mental impressions. Clairvoyance is the ability to see mentally beyond the normal range of physical vision.

Now, since there are only twenty-five cards and only five symbols, it's easy to see that the laws of probability would indicate that the average result would be five cards (or symbols) correctly guessed per "run." Naturally, no one expected the deck to revolve in exact mathematical rotation. On some tests, the normal ups and downs might give a reader only four, or three, or two correct; on others the score might jump to ten; but over the long pull—say, possibly, five thousand runs—the odds said that the results would tend to pretty well average out to five correct guesses per run.

Of course, a slight variation couldn't very well be considered a great example of psychic phenomena. However, if, in a run of five thousand, the results were far off-base, then the researcher would have something to shout about. Say in a run like that, which would mean one hundred and twenty-five thousand cards had been guessed, the total score was fifty thousand correct. That would be hard to explain. The average for that number being twenty-five thousand, or twenty percent, what would be the answer if someone ran up a fifty thousand, or forty percent response? Well, neighbors, I can tell you that it would be pretty unlikely. And according to a man like Rhine, I imagine it would rank as pretty conclusive proof that there was something to the ESP bit. At least the results he has gotten have completely convinced him that such powers are scientific fact.

Today, more than thirty years later, Dr. Rhine has enormously expanded his investigations, since he considers telepathy and clairvoyance established truths. His more recent experiments have dealt with psycho- or tele-kinesis—the ability to move physical matter with the mind. Today, as he has been for a long time, J. B. Rhine is still the top man in the ESP department—that is, the investigating end.

At this point let me take a moment to give my personal opinions about Dr. Rhine. Having met this man, and having corresponded with him a few times, and having met dozens of people who know him much better than I do, and having the opportunity of knowing their opinions of Dr. Rhine, I've come to the conclusion that he is one of the most sincere men in the field of psychic research, and an extremely bright man. And although I do not buy ESP myself, I have a sneaky suspicion that there may be something to it; and the man who will be responsible for discovering this unknown phenomenon will certainly be Dr. J. B. Rhine.

To get an even half-way clear picture of this tremendously complicated field, it's a good idea to become familiar with some of the terms employed. The following is far from a complete off-beat vocabulary, but it explains some of the more important terms—words which will give you a general idea of the major areas covered by this kind of investigation.

TELEPATHY ....the transference of thought from one mind to another.

MENTAL
TELEGRAPHY ....an old phrase which was supplanted by the word "telepathy."

CLAIRVOYANCE ....seeing mentally beyond the natural limitations of physical vision. This is its proper definition. Today it has come to be generalized to include many areas of psychic phenomena.

CLAIRAUDIENCE ....hearing mentally beyond the natural limitations of the auditory system.

TELEKINESIS ....the movement of objects without physical contact.

PARAKINESIS ....the movement of objects without sufficient contact to explain the motion.

PSYCHOKINESIS ....the movement of objects through non-physical, mental (psychic) force.

LEVITATION ....the raising of objects, or individuals, into the air with no physical aid or explanation.

TELEPORTATION ....the instantaneous transmission of an object, or individual, from one point to another—usually over a considerable distance—regardless of intervening physical matter.

ASTRAL PROJECTION ...the sometimes-instantaneous, sometimes apparently not, transmission of a human consciousness—or psyche, or "spirit"—

from one point to another, regardless of intervening physical matter. Also the ability to sustain the projection of this second self, or astral body, over a period of time, before it returns to become one again with the physical being.

PRECOGNITION ....the power of prophecy.

RADIESTHESIA (or
RHABDOMANCY) ....the power to operate a divining rod.

CRYSTALLOSCOPY (or
CRYSTAL GAZING) ......the use of a crystal ball to aid in clairvoyant concentration.

PSYCHOMETRY ....the sensing of remaining vibrations from an object so as to perceive information about a present or former owner of same.

APPORT ....foreign object made to suddenly appear in physical form, in the seance room, through the powers of a medium or collective mediumistic force.

MATERIALIZATION ....the producing of ectoplasmic matter by a medium or by mediumistic force.

ECTOPLASM ....a smoky or misty visible intangible, usually produced from some orifice of the medium, or occasionally simply appearing from thin air, or on other occasions materializing out of a "cabinet," which concentrates itself into a portion of a human body—a hand or a face, and on extremely rare occasions into a head, bust or torso, or even an entire figure. In most cases where the ectoplasm emanates from the medium's body it's claimed that it. has a specific weight, and that the medium becomes lighter during the time the ectoplasm is abroad, and that the medium regains the lost weight when the ectoplasm dissipates back into him or her.

DEMATERIALIZATION ....the ability of a medium to reduce the cellular or atomic structure of some portion of his body so that it's no longer physical in nature. It was claimed by Conan Doyle that the great escape artist

Houdini was able to reduce the physical aspect of some portions of his body, permitting him to perform extraordinary escapes from handcuffs, cells, chains, and what-have-you.

SPIRIT WRITING .... the writing or messages left during a seance, presumably evidence of the presence of spirit personalities during a seance.

AUTOMATIC WRITING ..as the name implies, it's the unconscious, automatic writing by a medium while in trance, when his or her subconscious mind and physical hand is controlled by another personality—usually someone long since dead.

OUIJA BOARD .... is a board of letters and numbers, upon which is placed a planchette—which is a triangle on three little metal legs. Several people sitting around the table place their fingers lightly upon this planchette; and in theory it moves about, stopping at one letter and another until it spells out an entire message.

VOICE MEDIUM .... one who is able to produce the voices of persons not present physically—almost invariably persons who have died. These voices usually are in some way related to someone sitting in the seance. However, frequently they may be of famous historical personalities who have come back to visit with people they never knew nor heard of.

METAGNOMY .... a term sometimes used in places of "clairvoyance," and in combination with other words used to cover most of the areas of psychic phenomena. It's a phrase which is preferred by some scientific investigators.

And one could go on indefinitely, describing various other forms of phenomena that are supposed to take place, frequently or rarely, in the field of parapsychology. There are those who divide the entire study into four or five slots. There are those who feel there are nine or ten major categories. Most investigators would accept that there were at least twenty-five or thirty possible manifestations of psychic power—or, I should say, so-called manifestations of so-called psychic power. Others would claim that this number would more properly be fifty or sixty. Essentially this depends upon just what you "include in" and what you "include out." And there are a number of things we haven't even mentioned. Poltergeist, ghosts, disappearing villages, the return of people who've lived forever—these are some of the stories you hear. But only a few.

One of the most fascinating experiments I ever had come up on the radio show was apparently a demonstration of several parapsychological powers blended together. In some respects it may be the most fantastic of all the things that have come to pass in Studio Six, twenty-four floors above the Square known as Times in (with apologies to Dick Kollmar) "little ol' New York."

The date was the morning of Friday, January 15th, 1960; the show was a jackpot—that is, an open discussion with no particular subject—and my guests included the Amazing Randi, Stewart Robb and Paris Flammonde. It was an easy, wandering, roving bull session, which had touched on about every phase of extra sensory perception, psychic phenomena and the occult. Then a telegram was delivered from the teleprinter which brings me messages all night long from the listeners who feel like they'd like to participate in the conversation of the morning.

The communication was signed "Mr. Adam Kennedy (Mr. W.)". Well, when I saw this kind of complicated signature I knew that this was going to be a great show. I heard from "Mr. W" on other occasions (although I must admit that at the time the "Mr. Adam Kennedy" part was new to me), and wild things had happened. Just to do a fast flashback for a moment, I'd like to mention the first time I ever was contacted by this anonymous person.

It was early in my broadcasting career—if that's what you call the kind of action I have going for me—and I was still doing the show from a small deserted (except for the engineer) studio out in the plains of New Jersey, called Carteret. It was a long, lonely haul; and I was glad when someone dropped out to kill the night with me from time to time. I don't mean guests, because I pretty much did a solo in those days, but friends and acquaintances. On this particular night, I was gabbing away with Sam Vandivert, who had looked in for an hour on his way back into New York from a late location shooting. We had been kicking around the telepathy bit, and I guess we had kicked it pretty hard, when a telephone call came in.

Now, in those days I didn't have the "beeper phone" setup I use today, where both sides of the conversation can be heard by my audience. The equipment was a standard cradle phone, and when I spoke with someone who called in I had to repeat his (or her) side of the conversation into my mike. For this reason I didn't accept calls too often when I did the bit from out there. However, on this particular night I decided to pick up the receiver when the phone light started flashing.

The caller was a man who insisted that he could only identify himself as "Mr. W.". He claimed that he was a very powerful telepath and he would like to prove to me once and for all that clairvoyance and telepathy were positive, absolute scientific facts. Naturally, I politely told him he was off his rocker, but I'd be happy to listen to his gaff if he could make it brief. He guaranteed me that it would take only a minute or two. He then proceeded to describe in detail a colored and patterned sports shirt my engineer was wearing and to read off, with no errors, the serial number on one of the lenses Sam Vandivert had in his equipment bag. He concluded by saying "Goodnight" very quickly and hanging up, before I could ask him a single question. Regardless of the fact that I could conceive ways the effect could have been accomplished, I have to give you a square count. It was pretty impressive.

However, I want to get back to the January 15th event.

"Mr. W.'s" telegram offered once again to demonstrate his extraordinary "powers" of clairvoyance by offering me the following proposition. If the panel would come to an agreement as to the random selection of a dollar bill, he, Mr. W., would attempt to "read" its serial number from where he happened to be at the moment. (The wire had a Connecticut point of origin.) He would then contact me via "beeper phone" and attempt to give me the number. The challenge was accepted, and the phone lines were cleared for Mr. W.'s call—which would be due about ten minutes after the selection of the bill.

We decided to choose the dollar in the following way. Each person present at the table extracted *two* one-dollar bills from his wallet or pocket and placed them face down in front of him. Someone came up with a paper bag, and the eight bills were placed inside of it. The contents were really shaken up, and Mr. Robb put his hand into the bag, as he looked in another direction, and picked one of the bills. The chosen dollar was then silently passed around the table, and everyone had a chance to write the number down. Then, with only the persons at the table knowing what the number was, we sat back and waited for Mr. W.'s phone call.

Seven minutes later in came through, and as I answered it my guests put on headsets so they'd be able to hear the entire conversation in the studio just as the listeners would. It was quickly agreed that there would be no build-up bits. Mr. W. would simply attempt to "read" off the serial number of the dollar bill which had been selected completely at random.

There was about a three-second hesitation, and he began to speak the numbers slowly, about a second apart, and clearly. Almost in rhythm, but not quite a chant. Sort of like a monotone. The whole routine was extremely impressive. But, of course, you want to know if he was correct in his "reading." Unfortunately, for the first time Mr. W. failed. Of the ten symbols on the selected dollar bill—that is, the initial letter, the eight numbers and the last letter—he got only *nine out of ten!*

As he named them one by one, he read the sixth numeral as a "9," when it actually was an "8."

At my pretty insistent request, the "psychic" agreed to try the same test once more. Mr. Robb pulled another bill "blind" from the paper bag, noted the number and passed it around the table. Each of us marked the numerals down, and I told Mr. W., who was hanging on the other end of the wire, to go ahead whenever he felt the "message coming through."

Almost immediately the voice began to read the symbols off. Much more quickly than before. In about five seconds he was finished. But for good measure he rattled the number off a second time.

What can I tell you, friends. It was absolutely accurate. Letter-number-number-number-number-number-number-number-number-letter. One hundred percent correct!

The Amazing Randi, who is one of the few people as skeptical as I am, had no immediate answer; and I certainly wasn't in any position to top him in that department. Steward Robb, while not claiming that the results *conclusively* proved the existence of ESP, announced that "everything definitely points to something psychic being afoot." Paris Flammonde merely asked what had happened to the paper bag with all the money.

Calls and telegrams began to pour into the studio; by the end of the morning twenty-two states and over a hundred communities had been heard from. Belonging in neither category, but also heard from, was my regular panelist Ben Isquith, the cyberneticist. He announced he was on his way to the studio.

"Hold everything," he exclaimed. "This idiocy has to be straightened out, John. You and Randi sound like you've fallen out of your ever-loving skulls. Why didn't you denounce that fraud?"

"How did he do it, Ben?" I challenged. "So, if he was a fake, how did he do it?"

"I don't know, but tell him to call back in half an hour. I'm on my way up. We'll have a *clinically controlled* experiment. Then we'll see what this psychic can do."

When Ben arrived the following test was arranged. Each member of the panel, which now numbered five, and I picked a random number from what my psychologist friends call our subconscious mind. Everyone wrote his number on a small slip of paper, and these were all dropped into the paper bag. Three of the panelists had the bag held over their heads, and each selected a slip. These three numbers represented a page number. Then I chose one of the two remaining slips and the number on it indicated the word on the page selected.

Looking around the room, Ben decided that the book to be used would be the Collegiate Merriam-Webster Dictionary, 1943 edition. The test continued, and the page number turned out to be seven-twenty-six (726). The word was "pointed arch." But no one knew this except Isquith, who had opened the dictionary and located it in accordance with the numbers we all had picked at random and thrown in the bag and pulled out again.

I announced over the air that we were ready and that Mr. W. could send in the word any time he thought that he had "received" it clairvoyantly. Within ten minutes his reply came into my studio. It consisted of only two words which were, as you've already guessed, "pointed arch." The Amazing Randi could offer no explanation. Ben Isquith said that the probability of such a result was almost incalculable. And I have to give you a fair shake, neighbors; for once in my life I didn't say "I don't buy it." I just sat there and wondered.

CHAPTER 14

"For I dipt into the future, far
as human eye could see . . ."
—Alfred, Lord Tennyson

PROPHECIES, PHILOSOPHIES AND A WRAP-UP

BEN GROSS, of the *New York Daily News,* the dean of radio and TV commentators, whom I've had the pleasure of interviewing many times, once said to me: "John, everyone is so concerned with the future they have no time for today." The obvious wisdom of the remark struck me at the time; but whenever I think of the mystics and seers and fortunetellers, and their clients, I realize even more how pointless it all can be. However, there is one man who belonged in a class by himself. His name was Michel de Notre Dame, usually called Nostradamus. This French physician was born in 1503, began writing prophecies in 1555, and died in 1566. He was the rare exception, a prophet with honor in his own land. People came from all over Europe to consult Nostradamus.

It's been claimed by his admirers that he saw hundreds of years into the future, and that he slipped the occultists who are in the know today a little bit of the knowledge he had about what was to come. His messages are found in endless quatrains, or brief poems. But, naturally, they have to be interpreted.

I have to say one thing, though. I've heard the Nostradamus expert, Steward Robb, go through the full explanation of many of these coded messages, presenting his interpretations, and my feeling is that there's something about the whole bit we don't undertand anything about. But don't mistake me. I'm not in the market for the future-telling gaff either, any more than any of the others.

Andy Sinatra, the Mystic Barber of Brooklyn, has sent me dozens of prophecies over the last few years, and his record is almost completely unblemished. None of them have ever come true. But that doesn't discourage him; he keeps sending them in, and sooner or later he's going to hit one right one the head.

In the last couple of years I've been bombarded by "yogis" and believers in yoga to do shows on this Eastern philosophy. On several occasions I've booked one in, but for the most part they just bombed out. However, there were a couple of interesting exceptions. One in particular. This individual referred to himself as the "Infinite Master of Applied Yoga—Western Division."

My first contact with him was via phone. It was just prior to air time. My staff was setting up the show when a call came in, and so I took it myself.

"Hello, John Nebel's office," I answered.

"Good evening. I am the Infinite Master of Applied Yoga—Western Division. I am ready to appear on your program."

"Well, that's fine, friend," I replied. "Just send us a letter telling us all about yourself, and we'll think about it."

"Ooooooooommmmmm," moaned a controlled howl over the receiver, followed by a "click."

I must admit that I was just a little shook up by the bit, but I soon forgot about it as I got the show rolling that morning.

About an hour later, I was wrapping up a commercial when I looked up into the engineer's control room and saw one of the station's elevator men standing there. I got the discussion rolling again and went out to see what the problem was. It was obvious to me that someone was trying to get up to the twenty-fourth floor, where the studio is located, but had no pass.

"What's the problem, Billy?" I asked, as I stepped into the engineer's booth.

"John, there's a really weird one downstairs this time. What I mean is, he's just about the strangest looking character who ever tried to crash the show. So, of course, I wanted to check him out before I brought him up."

"Well, who is he? Did he give you a name?"

"Just this slip of paper. I guess it's his name."

I looked at a dirty little wrinkled piece of paper. It looked like half of the back of a hundred-year-old envelope. In it were two words: "Rama Hathabata."

"What does he look like, Billy?" I asked.

"He's about five feet tall, thin. Big black eyes that pop out a little. He's wearing faded old blue jeans which are cut off above the knees, and a dirty shirt that used to be white. And . . ."

"And what? You stop like he had horns."

"And one of those hats the Bengal Lancers wear in movies with Ronald Colman! Sun helmets, they call them."

"You're kidding," I exclaimed. "No one could possibly look like that. Not even coming to this show."

"That's the way he looks. Shall I bring him up?"

"Bring him up," I agreed.

About five minutes later he came into the studio. He was at least twice as weird as Billy had described. Square count, friends, but nobody ever looked like this fantastic little man. If he had told me he was from Mars, I swear I might have almost fallen for the kook's story. Actually, all he did do was to look up at me and say:

"Nebel, John?"

I could only nod. He slapped a rolled-up piece of paper, tied with a red string, into my hand. Then, bobbing his head, he smiled and scooted off through the door and down the hall.

Slipping off the red string, I unrolled the sheet of paper. It turned out to be an almost three-foot-long piece of white wrapping—the kind they often use in candy stores. At the top it said: "To Señor Juan Nebel"—and just under that: "Monsieur"; and if you can figure that out, please write. But that was just the beginning. The message continued.

"Per, as following your suggestion to forward messages to yourself. That I am doing at this time now. I think you have need of knowledge regarding something about me since you wish me to be an honored guest when on your program. Thank you.

"I am a famous yogi.

"I am willing to let you in on some first class absolutely must not be revealed occult knowledge.

"You're welcome.

RRR

Infinite Master of Applied Yoga—

—Western Division (his phone number)"

All of the rest of the page was covered with what looked like Chinese or Japanese characters. Unfortunately, I only read Korean, and so I didn't have any idea what the gibberish was all about. Anyway I decided to call the kook, because if he was as crazy as all the rest of this business it would probably make a really great show. I figured if he worked out on the radio bit he'd be sensational on television. You never saw anything that looked like him in your entire life. Really fantastically weird.

On the next afternoon I called the number and spoke with the "famous yogi." The conversation was brief, since I didn't want to kill any of the material before I got him in front of a microphone. He was booked in for the following week.

On the night "RRR" was supposed to appear, a couple of the panelists were sitting around with me having coffee before the show when the guest arrived. I should mention that he refused to give, or answer to, any name but "RRR" (if that can be called a name) or just plain "Yogi." Well, the gang and I were sitting around cutting up a few jackpots when this figure suddenly appeared in the doorway of the studio without a sound and said in a voice out of a "Wolfman Meets the Man from Outer Mars" movie:

"R . . . R . . . R . . . is here."

After a couple of the guys climbed back into their skins, I went over and gave him the conducted tour into the studio, introducing him to the panel. Of course, as some of you may have figured out, this was not the strange little scroll messenger. "RRR" was almost as tall as yours truly L. J., and that's 6'4", but he was thinner. I don't think that this character could have weighed more than a hundred and twenty pounds. He was a real living and walking rail. His eyes stared out of his head as though they were painted on the inside of the back of his skull. And, I'm levelling with you, neighbors, he wore a turban with a big hunk of glass in the middle, and a pair of white pajamas. He was, to quote a later generation than mine, "a real gasser."

He asked if he could spend the ten minutes before the program "meditating," and I assumed that he'd go over in the corner, sit down, close his eyes, and—meditate. Instead he walked over beside the piano, stepped up on the bench, and lay down on the top of the instrument. Fortunately, the top was closed.

I was so surprised I couldn't think of anything to say. I figured that whatever he did might be even kookier, so I just let things—I mean him—lie until the clock hit midnight and we went on the air.

A few minutes later the engineer hit the theme and the show was under way, for better or for worse, and this time I wasn't sure which it would be. I should mention that the yogi had gotten up the minute I called him and had taken his place at the table. My first question really got us off to a great start.

"Mr. RRR, when I received your . . . by the way, is that the way you wished to be referred to or addressed . . . as 'Mr. RRR,' that is?"

"You do not have to employ the full name of which I am called. You may speak to me merely as 'Mr. R,'" he replied.

"Just so that I'll understand," I continued, "that would be the third 'R', I suppose."

"No, that is the first 'R'," he countered.

"But we certainly want to give you your proper title. Possibly you wouldn't feel comfortable if we referred to you by your first name . . . or should I say your first 'R'," I suggested.

"You are not such doing," he explained. "That is the formal custom in India of my part. The last name is the first name and the first name is the last name. It is as though in this your country your name was Nebel John."

"I see," I lied. "But just one other point before we get into the art and science of Yogi. When I received your letter I got the impression that the small man who delivered it was you."

"No, I am me," was his answer.

I never did find out anything else about the little fellow in the Ronald Colman pith helmet, until about a year later. I saw him getting into a cab late one night. He was wrapped in a red cape that covered all of his outer clothes, and he was wearing a white thing that looked like a baseball cap. To this moment I think he was the oddest person I ever saw or met. But, who can tell, possibly there was a perfectly rational explanation for him both of those times. It's just that I have never been able to imagine what it could be.

Anyhow, getting back to "Mr. RRR," or rather "Mr. R," I asked him about the strange writing all over the message he had sent me, and I was told that all of it had been "spirit writing." Actually, what the yogi really meant was "automatic writing," since it came out of his "unconscious hand." Or, to more or less put it into his words:

"A message it is for you from other places not known. It is sent by the force of a mentor of mine Chin Ling."

"Then it is Chinese."

"It is. However, don't ask of me to read it. I don't understand Chinese."

"I see. You only speak English and your native tongue. Is that correct?" I inquired.

He nodded several times.

"Is one of the Indian languages your native tongue, Mr. R?"

"No," he said, "Swedish."

And that was just about the way it went for the next couple of hours. I could hardly match up any of his answers with any of my questions. The rest of the panel was even worse off than I was. If I measured this show against any of the other weird ones, it would have to come out on top in the no-one-could-even-re-motely-understand-this-routine department. It was really completely gaffed. So much so that even I couldn't read this kook or con. I wasn't positive which he really was at that point.

I decided to see if I could get an experiment going, since the guest had spoken of his ability to duplicate anything described in yoga books. He seemed a little surprised when I asked him if he'd care to demonstrate one of these remarkable feats, but said he thought possibly we could try some. I asked him what he had in mind, since we unfortunately had no earth immediately available to bury him in. And even if we had had a grave for him to use, it could only have been until the show was over that morning. This would have meant a couple of hours, which wouldn't have been very impressive since "The Amazing Randi" could do the same thing for the same length of time by purely explainable (but, to the public, secret) means.

Finally he suggested that he stop his heart. I wasn't too sure what he meant and he said he meant what he said. He would stop the beating of his heart. It was agreed that each of the panel and yours truly would come over and check his results when he felt he had succeeded in his test.

He straightened in his chair and closed his eyes. His breathing became a little more regular, then slower and slower. Finally he was inhaling and exhaling very quietly. What I'd consider would be about like the breathing of a man sitting very quietly. Then

216

his head nodded very slightly, which was our agreed-upon signal.

I pointed to one panelist after another, and each guy went over to the guest. Three put their hands lightly on his chest, one leaned over and listened with his ear. I reached over and felt his pulse. When everyone was reseated, I suggested that Mr. R might come back to his normal state (although I must admit that I seriously doubted that he had one).

One by one, I asked each of the regulars what his opinion of the experiment was. One by one, they announced that they weren't terribly impressed, since they heard or felt the heart beating loud and clear. I admitted that I had no problem finding a strong pulse.

Without a word, Mr. R rose from his chair, walked to the door and opened it. Pausing, he announced:

"If you weren't going along with the bit, I don't know why you had me come up. Now you've blown the whole damn gaff. Thanks for nothing, dads."

All this went over the air. I was flipped. Not that I didn't realize that he might be an operator, but it never occurred to me that he'd crack to the con right to the hot mikes. Of course, actually I suppose he was trying to break it off on me. In reality he just killed his own routine. I sometimes wonder what ever happened to Mr. R. I never saw or heard of him again.

On other occasions, as I mentioned before, I had other yogis on the show. Several seemed fairly legitimate. But, outside of one who got in the lotus position on the table and stood on her head in the corner during the coffee break, none were anywhere near as fascinating as the Infinite Master of Applied Yoga—Western Division.

Another Eastern philosophy I had represented on the program on one occasion was so-called Zen. I say so-called because I've been told that none of the stuff the guest spouted had anything to do with the true Zen philosophy. As a matter of fact, the program wasn't actually about Zen itself—it was about the "beat" generation.

After going through about twenty-five applicants, I decided upon a younger man who wrote stuff he called poetry, pitched what he called Zen, and believed that everyone should smoke marijuana. The guest really came on strong, and I have to admit that I came on even stronger with him. By the coffee break, I'd just about had it and off into the night he went. And that was that.

Martinus Cosmology provided me with another great show.

This is a mystical philosophy whose center of activity is Denmark. It's named after its founder, Martinus, who began the whole thing by having visions early in life. He went on to write some very esoteric books. The two gentlemen who came on the show to present this philosophy did a magnificent job of explaining the bit. They were articulate and extraordinarily gracious. The printed matter, the books and pamphlets, were beautifully designed and even more beautifully published. There was only one problem. After five hours of detailed teaching, of careful explanation of the many colored graphs and charts, of penetrating questions and exact answers—no one had the slightest idea what Martinus Cosmology was all about. Lovely, sincere, humanitarian, these we were all sure it was. But intelligible it wasn't.

Voodoo has also had its fair share of airtime with me. On two or three occasions I had the privilege of talking to the noted experimental film maker Maya Deren, who's also a noted authority on the dark magic of the Caribbean.

And that's the way they come and go. The kooks and the seekers, the cons, the pitchmen and the serious researchers. The salesmen and the liars; the fools and the demented and the deceived. Night after night they come. Believers in anything—in all things. But why? Why do they believe?

Lord knows, I'm no psychologist or philosopher; and so I thought I'd throw that question—why?—at my old friend, and many-time guest, psychologist Dr. Emerson Coyle, and see what he had to say.

"John, it would take a substantial volume to give a superficial evaluation of these curious sub-culture worlds," Dr. Coyle remarked, "but very briefly you will generally find that the person who truly devotes himself to any of the off-beat enterprises described in your book is a cultural deviant. I have found many of his kind to be completely sincere and convinced of his assertions, as leaders and followers of orthodox causes often are. Frequently the acceptability of any of these systems is contingent upon the acceptability of some of the off-beat individual's personal experiences. One important difference between the on-beat and off-beat is that of integration, both intra-physically and intra-personally. In the normal individual the personality is better organized; it is somewhat like a chariot driven by the Ego, with the yea-saying Id and the nay-saying Super Ego functioning as the steeds. In the pitchman or practitioner of the occult, off-beat and eccentric, the Super Ego seems to assume the role of

218

driver. I have often noted that the person of this type displays a virtually ascetic and monkish morality. He is not merely good, but too good; not moral, but too moral. In short, he usually suffers from an overdeveloped Super Ego. Often the only girl these young, middle-aged and older 'kooks' have ever related to is 'Mother.' In fact I recall several guests who gave the distinct impression that they considered 'girl' a dirty four-lettered word.

"With few exceptions, the true off-beat leader or follower personifies personal and social inadequacy. Having failed to mature and/or find success, he is lonely, frustrated, unhappy, dishonored, and, usually, unloved. Three courses have been open to him: get in step, withdraw from the life game, or change the rules. The real 'kook' selects the latter road, and focuses his attention and effort on some esoteric art, science or faith. By associating with fellow-believers, he gains almost all of these things he has previously lacked. He has become somebody.

"However, let us never forget that the critical difference lies in the criterion used. In their own time there were few greater 'kooks' than the man who believed the world was round, that boats could sail under water, that man could fly, that men could reach the moon, that travel between the planets was possible, that . . ."

I have to give you a square count, neighbors, I had to hold on tight when Dr. Coyle got to that part about the Id, and the Ego, and all like that, but as the old kook-master I had to agree with pretty much everything he had to say about the offbeaters. After talking with the great psychologist, I figured that I ought to get a top professional science opinion from "The Magnificent," as his friends call him, Lester del Rey. It seemed to me that as author of dozens of fact and fiction science books he certainly would have a definite and valuable idea about all of these strange ones. I was right. He had an opinion, all right.

"The thing I find hard to take," he began, "from our modern irrationals is their presumptuous demand for an 'open mind.' This is ridiculous!" del Rey exploded. "During our six thousand years of history irrationality was studied and accepted as a science until almost the modern era—and is even being studied now. Yet out of this study and acceptance not one single aid to man's development, or to civilization's progress, was adduced. The closed mind of science, which demands hard facts before theories, rejected irrationality less than five hundred years ago, and has since re-built the world at least a dozen times. The cults had their chance, and couldn't make it. Now, because of their own narrow minds, they cannot understand why the world had left them behind and they cry to science, which has replaced them, to prove what they could never prove. Let them open their own minds and accept the world or—and this I prefer— let them close their minds," he concluded, "in death, and improve the world."

As usual, Lester del Rey gave me what I asked for—a strong opinion. But when it comes to the science department, I just don't argue with "The Magnificent."

The next facet I decided to add to the conclusion of this kookological report was the political. Naturally, for this point of view, I called upon Robert Eric Norden, political writer and analyst who has appeared on the show so often. His reply was direct and to the core of the question.

"John, there is absolutely no question that threads of many political colors are woven into the whole cloth of off-beatism. In the flying saucer field alone, a number of people formerly associated with neo-fascist organizations have leaped to prominence; while others have more discreetly remained in the background, pulling some of those political threads and making the front-men puppets dance. As you know even better than I, John," Norden continued, "an uncommon number of the 'contactees' describe all of their friends from other planets as fair-skinned, fair-haired, blue-eyed Aryan types, and go on to leave little distinction between their ultra-persons from super-planets and the Nazi concept of the perfect race type. Also, of course, there is the frequent allusion to the fact that all of these visitors from other planets wear uniforms and are militarily oriented, some carrying it a little further and claiming royal titles.

"On the other hand, there are groups moving in the other direction, where the accent has been placed on the 'one world' dream, where the national and patriotic impulses are denigrated. The orientation in these cliques seems to be at least strongly socialistic, and frequently even further left than that.

"However, it would be my opinion that, except as a possible hiding place for foreign agents, the so-called 'kooky' organizations would be of hardly any value to the serious political subversive. They are too many in number and too scattered in allegiances to offer a very effective political machine, let alone white horse."

Turning from Mr. Norden's political evaluation to a legal

perspective, I contacted the prominent New York attorney and frequent guest, Martin Berger, for the lawyer's opinion. He immediately made his position clear by noting that "lawyers are, in popular belief, a sceptical lot; and I must plead guilty to the charge, at least with respect to most of the claims of those frequenting the strange world of Long John Nebel. The failure," attorney Berger continued, "of those advancing their stories of cures by methods unknown to medical science; the unworldly, otherworldly experiences not granted to us ordinary mortals; the new scientific discoveries unverifiable by scientific methods, and the like; to offer corroboration in evidence verifiable by all, impels disbelief. The credulous may not need evidence, but to establish the truth of a claim of any nature the essential precondition is that the experience or the experiment may be repeated by objective witnesses. One must conclude that those who advance their claims without such evidence and request that we accept their stories on faith are either charlatans or possessed of diseased minds," finished Martin Berger.

The pychological, the scientific, the political, the legal attitudes are all part of the sociological one, and so I decided to tie this group of observations together by asking my old friend, famous sociologist, and author of *The American Funeral,* Dr. Leroy Bowman, for his thoughts on the whole bit. Or, more accurately, I asked what he thought about the thousands of hours I had spent interviewing these odd-balls.

"The unorthodox approach of your show, John, to unorthodox subjects, has a very distinct value in a society as regularized and conformist as ours. It serves to broaden the possibilities of knowledge of the individual and to stimulate adventurous thinking so sadly lacking in every-day routine. Further," Dr. Bowman elaborated, "the sheer implausibility of certain of the tales heard is an escape from rational thinking that to many of us becomes arduous at times.

"The mere fact," he went on, "that a group of persons sit around and talk for five hours a night is a comforting thought to persons who must organize their lives according to the hectic demands of city living. Impersonality, so often charged to urban contacts, is less onerous when five discussants agree, disagree, become excited or banter as if nothing else mattered. It is different in the dreary succession of sameness. It is spontaneous, natural and uninhibited in the compulsive requirements to play a role."

And so there you have the thoughts of five of the top men I

know in the brain department on the general subject of kookery. And, as far as I can see, they all agree a little, but maybe disagree more. It seems fairly likely even astute men may open new doors eventually, but it would be my guess that they'd be operating in the sciences or arts, not where the kooks congregate. But I could be wrong. Who knows, maybe telepathy is the answer. Possibly the first contact with Mars will be from their end. I certainly am not the one to guess. However, I must punctuate this book by saying one more time, "I don't buy it." But it has been a great experience writing it, almost as great as living it was. Maybe in another five years I'll have a whole new bunch of off-beat characters to tell you about. Maybe, by then, I'll have become a believer. I'll leave that to the prophets I have the pleasure of talking to from time to time. But until that day, if and when it comes—

If you're getting up, have a wonderful day; and if you're going to bed, sleep real good. Bless you.

THEME